New Essays in Technical and Scientific Communication: Research, Theory, Practice

Edited by:

Paul V. Anderson
R. John Brockmann
Carolyn R. Miller

Baywood's Technical Communications Series:
Volume 2
Series Editor: JAY R. GOULD

Baywood Publishing Company, Inc.
Farmingdale, N.Y. 11735

Copyright © 1983 by the Baywood Publishing Company, Inc.
Farmingdale, New York. All rights reserved. Printed in the
United States of America.

Library of Congress Catalog Card Number: 83-2568
ISBN: 0-89503-036-5

Library of Congress Cataloging in Publication Data
Main entry under title:

New essays in technical and scientific communication.
    (Baywood's technical communications series ; v. 2)
    Includes bibliographical references.
    1. Technical writing—Addresses, essays, lectures.
I. Anderson, Paul V. II. Brockmann, R. John.
III. Miller, Carolyn R. IV. Series.
T11.N46 1983   808'.0666   83-2568
ISBN 0-89503-036-5

Acknowledgements

For assistance they have given us in preparing this book, the editors wish to thank Rick Bastyr, Susan Evans, Diane Gerler, Lisa Hoopes, Jennifer Kerch, Mary Jean Northcutt, Deb Schoenberg, and, especially, Professor C. Gilbert Storms. We are also grateful to Norman Cohen, President of Baywood Publishing Company and Professor Jay R. Gould, Executive Editor of Baywood's Technical Communications Series, for their continuous support, encouragement, and patience.

Table of Contents

PART IV: HISTORICAL PERSPECTIVES

PART V: REDEFINITION

Introduction

PAUL V. ANDERSON
R. JOHN BROCKMANN
CAROLYN R. MILLER

RESEARCH IN
TECHNICAL AND SCIENTIFIC COMMUNICATION

In 1963, the authors of an NCTE report, *Research in Written Composition*, openly lamented the state of research in that field: they found research in composition in the same state as "chemical research as it emerged from the period of alchemy." [1, p. 5] Much the same can be said for research in technical and scientific communication today. To understand the current state of research, and thus the contribution we hope this collection of essays can make, it is useful to consider technical and scientific communication as consisting of three subdisciplines: the theoretical, the pedagogical, and the professional. As one of us has earlier argued, only the professional subdiscipline has a vigorous tradition of research; the least healthy is the theoretical [2]. And despite its vigor, research in the professional area has often been repetitious, unmethodical, and trivial. There seem to be two reasons for the general weakness of research in technical and scientific communication, one traceable to the inheritance of previous theory, the other an accident of the way colleges and universities have organized themselves in the twentieth century.

The first reason has to do with the way that the language of science and technology has traditionally been viewed. Such language has not seemed amenable to scholarly research, in part because of a distinction drawn by

7

Aristotle between rhetoric and science, a distinction which has since taken several forms but which remains central to our understanding of both language and science. As S. Michael Halloran summarizes the problem, there are two bases for the distinction [3]. The original Aristotelian position is that rhetoric addresses the ordinary citizen using arguments that are available to anyone, and the sciences address expert practitioners using specialized or esoteric arguments. A later position, elaborated in the Renaissance with the development of modern science, is that rhetoric is the art of managing language to influence minds, and science is a method of apprehending truth in the material world. Rhetoric became the practice of verbal ornamentation to affect belief, and science an enterprise that eschews the distortions of both language and belief. In principle, then, scientific discourse (and by unexamined implication, technical discourse) has not been of scholarly interest either as science or as language. To science, language has been an unfortunate encumbrance, not a medium central to the pursuit of truth. As language, scientific discourse has seemed inconsequential because it is assumed to correspond directly and unambiguously to the factual world [4].

A second and more recent reason for the failure of research in technical and scientific communication involves the historical accidents of the organization of the academy, where one might expect to see most serious research being undertaken. In colleges and universities, technical and scientific communication has been one of the casualties of the dissociation of English and speech, which William Riley Parker dates to 1914 [5]. This separation had two manifestations: the distinction between literary art and persuasive or functional discourse, on the one hand, and the distinction between written discourse and spoken discourse, on the other. What fell between the cracks was discourse that was both functional and written. The consequences for freshman composition, in terms of academic status, research, and pedagogical accomplishment, have been widely noted. Written composition survived in English departments, according to Parker, largely because of social pressure from outside the academy and raw necessity within, not because of any sense of responsibility or interest on the part of English departments. Again, much the same can be said of technical and scientific communication. It finds itself most often in departments of English because, as Parker puts it, they "became the catchall for the work of teachers of extremely diverse interests and training, united theoretically but not actually by their common use of the mother tongue." [5, p. 348] Because technical and scientific communication is newer than freshman composition and more aggressively functional, its status within belletristic departments of English remains shakier than that of composition. Without the promise of collegial support and academic prestige, then, technical and scientific communication has been hampered from developing a tradition of scholarly research.

In sum, scholarly research in technical and scientific communication has lacked both the theoretical rationale that provides problems and methods and the academic standing that provides motivation. As a result, very little serious scholarly work has been produced. What has been produced is practical research by the pedagogical and professional subdisciplines. The pedagogical subdiscipline emerged at the beginning of this century, when textbooks in the subject began to be published [6]. Until a few years ago, its research was strictly practical, relying primarily on common sense and personal experience for strategies to solve problems of the classroom. The professional subdiscipline is much younger, dating from World War II. Although it has developed a strong research tradition, its research also has been practical, directed at discovering *ad hoc* solutions to the problems of the marketplace. Without the depth and breadth of inquiry that theory can supply, this practical tradition of research has produced work that is largely intuitive and often repetitious. Furthermore, the practical concerns of the pedagogical and professional subdisciplines have created an environment inhospitable to the speculation and skepticism that scholarly research requires. For that reason, until very recently it would have been an exaggeration even to talk about a theoretical subdiscipline.

At the same time, however, the growth and vigor of the pedagogical and the professional subdisciplines have created both the need and the opportunity for development of the theoretical subdiscipline. The academic standing of technical and scientific communication has improved recently, if only because of increased pressure for more and better teaching. More and better scholars with more and better preparation are entering the field, and many are now willing to put serious intellectual energy into the study of technical and scientific communication. Their efforts are fostered also by recent challenges to the traditional distinction between rhetoric and science. These challenges come from a new interdisciplinary tradition of language study, based not in literature and philology, but in modern linguistics, anthropology, cognitive psychology, sociology, philosophy, and a new, non-Aristotelian rhetoric. Correspondingly, some literary scholars have begun to question the definition of their own discipline and its presumed insulation from the study of other forms of language, such as referential or scientific language. The literary critic Stanley Fish, for example, has challenged the positivist opposition "between a basic or neutral language that reflects the world of objective fact and a language that reflects the uniqueness of individual or subjective perception." [7, p. 10] As a result of such changes in perspective, researchers in technical and scientific communication are finding serious intellectual challenges in the very relationships between language, science, and technology that hitherto had been presumed not to exist.

Recent work in technical and scientific communication includes scholarly attention to a variety of theoretical and practical issues, as well as scholarly use of a broad range of methods and concepts. It is based on established research in other fields, such as those mentioned above, and not merely on an author's own practical experience or on the previous literature in this field. It questions the adages and commonsense assumptions that have constituted much of this prior literature. Scholarly research such as this, we believe, can contribute to all three subdisciplines of technical and scientific communication: scholarship can build further theory, which is the foundation of a coherent and vigorous discipline; scholarship can both support and correct teaching strategies and curriculum design, as Richard VanDeWeghe has shown for composition [8] ; and finally, scholarly research can inform the practices and problem-solving strategies of the communication professional.

CONTENTS OF THIS COLLECTION

The twelve essays in this collection, all previously unpublished, were submitted in response to a general call for papers. They represent, in our opinion, the best scholarly work that is being done today, and their diversity reflects the vitality of that work. Some of the essays concern themselves primarily with the theoretical subdiscipline, by addressing such questions as what technical writing is and whether technical and scientific writing are the same. Others concern themselves primarily with the pedagogical and professional subdisciplines, addressing such questions as what is the most effective style for technical and scientific communication and what is the most effective way to design functional documents. We have arranged the twelve essays into five sections, each representing an important type of inquiry.

We begin with three essays that describe research using empirical methods, both quantitative and non-quantitative. This style of research, in which the behavior of actual writers and the responses of readers are observed and analyzed, represents a vigorous and promising new trend in research about writing, one especially appropriate for technical and scientific communication. The first of these essays is "Studying Writing in Non-Academic Settings" by Lee Odell, Dixie Goswami, Anne Herrington, and Doris Quick. Wary of the assumption that writing, as it is taught in the academic classroom, is adequately attuned to practices in the working world, these authors have used three different techniques for examining writing that workers do on the job. Their research is designed specifically to explore the extent to which workers adapt their writing to the rhetorical context in which it occurs and the ways they adapt it. The authors of the next essay also used a variety of research techniques. In "Revising Functional Documents: The Scenario Principle," Linda Flower, John R. Hayes, and Heidi Swarts report on a series of studies they conducted in order to develop a principle to help writers prepare functional documents (such as contracts or regulations) that can be readily used by their readers. In one study, they gathered transcripts of what readers said as they reported on their efforts to understand a government regulation. From these transcripts, Flower, Hayes, and Swarts drew inferences about the kind of structure and information readers want in functional documents — and consequently the kind of structure and information writers should supply. And finally, in "Topical Focus in Technical

Writing," Lester Faigley and Stephen P. Witte describe their efforts to determine how the assignment of topics as grammatical subjects in a passage of connected prose influences what readers perceive to be the main idea of the passage and how much they remember from it. Their work addresses issues of style and comprehension in a way that little previous research in technical and scientific communication has: it concerns the effect of relationships among sentences, not the structure of single sentences.

The second section contains two essays that provide a new look at one of the most frequently discussed topics in technical and scientific communication — readability. In the first, "What Constitutes a 'Readable' Technical Style?" Jack Selzer assails the widespread belief that readability research provides a sound basis for advising writers to use short sentences and short words. Selzer reviews a large number of controlled experiments in psycholinguistics and comprehension, work that has been almost entirely ignored by people working in technical and scientific communication. In the next essay, "A Cognitive Approach to Readability," Thomas N. Huckin suggests a promising new source of advice about style: research by psychologists into the processes by which people read and understand. Huckin explains several distinct concepts in cognitive processing that have a direct bearing upon the comprehension of technical and scientific prose. He then provides eight guidelines for writers, each founded upon this research, each richer and more plausible than the counsel to use short words and short sentences that Selzer criticizes.

The next section, "Approaches from Rhetoric, Discourse Theory, and Sociology," contains four essays that are almost so diverse as to defy classification. Nevertheless, as a group they show how greatly research in technical and scientific communication can be enriched by other disciplines. In the first essay of this section, "The Role of Models in Technical and Scientific Writing," Victoria M. Winkler examines the theoretical models of writing that inform the two main approaches to teaching writing: the product approach and the process approach. She notes that although much technical and scientific writing pedagogy emphasizes the analysis of audience and purpose, which bespeaks a process orientation, nevertheless, most teaching relies on formal, or structural models of writing, which underlie a product-oriented pedagogy. Winkler's discussion of these two basic models shows that they play different but not incompatible roles in the creation of discourse. In the next essay, "A Rhetoric for Research in Sciences and Technologies," James P. Zappen draws upon two traditions, those of philosophy and rhetoric, to test the widely held belief that scientific writing is fundamentally different from technical writing because science and technology have each developed their own rhetorics. Zappen's strategy is to compare, in rhetorical terms, communications that scientists and technologists have written about their research projects. Through these comparisons, Zappen leads us to a novel account of relationships among science, technology, research, and rhetoric. In "A Theoretical Perspective on

'How To' Discourse," Elizabeth Harris applies a semiotic analysis to one of the most common forms of technical communication. She examines "how to" discourse syntactically (in its constitution and characteristic internal relations), semantically (in its characteristic relations to the world its signs "stand for"), and pragmatically (in its characteristic uses by writers and readers). Her detailed study turns up some unexpected complexities in what seems superficially to be a very simple form of communication. Charles Bazerman opens his essay, "Scientific Writing as a Social Act: A Review of the Literature of the Sociology of Science," by presenting several models that historians, philosophers, and sociologists have developed to describe the activities of scientists and scientific disciplines. As Bazerman explains, each model entails an account, either explicit or implicit, of the functions and characteristics of scientific writing. Bazerman then reviews more than fifty sociological studies of scientific communication. Despite the usefulness of these studies, few are known to teachers, practitioners, or researchers in technical and scientific communication.

The fourth section, "Historical Perspectives," contains two essays that examine the origin and development of two long-standing traditions in technical and scientific communication, both of which began in the Renaissance. In "Style as Therapy in Renaissance Science," James Stephens tells how and why scientists first began using popular, non-scientific knowledge (derived from alchemy, classical mythology, and Christianity) to present their radically new views of the world. As Stephens shows, the scientists who developed and employed this rhetorical strategy — some with more success, some with less — include many of the major figures in the development of modern science: Paracelsus, Copernicus, Galileo, Kepler, and Bacon. In the next essay, "Early Language Reform in the Sciences," James Paradis describes a contrary movement: the creation of modern scientific lexicons in which, for the sake of precision, words are stripped of the meanings they have acquired in the vernacular or in such received traditions as alchemy. The major figures in Paradis's essay are Bacon, Linneaus, and Lavoisier. Together, the essays by Stephens and Paradis show how various and complex is the heritage of technical and scientific communication and suggest how our understanding of current practices and problems can be deepened through historical studies.

Finally, because the diversity of current research invites rethinking our assumptions and because we believe that the weakness of previous scholarly research in technical and scientific communication can be traced to inadequate explanations of its nature, we conclude with a section entitled "Redefinition." This section contains one essay, David N. Dobrin's "What's Technical about Technical Writing?" Drawing from the traditions of philosophical inquiry, Dobrin classifies current definitions of technical writing, shows their short-comings, and then offers an alternative definition. The value of his alternative is demonstrated by its compatibility with the lines of thought pursued by several other essays in this volume, lines of thought that are fundamentally incompatible with earlier definitions. Dobrin's essay also gives the study of technical writing a new significance by showing its connection with the general texture of human relationships.

THE FUTURE

Because these twelve essays represent the best current scholarly work in technical and scientific communication, they indicate some of the characteristics of present and future work in this field. Certainly, the most obvious of these characteristics is the conviction that technical and scientific communication is worthy of concerted intellectual consideration. Other obvious characteristics are diversity and eclecticism: this research uses a wide variety of methods and approaches, many of them borrowed from other disciplines. Furthermore, it promises to recompense the disciplines from which it borrows by producing work of interest to them; several of the essays in this volume may be of interest to researchers outside the field of technical and scientific communication as traditionally conceived.

The essays in this volume also hint at certain themes that we might expect to become increasingly prominent in future research. One such theme is that technical and scientific communication should be studied contextually — in terms of the disciplines that employ it, of the historical circumstances in which it has arisen and developed, of the offices and laboratories and shops in which it is produced and used. Another theme is that research should focus on connected discourse, not on isolated words and sentences. And another is the difficulty of making clear and useful distinctions between scientific and technical discourse, and between them and academic writing, freshman composition, functional writing, and other commonly used categories. There are many more themes, of course; we hope that every reader of this book will come away with a long list, together with a variety of ideas about other research questions that are worth pursuing. Indeed, their suggestiveness is one of the qualities that most made this particular set of twelve essays appeal to us. None, even the most thorough, exhausts its subject; each lays the groundwork for future investigations. Each deserves to be taken seriously on its own terms. And together they delineate a field of inquiry that has an important place in contemporary scholarship.

REFERENCES

1. R. Braddock, R. Lloyd-Jones, and L. Schoer, *Research in Written Composition,* National Council of Teachers of English, Urbana, Illinois, 1963.
2. P. V. Anderson, The Need for Better Research in Technical Communication, *Journal of Technical Writing and Communication, 10:*4, pp. 271-282, 1980.
3. S. M. Halloran, Technical Writing and the Rhetoric of Science, *Journal of Technical Writing and Communication, 8:*2, pp. 77-88, 1978.

4. C. R. Miller, A Humanistic Rationale for Technical Writing, *College English*, *40*:6, pp. 610-617, 1979.
5. W. R. Parker, Where Do English Departments Come From?, *College English*, *28*:5, pp. 339-351, 1967.
6. G. H. Alred, D. C. Reep, and M. R. Limoye, *Business and Technical Writing: An Annotated Bibliography of Books 1880-1980*, Scarecrow Press, Metuchen, New Jersey, 1981.
7. S. Fish, *Is There a Text in This Class?*, Harvard University Press, Cambridge, Massachusetts, 1980.
8. R. VanDeWeghe, Research in Composition and the Design of Writing Programs, *ADE Bulletin*, No. 61, pp. 28-31, May 1969.

PART ONE
Empirical Research

CHAPTER 1

Studying Writing in Non-Academic Settings

LEE ODELL
DIXIE GOSWAMI
ANNE HERRINGTON
DORIS QUICK

This essay is based on two principal assumptions. The first is that teachers of writing must also be students of writing. Whether we teach "composition" or "technical writing," we need to examine critically our classroom procedures and the theory that forms the basis for our discipline. We must be continually asking such questions as these: Are my theory and teaching procedures consistent with what writers actually do? If I analyze written products and composing processes, do I find corroboration of my theoretical assumptions and classroom practices? When composition teachers and researchers have asked these questions, the answers have often been disconcerting. When researchers have attempted to find out what writers actually do, they have called into question widely held assumptions about the value of outlining [1], the necessity of topic sentences [2], and the importance of such "basic" methods of paragraph development as comparison and contrast [3].

One might assume that the teaching of technical writing would be more in tune with the practice of writers, since such courses are designed to equip students to meet the specific writing demands they will encounter when they enter business and industry. Yet there are at least some bases for questioning this assumption. For one thing, textbooks are often derived from other textbooks, and teachers of writing tend to reflect the values of their own teachers rather than their understanding of what writers actually do. Further, a recent study by Paul Anderson notes several disparities between the technical writing done in some university classrooms and that done by workers in several fields [4]. Anderson's study indicates that many of these workers have to write to different types of readers: to some who are quite well-informed, to others who are not; to some readers who are at the writer's own level in an organization and to others who are at levels higher or lower than the writer's. Consequently, Anderson questions the practice of those technical writing teachers who insist that students address all their writing to a single type of audience, "the intelligent but uniformed layman." In addition, the study indicates that writers have to do a number of different types of writing (e.g., memos, letters, instructions) much more frequently than they have to write formal reports. Thus Anderson suggests that technical writing teachers who place a great deal of emphasis on the writing of formal reports may not be preparing students to handle the demands they will encounter in business and industry.

Our second principal assumption is that when we attempt to find out what writers do, we should not rely solely on teacher-designed, experimental tasks. We should also be concerned with the writing tasks people actually do as a normal part of their day-to-day work. We think experimental tasks are attractive, especially those in which researchers stipulate a rhetorical context — a purpose (e.g., to inform or persuade) and a specific audience (e.g., readers of a particular magazine), by manipulating such important variables as audience and purpose. Moreover, such tasks have been useful in testing basic assumptions from discourse theory. By carefully varying the rhetorical purposes of a series of assignments, and by asking writers to do those assignments in a setting where the composing process could be videotaped and timed, Ann Matsuhashi [5] has provided important support for James Kinneavy's claim that "The aim of a discourse determines everything else in the *process* [our emphasis] of discourse." [6] Prior to Matsuhashi's study, this claim about purpose and process had been supported solely by analysis of theory and written products. In addition to helping researchers test theory, experimental tasks can be very useful in studying the development of writing abilities. By giving the same experimental task to children, adolescents, and adults, researchers have been able to record developments in syntactic skills [7], persuasive strategies [8], and ability to anticipate the information needs of readers [9]. Furthermore, Linda Flower and John R. Hayes have shown that it can be useful to present writers with novel tasks, tasks that make it difficult to rely on "stored plans" or routine strategies for producing a piece of writing [10]. Such tasks can, for example, let us see how the composing process of skillful writers differs from that of less skilled writers.

While recognizing these uses of experimental tasks, we think that teachers and researchers should also get outside the classroom and look at the writing people do in non-academic settings, writing that is rarely published or distributed widely but that is central to one's success in a given job or profession. Our experience in working with writers in non-academic settings suggests that the contexts for and the consequences of this writing can be substantially different from what one encounters in experimental tasks designed by a teacher or researcher. In this latter type of writing, especially when the experimental task stipulates an audience other than the teacher or researcher, the writer may have had little prior experience in writing for the assigned audience and has little reason to believe that the writing will ever have its intended effect on the assigned audience or that the writing will have any consequence beyond earning a grade or satisfying a teacher's or researcher's request. By contrast, our experience suggests that writers in non-academic settings experience the writing situation quite differently. They often have detailed knowledge about their audiences and have developed a repertoire of strategies for dealing with their audiences. Further, these writers can usually assume that their writing will actually be read by someone who can, in fact, be informed or persuaded and that the reader may very well be dependent on the writer's ability to inform or persuade. Finally, these writers know that their writing will have important consequences; if they do not write reasonably well, they may not obtain what they want; they may have the additional trouble of dealing with an angry or confused reader; they may not be promoted or given merit raises; or they may lose their jobs. Since we assume that context and consequences can have an important influence on written products and the writing process, we think it important to examine the routine, non-experimental tasks that continually confront writers in non-academic settings. As we shall argue in the final section of this essay, we think that the study of writing in non-academic settings has implications for teaching and for learning.

In the next three sections of this essay, we shall introduce three research strategies which we have developed in the course of our own study of writing in several different non-academic settings. Each focuses upon a different type of data: one examines the linguistic features in samples of work-related writing; another examines workers' criteria for evaluating the writing done by someone else; a third, the discourse-based interview, examines the reasons writers give for making a particular stylistic or substantive choice in their own writing. We have developed these three different strategies because we believe that in order to understand writing in non-academic settings (or, indeed, any subject matter) one must be able to draw upon a repertoire of complementary investigative strategies. Our decision to use a particular strategy or combination of strategies has depended upon the setting we have been working in and upon the types of questions we have wanted to answer.

As we discuss each research strategy, we shall explain how that strategy was used in a particular non-academic setting to answer a particular question. Further, we shall suggest additional questions which arise from our use of a given procedure. Since we are primarily interested in encouraging further study of writing in non-academic settings, we shall, for the most part, be less concerned with reporting our findings than with describing research procedures. The one exception to this plan will appear in our discussion of our third research strategy — analysis of the reasons writers give for making a stylistic or substantive choice. In this discussion we shall present a more thorough discussion of findings from one study since those findings are not available elsewhere.

Although we shall discuss each strategy separately, we want to emphasize at the outset that they are complementary; moreover, each has provided support for one basic conclusion about writing in the non-academic settings where we have worked: for the writers we have interviewed, this writing is not rule-governed. There are very few instances in which these writers rely solely upon a particular stylistic maxim that says, in effect, "Always do X" or "Never do Y." Instead, each of our strategies shows that when these writers make choices of style and substance, those choices reflect a complex awareness of rhetorical context, of the interrelations of audience, persona, and subject matter.

WRITING SAMPLES

One way to assess writers' sensitivity to rhetorical context is to ask this question: When writers in non-academic settings address different audiences in an attempt to accomplish different purposes, does their writing show variation in such linguistic features as, say, syntax? In an attempt to answer this question, we analyzed an extensive collection of writing done by administrators and caseworkers in a county bureaucracy, a Department of Social Services [11].

In gathering this writing sample, we departed from the usual practice of devising a series of experimental tasks which asked people to write for different audiences and purposes. Indeed, we did not attempt to give any writing assignments at all. Instead, we began by trying to determine what kinds of writing were actually done by workers in the agency. At our initial interview, we asked workers to keep copies of everything they wrote during a two-week period. This provided an extensive writing sample, which we supplemented in the following ways: we tried to notice what types of written materials were on people's desks; we accepted some participants' invitations to rummage through files in which they kept copies of everything they wrote; we asked for copies of materials when participants occasionally approached us in the hallway or interrupted an interview, saying, "Here's something else you might be interested in." Such procedures, obviously, are not systematic, and they rely heavily upon the good will and interest of the participants. In all our studies, however, we have found that researchers may expect a good bit of cooperation and interest from participants, especially if we make it clear that we are not interested in evaluating their work but, rather, are interested in identifying the skills they have developed as a result of writing repeatedly on the job. Consequently, we have found that participants can often identify types of writing that we would not have anticipated. As participants mention such pieces of writing, it is a simple matter to check back with other participants, asking if they, too, do that sort of writing. This procedure does not guarantee that we can identify every single type of writing done in a given non-academic setting. But it does let us identify several types of writing that are done by a number of people at a particular site and that participants themselves have identified as having different functions and audiences.

In our early interviews at the Department of Social Services, administrators described and provided examples of three types of writing done by all administrators in the agency:

- *pink memos* – relatively short, informal pieces of writing (written on 8½ by 6 inch sheets of pink paper) that usually serve a routine function such as making a request or responding to someone else's request; these memos are usually addressed to a small audience, most often one or two specific persons;
- *white memos* – longer, more formal statements (written on plain white 8½ by 11 inch paper) such as official directives or explanations of agency policy; typically these are addressed to a rather general audience such as "All Supervisors" or "All Caseworkers"; and
- *letters on agency letterhead stationery* – these seem to have several different functions; they are usually addressed to specific persons; unlike pink and white memos, which are sent only to workers in the agency, these letters are sent only to people outside the agency.

We chose to examine these types of writing because we were interested in the extent to which writers in non-academic settings varied specific features of their writing according to the rhetorical context for their writing. We took each of these three types of documents to represent a different rhetorical context. In each type, we examined specific features of syntax that other studies had shown to vary according to rhetorical context. Specifically, we examined T-unit length (T-unit is a main clause plus all of its modifiers), clause length, number of clauses per T-unit, and the number of passive constructions per T-unit. In addition, we used M. A. K. Halliday and Ruqaiya Hasan's discussion of cohesion to identify the different types of cohesive ties (lexical cohesion, conjunction, substitution, and reference) that appear in each type of writing [12].

We found that administrators' writing did, in fact, vary according to rhetorical context. The pink memos differed from white memos in several ways that were statistically significant. The relatively informal pink memos had, on average, shorter T-units, fewer passive constructions per T-unit, and fewer instances of lexical cohesion, reference, and conjunction. Although we found only one statistically significant difference between memos and letters (the letters contained more instances of substitution than did the memos), our analysis of these written products indicates that features of certain types of written texts do vary according to rhetorical content. However, a number of questions remain unanswered.

1. Why did the writers make the different choices they did? Is there a difference in intention that accounts for the differences in types of writing? And do those differences have different effects on the readers of those types of writing?

2. All of the writers we have mentioned here were administrators who had had a great deal of experience in the agency where they were employed at the time of our study. Would one find comparable results if one were to study the writing of administrators in other types of institutions — large corporations, for example? Would one find that other Social Service personnel (e.g., caseworkers) also vary the features of their writing according to rhetorical context? Would they vary the same features as did the administrators? Would one find that inexperienced workers in the agency vary the features of their writing to suit their audience and purpose?

3. In analyzing writing samples for our study, we looked for features of syntax that have been widely used [13], but it turned out that a less widely used procedure, analysis of cohesion, let us find statistically significant differences between two types of writing. This makes us wonder whether researchers ought to be looking for still other features of style that might let us make distinctions among different types of writing. Joseph Williams, for example, identifies a number of characteristics of style, many of which could be counted reliably [14]. Would analysis of some of these features let us make distinctions among types of writing?

4. In deciding what types of writing to analyze in the Social Services agency, we depended heavily upon the intuition of agency personnel, all of whom indicated that pink memos, white memos, and letters really were different types of writing. Yet we suspect that audience and purpose might vary within each of the three types of writing. This possibility seems especially likely in the case of letters; in some, the speaker-audience relationship appeared rather formal and distant, in others it seemed rather informal. Consequently, we suspect that it might be informative to have judges group writing according to their perception of the purpose or speaker-audience relationship in specific texts. Would we find significant differences among these groups of texts? What types of syntactic, cohesive, or stylistic features would be most useful in differentiating these groups of texts?

DRAFT EVALUATIONS

As a result of analyzing workers' writing, we can make some inferences about their sense of what constitutes effective writing. To complement these inferences, it seems useful to elicit writers' explicit statements about the criteria by which they judge writing. What are these criteria? To what extent do these criteria suggest that writers rely upon a set of maxims or stylistic principles that are to be followed in all contexts? To what extent do writers' statements corroborate our inference that writers are sensitive to rhetorical context?

We raise these questions with some misgivings, for it seems only too likely that writers might be influenced by their assumptions about what writing teachers want or expect to hear. Furthermore, writer's statements may be inconsistent with the writers' own practice. For example, in our study of writing in a Department of Social Services [11], we wanted to test participants' sense of what constituted "acceptable style." Adapting a procedure described by Rosemary Hake and Joseph Williams, we rewrote several of the pink memos, white memos, and letters that we had collected in our writing sample [15]. Without altering substance or organization, we created three versions of each piece of writing. One version contained a number of nominalizations and passive constructions. Another version contained passive constructions but no nominalizations, and a third version was written entirely in active voice, containing neither nominalizations nor passives. We asked participants to read the three versions of each piece of writing and rank them as to "acceptability" of style, using the categories "most acceptable style," "less acceptable style," and "least acceptable style." Our analysis of writing done by these workers had led us to expect that they would prefer the active versions of the pink memos and the passive versions of the white memos. This did not happen. They consistently gave the highest ratings to the passive or passive-nominalized versions, even when they were judging pink memos.

There may be several ways to explain this result. But we feel that the most compelling explanation is that we had altered not only the texts but workers' relation to those texts. To use James Britton's terms, we were inviting workers to abandon the "participant" role, in which they wrote and read job-related materials and to view our versions of these memos and letters from a "spectator" role [16]. Our interviews with these writers made it clear that when they wrote their own memos and letters they expected to accomplish a particular goal (to inform or to persuade, for example), and they were very conscious of the specific context for each piece of writing — of the events that preceded or followed from the writing of a given memo and of the personal characteristics of the person who would receive a given piece of writing. Although we used memos and letters that had actually been written in the agency, these writings had, for most of the workers, no functional context. With the exception of the person who had written the original version, workers had little personal knowledge about the subject matter being discussed, the audience being addressed, or the purpose the writing was originally intended to accomplish. Consequently they had neither basis nor reason for viewing this writing from the perspective of one who was participating in a real rhetorical transaction.

In an attempt to help workers evaluate writing as a participant rather than a spectator, we devised the following procedure. First we asked workers to give us the data on which they had previously based a piece of writing. After using that data to create our own piece of writing, we showed each worker the writing we had done and posed this question: "Assume that I am a subordinate whom you have asked to do this writing. Would you be willing to use the draft I have written?" We asked workers to read our writing aloud and pause and comment on any aspect of our writing that seemed acceptable or unacceptable. Even though the reading aloud process was unfamiliar to these workers, there was at least one respect in which this procedure was not at all unusual: we frequently find that writers in non-academic settings delegate writing to subordinates. Especially in the case of subordinates who are new to the job, this writing is likely to be carefully reviewed by the person who "assigned" it.

Although we had not devised this procedure when we were working in the county Department of Social Services, we were able to use it in a subsequent study of writing done by legislative analysts, non-elected employees of a state legislature [17]. Our interviews with these analysts indicate that their criteria for good writing reflect a rather complex understanding of the context in which the writing has been done.

When we interviewed these analysts, we focused on only one type of writing, "bill memos," in which a writer had to assess the weaknesses of pending legislation. Invariably, these assessments, which were the type of writing analysts did most frequently, were addressed to committees of legislators who were trying to decide whether a particular piece of legislation should be considered by the entire legislative assembly. When we interviewed the legislative analysts about our attempts to write these assessments, their comments helped us see that a "good" assessment would answer one or more of the following questions:

- What are the likely consequences of this legislation?
- How does it relate to existing laws or procedures?
- Will the legislation achieve the sponsor's intent?
- Does the legislation stipulate the procedures that are to be followed?
- What are the characteristics of the people who will be affected by the legislation?

All of these questions indicate that, for one type of writing, the legislative analysts were primarily concerned with one aspect of the rhetorical context; that is, they placed great value on a careful investigation of the subject at hand. However, we came to realize that their evaluations entailed more than simply determining whether we had or had not answered a particular question about the legislation we were analyzing. They pointed out that we not only had to try to answer these questions but we also had to anticipate readers' reactions to our analysis. One analyst, for example, reminded us that we might be criticizing a piece of legislation before a committee that included the legislator who had' drafted the legislation. Further, the analysts expected us to see how our answer to one question might influence the way we answered another question. And finally, their comments made it clear that one must consider the context for a given piece of legislation; occasionally, analysts would point out that prior events would make it unnecessary to raise a particular question.

Thus far, we have used our draft-evaluation procedure in only one non-academic setting, and we have not tried to shape our writing so that (in content or in style) it would seem likely to win a worker's approval or disapproval. We can think of several questions for further research:

1. Would workers in other non-academic settings judge writing by the same kinds of criteria as did these workers? If workers' criteria differ, how could we account for those differences?
2. Would workers at different levels of the same institution display the same set of criteria in judging writing?
3. If workers were asked to evaluate student essays and then to evaluate researchers' attempts to do workers' writing, would we find that the workers appeared to hold one set of criteria for one type of writing and another set of criteria for the other?
4. If we systematically varied the style of our writing (using, for example, a great many passive constructions in some writing and few passives in others), would workers comment on those variations? Would they consistently prefer one style to another?

DISCOURSE-BASED INTERVIEWS

Each of the research procedures discussed thus far has certain strengths and weaknesses. The analysis of written texts can be highly systematic and can enable one to use statistical procedures in trying to determine whether certain features of writing vary according to the rhetorical context for the writing. For example, our analysis of writing in a Department of Social Services showed that the formal white memos contain significantly more passive constructions than do the informal pink memos. But an analysis of a written product cannot help us see how a specific feature of a text (e.g., the use of a particular passive construction) relates to a writer's understanding of the audience being addressed, the persona he or she is creating, or the subject being dealt with.

This problem was partially solved in the second research strategy we have described. As workers read and evaluated our efforts to do some of the writing they had done, they focused on specific points in our writing and explained how their sense of rhetorical context led them to approve or disapprove of something we had written. However, this procedure is unsystematic. We could never predict exactly what aspect of our writing a legislative analyst would decide to comment on. Consequently, we had no way to insure that all writers would comment on the same features of our writing.

Our third research strategy, interviewing writers about their reasons for preferring a particular choice of content or style, attempts to give a relatively systematic way of exploring writers' perceptions of the rhetorical context for a given piece of writing. This procedure, described below, enables us to compare the reasoning of different groups of writers, asking such questions as these: Do we find that a particular feature of content or style leads writers to comment upon a particular aspect of the rhetorical context? When we interview workers at various levels of an organization's hierarchy, do we find that these groups tend to be conscious of different aspects of the rhetorical situation?

Conducting and Analyzing Interviews

To answer these kinds of questions, we interviewed workers about job-related writing which they had previously completed. To prepare for these interviews, we first read a number of pieces of writing done by workers in a given setting. As we read these writings, we looked for types of variations that appeared in the writing of each worker. For example, in reading memos and letters written by employees of a state Department of Labor, we noticed the following types of variations:

1. Form used in expressing a command or request. Sometimes, for example, writers would say "please do X"; in other situations writers would say "you must do X" or "it would be appreciated if you would do X."
2. Form used in referring to oneself. In some pieces of writing, workers would use the first person singular pronoun; in other pieces of writing workers would use the first person plural pronoun or a third person pronoun, even though *I* would have been grammatically correct.
3. Use of an introductory, context-setting statement. Some letters and memos would begin with a statement such as "As you will remember from our discussion of last Wednesday . . . ," whereas other letters would omit this sort of information.
4. Use of informative detail. Often, but not invariably, relatively abstract statements would be followed by elaboration in the form of a non-restrictive clause, a passage beginning "for example," a definition of a specialized term, or a parenthetical expression.
5. Justification of assertions. Often, but again not invariably, workers would provide a rationale for their conclusions, sometimes in clauses beginning "because" or "since."

Having identified these variations, we interviewed seventeen employees in the Department of Labor, posing one basic question: "In this memo/letter you do X (use the first person pronoun, begin with a context-setting statement, etc.). In other pieces of writing you do Y (use third person pronouns, omit the introductory statement). In this memo/letter would you be willing to do Y rather than X?" After assuring the interviewee that we assumed the original choice was appropriate and grammatically correct, we asked the interviewee to explain why he or she would accept or reject a given alternative. All of these interviews were tape recorded and, subsequently, transcribed. (For a more detailed description of the interview procedure, see Odell and Goswami [11]; for a detailed rationale for this procedure, see Odell, Goswami, and Herrington [18].)

In order to devise a way of categorizing the reasons workers gave, two of the authors of this article examined a set of categories devised for Odell and Goswami's study of writing in a Department of Social Services [11]. After reading randomly selected transcripts from the Department of Labor, these two authors modified categories used in the earlier study. Using this modified set of categories, two judges read the interview transcripts and assigned writers' statements to one or more of the following categories of reasons for accepting or rejecting a particular alternative:

I. AUDIENCE-FOCUSED REASONS

    A.   Status of the audience or scope of duties.
        Writer mentions reader's title or place in the hierarchy and expresses deference or lack of deference. Writer refers to appropriate duties or authority of reader.

> "Writing to *my boss* I try to pinpoint things a little bit more."

> "In dealing with these employer agents — they actually represent [employers] on a power-of-attorney basis — we have to be careful that we're not giving them anything *they may not be entitled to.*"

    B.   Actual prior dealings with this specific audience.
        Writer mentions a specific prior transaction between the audience and the agency or a communication from the audience.

> "I mean, *we had written before trying to clarify this whole thing,* this particular case, and I wanted to kind of emphasize that — that — you know, if he had read this [prior] letter, maybe the second letter wouldn't have been necessary."

> "*When you have something as personal as a phone call and a conversation back and forth and he asked me,* I feel free to use "I" rather than "we." You know, he called me; he didn't call the Department of Labor."

    C.   Characteristic of the Audience.
        Writer refers to a personal trait of the reader or to the reader's work-related experience or knowledge or lack of it.

> "We want them to realize that this is the reason because *they're usually pretty mad at this point.*"

"Today they get so many different publications or letters from different sources, and unless we can specifically identify what we're talking about, *they're* liable to think it's from some other part of the Labor Department. Attorneys and lawyers. . . . They *figure you should change your whole system around to accommodate them*."

"She's obviously someone new in the business who doesn't understand New York State Law. *She's in Connecticut,* so *they might not know what NYS Law is*."

D.   Anticipated action or change in the audience's feelings or state of knowledge.
Writer refers to anticipated action or change in feelings or understanding of either the immediate reader to whom the letter is addressed or another secondary reader, perhaps internal to the department.

"We always want them *to realize* they can call on us if they have questions."

"Now why I'm using the word 'may.' It gives me some sort of flexibility. Because see, *he might come along with a different routine*, which – a – say he comes back and shows 95% of our report requirements, so now, even though he didn't follow every one to the T, now I got to make a decision."

II.   WRITER-FOCUSED REASONS

A.   Writer's role or position in the organization or scope of duties.
Writer mentions him or herself and specifically refers to the scope of his duties or his position.

"*We have no authority to do this. . . . As an accounting section, we have no authority to waive that*."

"The law is not me. *I'm just someone who*, in the executive branch of government, *is executing the laws*."

B.   Ethos or attitude the writer wishes to project or avoid.
Writer uses a word or phrase that describes the personal quality or attitude he/she wishes to project or avoid.

"This is a bit more on *a personal level. . . . The other is* much too *formal*."

"Just to say 'Send his address,'" would, I think, be *a little too authoritarian*."

"It makes the letter sound *less stuffy*."

C. Writer's feelings about the subject or task at hand.
Writer refers to feelings or attitudes which are not conveyed in the writing.

> "When I wrote this letter, *my juices in my stomach were* sort of, you know, *flip-flopping.*"

D. Subsequent action the writer wants or needs to perform.
Writer refers specifically to his/her or the agency's need to perform a certain action.

> "We need this information so we can *adjust his account ...* "
> "In order *to make a determination*, on this particular section, we need this for review."

III. SUBJECT-FOCUSED REASONS

A. Importance or sensitiveness of the subject dealt with in the writing.
Writer refers to the subject requiring special attention because of its importance or some special circumstances surrounding it.

> "There's a story before this whole appointment. *It was a difficult situation.*"
> "This was a rush job. He wanted it done right away."

B. Desire to provide an accurate, complete, non-redundant record.
Writer refers to a concern for accuracy or for documenting something completely or for avoiding redundancy without referring to the reader's needs at all.

> "Well, I couldn't say that ['I'] because *I will not necessarily handle the reply to this letter.*"
> "*Anything that's said must be documented in writing.*"

C. Desire to document or justify a conclusion or decision of the writer.
Writer refers to a conclusion he/she wishes to justify without referring to the reader or himself.

> "Every position over Grade 18 has to be approved and that's why — you know, *you're justifying what you want to do.*"
> "That is to me an important part of the sentence as *why I wanted to say this is a workable thing*, and something that has merit."

D. Prior, on-going, or subsequent actions concerning or analogous to the subject.

> "Well, yes, because this is a difficult situation, all right. This fellow has been here since '72. This other fellow has

never worked in our office, and he's worked in the Labor Department for many years. . . . And *before this we had passed him by before, and he went to the people upstairs, complained that we were skipping him,* a forty-year-old employee. But he's never worked in our office . . . "

"What we're trying to emphasize here is that *we've gone back to Cynthia. We've talked to her at length.* We understand her problem. They don't . . . "

IV. TEXT-FOCUSED KNOWLEDGE

A. Office practice, policy, or genre.
   "That's *the standard thing* that is included in this particular type of letter."
   "*We definitely are instructed to stay away from the personal in our letters.*"

B. Intra-Textual Concern, exclusive of any other rhetorical concerns.
   "Well, I do mention the Regulations up here, and *if I mention it here I'm tying my argument to what I said before.*"

Using these categories, two readers analyzed the interview transcripts. Working independently, these judges achieved 80 per cent agreement in categorizing the reasons writers gave for accepting or rejecting a particular alternative. After these readers had made their judgments, they discussed their results with a third reader, and the three readers discussed and resolved points upon which there had been disagreement.

Findings

As we analyzed our interviews with the seventeen participants in our study, we discovered ways in which workers' choices reflected their perceptions of specific aspects of the rhetorical context for their writing. These workers were especially concerned about their audience; they frequently mentioned some prior contact with their readers, remarked upon the characteristics of their audience, and speculated upon ways their readers might respond to a particular choice. These writers also related their choices to the persona they wished to create (or avoid) and justified some choices by citing the need for accuracy in dealing with the subject at hand. (Writers referred to other aspects of the rhetorical context, but these references occurred, on average, in less than 5% of their comments.) These results are interesting in part because they are consistent with what we found in our interviews with workers in an insurance company [19] and in the county Department of Social Services [11] : some writers in non-academic settings are quite sensitive to rhetorical considerations and mention those considerations when justifying a particular choice of style or content. Perhaps more important, the interviews with Department of Labor workers helped us understand how writers' considerations of rhetorical context might vary according to: 1) the type of choice writers were making; and 2) a writer's experience and status in an organization.

As we discuss these variations, limitations of our sample size will make it impossible for us to say whether the variations are statistically significant. Thus we can only report general trends, measured in percentages. In all cases, we shall report only those trends that are displayed by a majority of the workers in our study, or by a majority of the workers in a given sub-group of participants in our study.

Type of choice — We had expected that different types of choices might prompt writers to comment on different aspects of the rhetorical context. This did indeed happen, but not exactly as we had anticipated. We had thought, for example, that in deciding how to phrase a command or request, writers might be particularly concerned with the characteristics of their intended reader, trying to choose the form that would be most agreeable to an audience that had a particular set of biases or expectations. Writers did mention audience characteristics in 27 per cent of the instances in which we asked them about alternative ways of expressing a command or request. But in 55 per cent of the instances in which we asked about this type of choice, writers indicated that they were concerned about the persona suggested by a given alternative. Thus, writers were most likely to reject certain alternatives for expressing a command or request because, for example, an alternative seemed too personal or too impersonal, too authoritative or not authoritative enough. For another type of choice, form of reference to self, we had anticipated that writers might be especially concerned with the persona they were creating. And in 36 per cent of the instances in which we asked about reference to self, this concern was mentioned. But in 63 per cent of the instances in which we asked about this matter, writers justified their choices by implying a need for accuracy. For example, one participant in our study had written a memo containing this statement: "It is my opinion that [X's] suggestion does have merit." He was unwilling to say "we think that . . . " or, "it is thought that . . . ," because "I don't take it up with anybody . . . I [make these judgments] on my own." The same concern for accuracy led another writer to prefer *We* to *I*: "I feel we shouldn't use *I* in this office because we don't necessarily handle the same material all the time. I will write this letter or respond to it, but [subsequent correspondence] doesn't come back to me. It comes to someone else. OK? [Also] all the central letters are signed by [someone else]. That's another reason we couldn't use *I*." Finally, when writers justified their decision to include or exclude introductory statements, informative detail, and justifications for their assertions, they were especially concerned with the response they anticipated from their readers.

Writer's experience and status – In our study of writing in a Department of Social Services [11], we found that different groups of writers tended to give different types of reasons for the choices discussed in our interviews. Administrators tended to favor audience-based reasons, while caseworkers tended to give subject-based reasons. However, we cannot make too much of these differences since the two groups of writers usually did quite different kinds of writing; the administrators typically wrote letters and memos, while caseworkers wrote reports of their meetings with clients. Furthermore, when we selected participants from the Department of Social Services, we did not categorize them according to the length of time they had worked for the agency. Consequently, our study of the Department of Social Services will not let us answer these questions:

1. Do writers of relatively high status, "management confidential" administrators, give different reasons than do workers of lower status? If so, will these differences appear even when the two groups are doing the same type of writing?
2. Do reasons vary according to the length of time a writer has worked in a given organization?

Our answers to these questions are based on interviews with three groups of writers at the Department of Labor:

1. management confidential administrators;
2. experienced workers (not classified as management confidential) who had worked at the Department for three years or longer; and
3. inexperienced workers who had worked for the Department for less than one and one-half years, a length of time that administrators considered necessary to thoroughly train a worker.

Although there are some similarities among these three groups (see Figure 1), we found several differences. Inexperienced workers appear to differ substantially from the administrators and experienced workers in these respects: references to prior dealings with the audience and to the personal characteristics of the audience appear much more frequently in interviews with administrators and experienced writers than in interviews with inexperienced writers.

Further differences appear when we sub-categorize workers' comments about the response they anticipate from their readers. For the most part (in commenting on 59 per cent of all the choices we questioned them about), inexperienced writers referred solely to two types of audience responses: improving their readers' understanding of the subject at hand and getting them to perform an action which, by law, the readers were obliged to do. When we asked one inexperienced worker if he would be willing to delete some detailed information about state tax law, he declined to do so: "Without that sentence, it would be assuming [the reader] is aware that he should report the remuneration

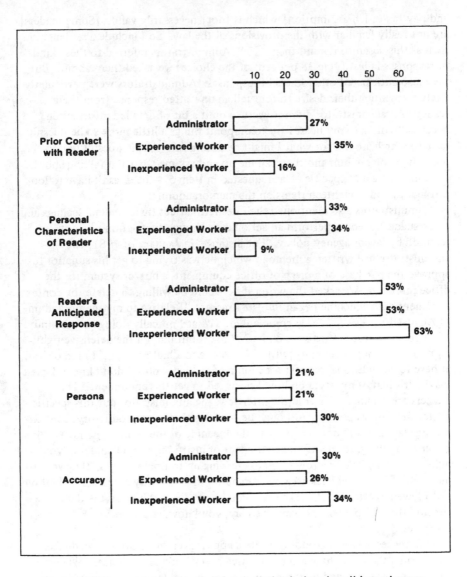

Figure 1. Types of reasons cited for stylistic choices by all interviewees. (Percentages were obtained by first determining the total number of choices discussed in our interviews with all seventeen participants, and then dividing the total number of choices into the total number of times a particular type of reason was mentioned.)

and pay taxes, [an assumption] which is [not] necessarily valid. [Some readers] are not really familiar with the provisions of the law. So I include a sentence such as this, again to remind them . . . " Administrators referred to these kinds of responses in justifying 38 per cent of the choices we asked them about. But they also anticipated other kinds of responses. Administrators were particularly likely to mention their desire to forestall an unwanted response from their reader. An administrator did not want to omit a bit of detailed information because "writing to my boss, I try to pinpoint things a little more so he doesn't have to search around for what I might be asking for. . . . He doesn't like to read my memorandum and then call me up and ask me what I'm talking about. . . . By being that specific — 'as requested in Item 5' — he doesn't have to look through the other eighteen items on the memorandum."

Administrators also mentioned their desire to affect their readers' feelings and to persuade readers to perform an action even though that action was not required by law or agency policy. For instance, in January of 1981, one administrator had written a memo in which he was trying to get his superior to approve the purchase of a piece of office equipment, a buzzer system for the office intercom. We asked the writer if he would be willing to delete the context statement with which he began the 1981 memo: "Relative to my memorandum of August 17, 1979 . . . " He commented: "What I'm really doing here is kind of zinging my boss a little bit, you know? . . . I put him on the defensive right away by referring to a memo [written] a year and a half ago. . . . I kind of lead in here to an additional request for equipment which — oh — I don't know. I guess maybe it's part of my style on how I managed to get this equipment. The buzzers are coming." Later in the interview, the administrator put this specific choice in a larger context. Although he observes that the introductory, context-setting statement is "not necessary to the meaning of the memo," he notes: "it's an on-going thing, it's justifying equipment or justifying people, and, oh, you build sort of a block or a row of blocks leading up to finally they gotta give it to me. And if I can trail back to a memorandum that's already a year and a half old and I haven't gotten what I asked for, you know, I've got him on the defensive already. It's just part of the game we play, you know, getting new equipment . . . "

Differences between groups of writers appear even more pronounced when we consider the ways these groups justified specific kinds of choices. When administrators explained why they preferred a particular way of expressing a command or request, they were particularly likely to refer to the characteristics of their audience. Administrators made this sort of reference in commenting on 39 per cent of the instances where we interviewed them about form of command/request; experienced workers referred to audience characteristics in only 29 per cent of their comments about command/request, and inexperienced workers referred to audience characteristics in only 9 per cent of their comments. On the other hand, both experienced and inexperienced workers were likely to justify their decisions about commands/requests by referring to the persona a particular choice seemed to create. Experienced workers mentioned this concern in 64 per cent of their comments; and inexperienced workers mentioned it in 77 per cent of their comments about command/ requests. Administrators, by contrast, mentioned persona in only 42 per cent of the instances in which they tried to justify a particular way of expressing a command or request.

Other differences appeared when groups of writers gave their justification for making other types of choices. When explaining why they would or would not include some informative detail, administrators made relatively frequent reference to the importance of accuracy. This concern appears in 25 per cent of administrators' comments about informative detail and in 28 per cent of experienced workers' comments. But it never appears when the inexperienced workers explain why they would or would not be willing to delete a specific bit of detail.

Even when overall percentages indicate a similarity among groups, more detailed analysis suggests differences. All three groups — administrators, experienced workers, and inexperienced workers — justified decisions about informative detail by referring to the characteristics of their audience. This sort of justification appeared in 44 per cent of comments made by administrators and in 46 per cent and 44 per cent of comments made, respectively, by experienced and inexperienced workers. Yet when we examined their comments about audience characteristics, we found that inexperienced workers were very likely to refer to one type of characteristic of the audience — the amount of information the audience had about the subject matter of the letter or memo. But the administrators and, to a lesser degree, the experienced workers commented on other types of characteristics such as the attitudes or habits of their readers.

Although we can find some overall patterns in the types of reasons elicited by different choices and in the types of reasons favored by different groups of writers, we want to emphasize the apparent complexity of the choices writers made. On the average, writers mentioned approximately two different reasons for each choice we asked them about. Thus one cannot reduce the choosing process to a rule-governed procedure that says, for example, "every time you decide how to phrase a command or request you should be primarily concerned about the persona you are creating."

Implications for Further Research

From this survey of our work in a state bureaucracy, one can begin to see how writers' perceptions of rhetorical context affect their choices. One can also see how concern for rhetorical context varies according to the type of choice being made and according to the group of workers being interviewed. We can think of several additional questions that might arise from this work.

1. How do we account for the ways inexperienced workers differ from experienced workers or administrators? Can their reasons be attributed to their lack of knowledge about the rhetorical context for their writing? Or can their reasons be attributed to the types of writing they are asked to do? We know, for example, that more complex writing tasks are likely to be assigned to experienced workers. If inexperienced workers were asked to do such tasks, would we find changes in their perceptions of the rhetorical context for their writing? Or would such changes come about only as the result of experience on the job?
2. How do these workers compare with workers in other types of institutions? Do these other workers justify their choices by emphasizing other aspects of the rhetorical context?
3. How do writers acquire their perceptions of and sensitivity to rhetorical context? What work-related experiences are influential? Are there colleagues who — officially or unofficially — serve as "writing teachers"?

These sets of questions focus our attention on writers. But we think it would also be useful to focus on the audiences who receive workers' writing.

4. How do readers respond to the alternatives we have discussed with writers? If, for example, a writer has told us that a given alternative is inappropriately formal, would the reader share that view?
5. How accurate and useful are writers' perceptions of their audience? Would a reader agree, for example, that a given piece of information was unnecessary because, in the writer's view, that information was already known to the reader? What kinds of difficulties or misinterpretations arise when readers read materials they have been sent?

IMPLICATIONS FOR TEACHING AND LEARNING

As we have begun to understand the writing that goes on in certain non-academic settings, we have found specific ways in which that understanding can influence our teaching of writing. As Anderson points out, we can have a better sense of the types of writing and the different types of writer-reader relationships we ought to emphasize in our courses [4]. Further, results of our own work are useful in devising specific teaching procedures. We have been able to provide students with the same data that a worker has written about, ask students to write about those data, and then we ask students to compare their work with that of the original writer. We have also been able to re-type materials we have discussed with workers, expanding each piece of writing to include all the options which writers commented upon in their interviews. We have asked students to justify their preference for a given option and then compare their justification to that of the person who wrote the document. This procedure introduces students to the importance of rhetorical context, shows them how rhetorical context bears upon specific choices of style and substance, and provides students with a persuasive rationale for our emphasizing rhetorical context.

In addition to these uses in our own classes, we think the study of writing in non-academic settings may help us see how to make connections between the process of writing and the process of learning. In the study mentioned earlier in which we worked with legislative analysts, we also interviewed university students majoring in history, economics, and political science. Legislative analysts hold jobs that university graduates might obtain without going through a master's or doctoral program, and many students in history, economics, and political science aspire to government jobs that entail some of the same types of writing as do the jobs held by the legislative analysts. When we interviewed the two groups and when we analyzed their writing, we found substantial differences in their degree of understanding of the context for their writing and in the conceptual strategies they brought to bear on the subject matter they were writing about.

Frequently, the legislative analysts made some comment about the way a particular piece of writing fit into a sequence of events that had preceded or seemed likely to follow as a result of a given piece of writing. Furthermore, they usually displayed a clearly defined conception of their audience, a conception that influenced not only the way they said things but also the care with which they explored a given topic. Although the specific characteristics of these audiences might vary, all the analysts reported that their audiences were likely to:

1. be less well-informed than was the analyst;
2. depend heavily on the analyst's careful exploration of a given subject; and
3. feel free to confront the analysts personally and insist upon further elaboration or clarification.

These audience characteristics seemed to have a great influence on analysts' thinking. The analysts repeatedly indicated how important it was to explore their subject thoroughly, often going well beyond their present understanding of a topic in order to insure that they and the reader would not be embarrassed by the analyst's treatment of a topic.

The undergraduates had a quite different conception of their audience. Although they repeatedly claimed that their writing had to be comprehensible to a very uninformed reader, their comments made it quite clear that they knew they were writing for a reader that was far more knowledgeable and authoritative than were they. Furthermore, the undergraduates were relatively unlikely to locate their writing in a sequence of events. Specifically, they never mentioned the events in the course that led up to the writing of a particular paper; nor did they indicate that their writing was likely to have any consequence beyond eliciting a particular value judgment from the professor.

Another set of differences appears when we consider the conceptual strategies, in effect, the types of questions, the two groups appeared to rely upon.

When analysts commented upon their own writing or the texts (usually drafts of legislation) they were writing about, they were likely to ask questions of the sort we mentioned earlier: What are the consequences of my writing? What are the consequences of the text I am writing about? What events preceded my own writing? What events preceded the text I am writing about? How will people be affected by my writing? How will they be affected by the text I am writing about? The undergraduates, by contrast, were likely to ask such questions as these: Have I justified my conclusions? Have I defined key terms? Have I summarized my sources accurately?

The undergraduates' questions are, of course, useful, especially when one has produced a draft that needs to be evaluated and revised. But the undergraduates' questions do not seem as useful when a writer is in the early stages of the composing process, trying to explore information and generate ideas. The legislative analysts' questions, however, seem useful throughout the composing process. Whether beginning their exploration of a subject or evaluating a draft, writers may need to ask themselves whether, for example, they have carefully considered the consequences of the material being discussed.

As we have argued in our report of this study [17], we believe that these differences are important, not just for teachers of "composition" or "technical writing," but also for all teachers who want writing to play an important role in their courses. We believe that students would explore materials more thoroughly if they had a set of strategies that would help them with the process of formulating ideas as well as with the process of evaluating a draft. We also expect that students would acquire these strategies more readily if:

1. they understood how the intellectual work of a given piece of writing related to a sequence, a progression from the knowledge and skills with which they entered the course to the knowledge and skills the instructor hoped they would have when they completed the course; and
2. their audience were to provide the immediate, insistent feedback of the sort the legislative analysts anticipated from their readers.

Finally, we believe that students would be more highly motivated to learn these strategies if they felt that their audience was someone who was genuinely willing to be informed or persuaded by the writing rather than someone who was simply interested in identifying the formal features of the writing or in determining whether students' understanding of the topic was consistent with the reader's own understanding.

We realize, of course, that the words *believe* and *expect* figure rather prominently in the preceding paragraph. Further, we acknowledge that our study includes only one group of undergraduates and one group of non-academic writers. However, all of our beliefs and expectations are testable; they can be refuted or confirmed, as can our finding about differences between writers in academic and non-academic settings. However, at present we have little refutation or confirmation. Consequently, we reiterate our basic assumptions. Teachers of writing must also be students of writing. Whether teachers of "composition" or "technical writing," we must go outside our classrooms, testing our conceptions of what writers actually do and refining the theoretical assumptions upon which our discipline is built.

REFERENCES

1. J. Emig, *The Composing Processes of Twelfth Graders*, National Council of Teachers of English, Urbana, Illinois, 1971.
2. R. Braddock, The Frequency and Placement of Topic Sentences in Expository Prose, *Research in the Teaching of English, 8,* pp. 287-302, 1974.
3. R. Meade and W. G. Ellis, Paragraph Development in the Modern Age of Rhetoric, *English Journal, 59,* pp. 219-226, 1970.
4. P. V. Anderson, Research into the Amount, Importance, and Kinds of Writing Performed on the Job by Graduates of Seven University Departments that Send Students to Technical Writing Courses, Xerographic copy, Miami University, Oxford, Ohio, 1980.
5. A. Matsuhashi, Pausing and Planning: The Tempo of Written Discourse Production, *Research in the Teaching of English, 15,* pp. 113-134, 1981.
6. J. Kinneavy, *A Theory of Discourse*, Prentice-Hall, Englewood Cliffs, New Jersey, 1971.
7. K. W. Hunt, *Grammatical Structures Written at Three Grade Levels*, NCTE Research Report No. 3, National Council of Teachers of English, Urbana, Illinois, 1965.
8. D. L. Rubin and E. L. Piché, Development in Syntactic and Strategic Aspects of Audience Adaptation Skills in Written Persuasive Communication, *Research in the Teaching of English, 13,* pp. 293-316, 1979.
9. B. Kroll, The Development of Audience-Adapted Writing, Xerographic copy, Iowa State University, Ames, Iowa, 1981.
10. L. Flower and J. R. Hayes, The Cognition of Discovery: Defining a Rhetorical Problem, *College Composition and Communication, 31,* pp. 21-32, 1980.
11. L. Odell and D. Goswami, Writing in a Non-Academic Setting, *Research in the Teaching of English, 16,* pp. 201-223, 1982.
12. M. A. K. Halliday and R. Hasan, *Cohesion in English*, Longman Publishing Company, London, 1976.
13. M. Crowhurst and E. L. Piché, Audience and Mode of Discourse Effects on Syntactic Complexity in Writing at Two Grade Levels, *Research in the Teaching of English, 13,* pp. 101-110, 1979.
14. J. M. Williams, *Style: Ten Lessons in Clarity and Grace*, Scott, Foresman and Company, Glenview, Illinois, 1981.
15. R. Hake and J. Williams, Style and Its Consequences: Do as I Do, Not as I Say, *College English, 43,* pp. 433-451, 1981.
16. J. Britton, The Composing Processes and the Functions of Writing, *Research on Composing: Points of Departure*, C. R. Cooper and L. Odell (eds.), National Council of Teachers of English, Urbana, Illinois, pp. 13-28, 1978.

17. L. Odell, D. Goswami, and D. Quick, Writing Outside the English Composition Class, paper presented at the University of Michigan Conference on Literacy for the Eighties, Ann Arbor, 1981.
18. L. Odell, D. Goswami, and A. Herrington, The Discourse-Based Interview: A Procedure for Eliciting the Tacit Knowledge of Writers in Non-Academic Settings, *Writing Research: Methods and Procedures*, P. Mosenthal, L. Tamor, and S. Walmsley (eds.), Longman Publishing Company, London, forthcoming.
19. L. Odell, Business Writing: Observations and Implications for Teaching Composition, *Theory into Practice, 19*, pp. 225-231, 1980.

CHAPTER 2

Revising Functional Documents: The Scenario Principle

LINDA FLOWER
JOHN R. HAYES
HEIDI SWARTS

Writers working in government and industry are often asked to write — and even more often to revise — documents which have goals beyond those of simple exposition. Expository prose, such as an essay or report, is typically designed to lay out a body of ideas so the reader will understand and remember them. However, the class of writing we will call "functional documents," which includes regulations, contracts, manuals, and procedures, has an additional overriding goal. People read these documents not merely to learn information, but in order to do something. For example, a reader's primary goal in reading may be to apply for a loan from the Small Business Administration, decide if he is eligible for Blue Cross benefits, sign her first apartment lease, make an insurance claim if he's covered, or clear a paper jam in the office's new copier.

For such purposes, the structure of the documents must do more than reflect the internal organization of the writer's information (e.g., offer a description of the copier). It should be designed around both the readers' goals and the reading strategies people bring to functional documents, which they read only in order to act. Are there then any clear principles which can guide writers in the writing and revision of such documents? As Thomas Huckin and Jack Selzer demonstrate in this volume, although readability formulas are often seen as the basis for revision, they can't deal with the overall information structure of a text; in focusing on the readability of sentences, they ignore the larger problem of comprehensibility a reader faces.

A more inclusive principle for revision, then, would need: 1) to deal with the logic behind the structure of a text — from syntactic structures which determine the focus of a sentence, up to the top-level organization of ideas, and 2) to be a reader-based principle, responsive to the practical needs and the comprehension processes readers bring to functional documents.

This article describes a research project intended to uncover some of the things readers need in order to process, or comprehend, a functional document. Our research was guided by two questions:

1. What would a reader-based revision of a Federal regulation look like? What do readers need?
2. What kinds of revisions do expert writers make when they revise a Federal regulation? How do they meet the readers' needs?

To answer these questions, we conducted two studies, one of which analyzed reading strategies people brought to a difficult Federal regulation, and the second of which tested our hypotheses about the role of "scenarios" on a set of good and poor documents. We hoped that this research would suggest a practical, powerful principle for revising Federal regulations and, by implication, other functional documents. And indeed it did. We call this principle the "scenario principle," which states that functional prose should be structured around a *human agent* performing *actions* in a particularized *situation*. On the face, this may seem like a very commonsensical proposition, yet it would be a radical departure from the current logic and structure of Federal regulations and most contracts.

STUDY 1: ANALYZING THE NEEDS OF READERS

Our approach to answering the first of our two questions was straightforward exploration: to learn what readers need in order to read a Federal regulation, we collected reading-aloud protocols (tape-recorded transcripts) of subjects reading and paraphrasing the meaning of a Federal regulation as they read. Protocol analysis has proven to be a powerful tool for uncovering cognitive processes in writing and other problem solving tasks [1] and has recently been used to study reading processes [2]. We turned to protocol analysis for this study because we wanted to observe the kinds of "revisions" readers actually had to make in a regulation in order to understand it.

Because regulation prose is so difficult to read, readers must often resort to conscious processing of the prose — we had observed this when the members of our research team first started discussing the meaning of a regulation. Each of us was literally "rewriting" the sentences in order to make sense out of them. Our working hypothesis, then, was that if there were consistent patterns to our *readers'* "revisions," these might suggest what sort of revisions the *writers* of these regulations should be making. Protocol analysis was well suited to this task, since it tends to capture just those places where readers encounter difficulty and have to resort to conscious processing of the prose [2], that is, where instead of reading fluently and automatically, they stop, reread, rephrase, and consciously think over what the passage might mean.

Method

Subjects were asked to read and interpret a text, simply trying to say aloud to a tape recorder everything that was going through their minds as they read. They were given sections of the regulation governing the Small Business and Capital Ownership Development Program (13 CFR Part 124 Section 121.1-121.3) under the jurisdiction of the Small Business Administration (SBA). We selected this regulation because it was ostensibly designed to aid the small-business person, the very person who probably couldn't afford legal interpretation of the regulations. We conducted a detailed analysis of the reading protocols of three representative readers: one was a successful entrepreneur with a graduate background in business, the second was a successful businesswoman who had had two SBA loans in the past, and the third was an Assistant District Director for the SBA who had worked in the management assistance office.

Coding System

We coded the readers' statements into two broad categories. The first was metastatements, which included the plethora of comments which didn't pertain to the content or meaning of the regulation, such as "This is going to be hard to read," "All right, I've seen this stuff before," and various other statements about the government, about regulations in general, and about the reader's own process.

Our second broad category covered all content-related statements. We divided them into two major sub-categories: content comments and content translations. The comments category was the more general and included any comment or inference as long as it in some way interpreted the meaning of the regulation (e.g., "All right. They want to keep all this money separate . . ."). But if a content statement was merely a restatement of a specific line or lines in the text, it was coded as a translation. Translations were, in effect, direct attempts to translate the meaning of some phrase, sentence, or group of sentences into another more understandable form. Comments and translations are complementary content statements: one expresses global, general meanings or interpretations, the other operates more locally. For our analysis this distinction was interesting but not crucial. What stood out in our analysis were the three distinctive kinds of content statements, which we labeled structural, retrieval, and scenario statements.

Structural statements – This category included any statement concerned with the structure of information in the regulation, whether the reader was using headings to actively search for missing information or using the structure to understand the document, as in "Now see then we go back to a second main point here."

Retrieval statements – In trying to understand a regulation our subjects often drew on their prior knowledge, including knowledge about the SBA itself or about business and economics, as in the comment, "Oh, they're trying to prevent chaining." Here, the notion of "chaining," which is familiar to people in business but not mentioned in the regulation, let our reader stand back and grasp the unstated, sometimes hidden meaning behind a specific part of a regulation. This category, then, included any statement that indicated explicit retrieval of such prior knowledge from long-term memory.

Scenario statements – The final distinctive kind of statement we saw was also the one which proved to be most interesting. This category included statements structured around a human agent performing actions in a particular situation. Some turned the meaning of a passage into a generalized condition/action sequence, others created a dramatized scenario with an example of somebody doing something, and still others did both. For instance, this is a reader's rewrite of the meaning of "ineligible concerns": "Say that if a fellow has a bar and he's selling moonshine which is not taxed, . . . " Since regulations so rarely express their meaning in this way, these scenario statements were particularly conspicuous as "revisions" which changed the text from one form of expression to another.

In coding the protocols, all content statements were classified as either a comment or translation. However, a statement could then receive multiple coding if it contained structural, retrieval, and/or scenario features. Our unit of measurement was the clause, with two exceptions. Speakers frequently use relative clauses where writers would merely use a noun, and we wanted to limit our units to clauses that were adding new, independent information. Therefore, restrictive clauses and clauses which were in the subject or object position of a sentence were simply coded as part of the main clause.

Results

Table 1 shows the results of our coding of the three dominant categories described above.

The presence of structural statements shows that the readers employed structure to read the document. In fact, structure may be especially important to readers who are trying to use a document, not merely understand it. For example, the large number of structural statements from Subject 2 may be due to her attempt to discover whether she was herself eligible for the program. Her concern with structure grew in proportion to her need to actively search for relevant information. (She was, by the way, never able to find the answer to her question.)

All three of our readers attempted to "retrieve" and use prior knowledge to understand the prose at hand. For example, the subject with graduate training

Table 1. Categories for Readers' Statements

		Content Clauses			
Subject	*Total Clauses*	*Total Content Clauses (Comment/Translation Ratio)*	*Structural*	*Retrieval*	*Scenario*
1	208	127 (49/78)	15	22	75
2	200	114 (70/44)	50	41	42
3	155	102 (28/74)	17	26	65

read pieces of the regulation in terms of economic and business concepts such as "pyramiding." Without that knowledge, parts of the regulation designed to close loopholes (but not explain them, of course) are very difficult to understand. As one might expect, the businesswoman often used her own past experience to interpret parts of the regulation, and interestingly enough, so did the SBA official, as in, "OK, we've made loans to technical schools and so forth, so they — they are eligible." Our coding of the explicit use of past knowledge probably reflects only a small portion of what was actually used.

The most dramatic result from this analysis was the frequency with which our readers resorted to scenarios in their "revisions" of the regulations. That is, in trying to understand the text they frequently recoded it in order to form a concrete story or event by creating a condition/action sequence or by supplying agents and action. As Figure 1 shows, for Subjects 1 and 3 scenarios account for over half of all their content statements (59% and 64%). Furthermore, scenarios account for 37 per cent of the content statements even for Subject 2, despite the fact that her desire for eligibility information led her to make an unusually high number of structural statements. Clearly, creating scenario statements is an important revision strategy for all three subjects.

The Role of Scenarios in Reading

Because scenarios account for such a large proportion of our readers' "revisions" (and, as we will see, for such a small proportion of the original prose of the regulation), they deserve more exploration. If the only problem with the text were its "readability," we might have expected our readers to break the prose into shorter sentences and to substitute simple words for hard ones: to *rephrase* the original sentences in simpler ways. Instead, we find them making

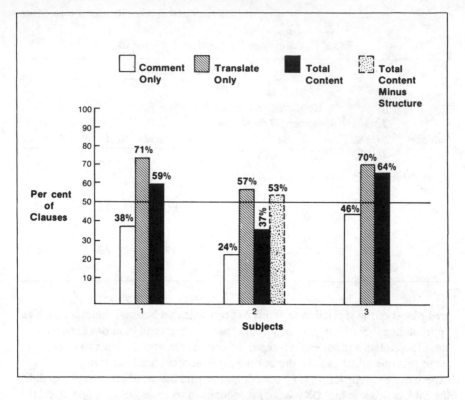

Figure 1. Percentage of scenarios in content statements.

these much more radical transformations in which a definition is turned into an action and embedded in a context. Below are some examples which compare three versions of the prose our readers produced: a reading of the original, a rephrasing, and a scenario.

1. Original: No part of such financing shall be used . . .
   Rephrase: Money can't be used . . .
   Scenario: If a borrower has that money on hand, . . . we won't make her a loan so that she can use that money on hand to purchase land or things like that.

2. Original: (Discussion of eligible concerns) Printing: A firm solely engaged in commercial or job printing, if there is no common ownership with a concern ineligible under this paragraph (d) (4) of this section and the printer has no direct financial interest in the commercial success of the material so produced.
   Rephrase: In other words they [this eligible concern] are strictly a job shop printer.
   Scenario: You have something that you need printed, you bring it in, they print it up.

Table 2. Frequency of Scenarios in Translate Statements

| | Translate Statements | | | | |
| | | | Scenario | | |
Subject	Word Only	Rephrase Only	Scenario Only	Scenario (+ Word or Rephrase)	Scenario Total
1	4 (5%)	18 (23%)	5	51	56 (72%)
2	11 (25%)	8 (18%)	8	17	25 (57%)
3	3 (4%)	19 (26%)	5	47	52 (70%)

As you can see from Figure 1, the majority of these scenarios occur in the translation statements and *not*, as one might expect, in the more global comment statements. Readers are using these agent/action and condition/action structures to restate individual clauses and sentences, not just to comment on or develop the meaning as a whole. That is, they are using scenarios in the activities that most closely resemble what writers usually do when they revise prose.

Table 2 shows the large role scenarios play in these translation statements. In order to compare readers' revisions with the changes suggested by readability formulas, we coded each reader's attempt to clarify a word, to rephrase a sentence, or to use a scenario. (In a few cases noted in the fourth column, the readers embedded a scenario in their attempts to rephrase or substitute words.) To our surprise, we found our readers spending relatively little time worrying over "hard words" or trying to phrase and restructure big sentences into little ones. Although our readers did use short, simple words and achieved a "standard" level of difficulty on Flesch's Reading Ease Scale (i.e., scores of 57, 65, 69), their sentences were long (around 25 words per sentence). But, because these long sentences took the condition/action or agent/action form of the scenario, they also seemed easy to understand. On Flesch's Human Interest Scale they only achieved scores of 20, 29, and 30 out of 100 points (mildly interesting to interesting). In other words, our readers' performance did not violate the canons of readability, but the protocols suggest that there are better ways to account for the ways they revised prose to make it understandable.

What conclusions could we draw from this exploratory study of readers' "revisions"? Manipulations to improve readability scores would certainly have improved the prose our subjects were reading, but their revisions suggest that they are looking for something more and something different in kind. As the final column in Table 1 shows, scenarios account for a substantial chunk of our readers' interpretive behavior, and in particular, as the final column in Table 2 shows, they account for a very high proportion of our readers' translation activities (72%, 57%, 70%), in which the readers are performing tasks very like revising prose. Scenarios represent a more radical kind of transformation than "readability" revisions, because they actually *restructure* the information. By creating situations, agents, and actions, they embed the abstract meaning of a regulation in particular contexts — they make meaning concrete enough to be *functional* for the reader.

Our study of the reader's revisions also suggests that there is a second kind of scenario that might be important to revisers of functional documents: the scenario of the reader using the document. In this scenario, the agent is the reader, the situation is the reader's desire for information he or she plans to use in a particular way, and the action is the reader's reading activity. By considering how the reader will approach a document, a reviser can structure the document so that the reader's scenario (the reader's reading activity) is as efficient as possible. For example, the reading activity of our second subject (who wanted to know whether *she* was eligible for the SBA program) suggests that she approached the document with a specific set of questions in mind. From her point of view, the regulation would have been more readable if her questions had been used as headings in the regulation, and if the regulation's contents had been organized accordingly. Because the regulation was not structured around her questions, she was forced to make a large number of structural statements in her effort to reformulate the contents of the regulation into answers for her questions.

The importance of this second kind of scenario can be explained from the perspective of cognitive science. According to that perspective, the best representation of knowledge on a given topic depends on how that knowledge will be used [3, p. 104]. One way of viewing the use of a document is to consider the way readers will read it. For example, readers can approach a text with a passive or "bottom-up" reading strategy in which they allow the text to direct their reading process. Or, they can take a more active or "top-down" processing strategy in which their own goals and motives direct how they read and represent the meaning of the text [4, 5]. It seems likely that readers normally approach functional documents with a top-down strategy. People rarely read such documents for pleasure or general enlightenment. They read them for a reason. They want to find information, make decisions, and act: to comply with a regulation, apply for benefits, sign or oppose rental terms, purchase or draw on an insurance policy. So from the reader's point of view, good writing is writing that structures information in a way that enables him or her to act.

This relationship between prose structure and the readers's use of a document has been looked at for other kinds of documents. In discussing general expository writing, Flower has argued that one of the key differences between writer-based prose and reader-based prose is its structure [6]. The narrative or descriptive structure of writer-based prose is often quite satisfactory from the writer's point of view, since it is based on the writer's own discovery process or the information before him. But it fails to meet the needs of the reader, who requires a hierarchically organized discussion focused on the topic, question, or problem. In a similar way, Kern, Sticht, Welty, and Hauke's excellent work on training manuals demonstrated that the key to effective revision of manuals is the revision of structure [7]. The function of a training manual is to tell someone how to do something; therefore a reader-based revision takes that function seriously and organizes information around the task the reader must perform, such as how to locate land mines, rather than around the general topic of land mines and their locations. Our study, then, suggests another strategy for reader-based revisions, a strategy that is appropriate for documents to which readers turn for the answers to practical questions. The strategy is to organize the text around the readers' search for answers to those questions.

STUDY 2: ANALYZING THE NATURE OF WRITERS' REVISIONS

Our study of reading protocols revealed a revising principle used by readers: they try to structure information around agents performing actions in specific situations. The next logical question to ask is: does this principle apply to written revisions? Do expert *writers* also use this principle? Therefore we used our scenario hypothesis derived from protocol analysis to compare two regulations: a regulation we knew to be difficult to read (the SBA regulation), and a revised regulation which had been generally praised as easy to read (the HEAL or Health Education Assistance Loan regulation). The question we wanted to answer was: do published revisions made by expert regulation writers reflect the heavy use of scenarios that we saw in the readers' revisions? To answer that question, we compared the old and revised versions of the regulations in two ways.

Analysis of Clauses

First, we compared the old and revised regulations by selecting comparable segments and counting the number of lines containing clauses with 1) a human agent and an action, or with 2) a human subject if the verb was a state-of-being verb. In essence, we were looking not simply for active verbs, but human-centered discussions, as in, "The borrower must repay . . . " and "The Commissioner agrees to pay . . . " or "A student must be: a citizen, national, or permanent resident in the United States." The alternative was clauses such as, "Eligibility is described . . . , " "Determinations will be made . . . , " or "Membership alone in any group is not conclusive that an individual is socially disadvantaged." We ran this test on two different parts of each regulation — first, on the initial 360 lines which described the program and eligibility (see Figures 2 and 3) and, secondly, on two smaller, more specific 160-line sections which told people how to apply for money. As it turned out, each regulation was consistent across its sections, differing by no more than two percentage points. However, the old and the revised regulations differed considerably, as Figure 4 shows. The SBA writers used agents and actions or human-focus on only about 33 per cent of the lines, whereas the HEAL writers focused on people and their actions about 59 per cent of the time. Clearly, the HEAL writers used a scenario strategy similar to that used by regulation readers.

Analysis of Headings

We examined old and revised documents in a second way because we wished to learn whether or not good writers use a human focus even in the headings of documents. Therefore, we ran a small test to see if readers could successfully discriminate the headings of old and revised documents from a scrambled list of headings. The headings came from four documents: an old (the SBA) and revised (HEAL) regulation and an old and revised version of a Personal Liability Catastrophe Policy. The readers were instructed to: mark as "old" any heading that appears to be trying to define a term that is of importance to the agency or company; mark as "revised" any heading which 1) contains an agent or action or

§ 121.1.3 Advance Payments

(a) *Definitions.* Advance payments are disbursements of money made by SBA to a section 8(a) business concern prior to the completion of performance of a specific section 8(a) subcontract for the purpose of assisting the said 8(a) business concern in meeting financial requirements pertinent to the performance of said subcontract. Advance payments must be liquidated from proceeds derived from the performance of the specific section 8(a) subcontract. However, this does

Figure 2. Fourteen lines of the 360-line passage from the "old" regulation.
(This regulation governs the Small Business and
Capital Ownership Development Program.)

§ 126.1 What is the HEAL program?

(a)   The health education assistance loan (HEAL) program is a program of Federal insurance of educational loans designed for students in the fields of medicine, osteopathic medicine, dentistry, veterinary medicine, optometery, podiatry, pharmacy, and public health. The basic purpose of the program is to encourage lenders to make loans to students in these fields who desire to borrow money to pay for their educational costs. In addition, certain nonstu-

Figure 3. Fourteen lines of the 360-line passage from the "revised" regulation. (This regulation governs the Health Education Assistance Loan Program.)

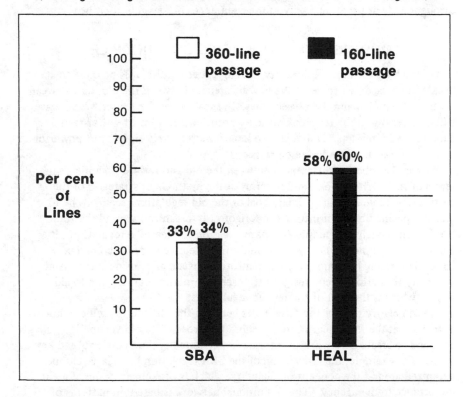

Figure 4. Percentage of lines with focus on human agent/action.

2) states or answers a question the reader would have. Examples of headings that define terms are: Personal Liability; Occurrence; Social Disadvantage. Examples of headings containing agents and actions or else stating or answering questions are: Who is an Eligible Student Borrower?; The Loan Application Process; Can This Policy Be Cancelled?

Out of a total of sixty-three headings, our four readers were able to identify correctly twenty of the twenty-seven headings from the revised versions. That 74 per cent of these headings could be correctly identified suggests that the writers of the more effective regulations used a human-focus even in their headings. Why couldn't 100 per cent of the headings be identified correctly? One possibility is that even revised regulations and policies aren't as good as they might be.

The Role of Scenarios in Revising

These two comparisons of old and revised Federal regulations lead us to a conclusion that, though simple, has broad implications for revision. Just as our readers interpret prose by organizing it around human agents and their actions, expert government writers and revisers seem to provide that human focus throughout their prose, not only in their sentences but even in their headings.

MOVING TOWARD A REVISION PRINCIPLE

On the basis of these exploratory but suggestive studies, it is possible to step back and characterize some of the key differences between the old, hard-to-read documents studied and the revised ones. In speaking of the revised versions we will be referring to the revisions made by both the government writer-revisers and our reader-revisers. Our goal is to look for a relatively simple but powerful principle for making reader-based revisions.

We can describe the differences between the old and revised documents in terms of their writers' goals and in terms of the methods or strategies of the writers (see Table 3). The primary goal of the old regulations seems to be to teach a specified body of information, rigorously organized around the topic itself, even though few people ever have occasion to "learn" a regulation. It would, for example, be ludicrous to study the effectiveness of income tax packets by seeing how much people remember a week after using them. And yet many regulations seem designed to teach information rather than to aid action, which is the goal of the revised regulations.

We can clarify further the differences between the old and revised documents if we look at the rhetorical strategy behind the prose. The old version is designed to create a network of information centered around concepts and key terms. For example, the old version of the SBA regulation has a large chunk organized around the concept of eligibility, which is of course a topic of great importance to the agency. This definitional network is based on patterns of

Table 3. Critical Differences Between Old and Revised Documents

Kind of Document	Writers' Goal	Strategy	Example	Consequence
Old Documents	To Teach Information	Develop a Concept-Centered Network	Focus on "Eligibility"	A Definition
Revised Documents	To Help the Reader Act	Develop a Human-Centered Network	Focus on "the Borrower"	A Scenario

classical definition with particular use of categorical definition and the listing of attributes. Nominalizations predominate along with passive constructions and non-human subjects of clauses. The revised regulations, on the other hand, try to create a human-centered network of information focused on human agents and their actions, such as borrowers who live in the United States and promise to repay loans; it is this strategy which we have been calling the scenario principle.

Although the scenario principle seems to be the height of common sense, it is not fully or commonly recognized in most revision methods. For example, a scenario structure is a more specific and rigorous constraint than the "human interest" factor scored by Flesch's readability formula, which counts the number of persons, personal pronouns, and gender-specific references. Scenarios are concerned with the active role humans play in the world that the regulation depicts. Furthermore, the scenario principle goes beyond the recommendations made by psycholinguists and technical writing texts, which urge writers to transform passive expressions. The research on passives generally pays little attention to whether the subject of the new active sentence is a person or a thing [8]. However, the scenario principle says that in documents such as regulations, or contracts which demand performance, expert revisers create a human agent.

To sum up, we think that this exploratory analysis of the use of agents, actions, and situations by both writers and readers points toward a principle for revising documents such as regulations. This principle, which we call the scenario principle, meets our goal of being simple and powerful — used alone this principle can improve prose significantly. In addition, unlike readability measures, it can deal with overall organization and can produce reader-based revisions. This is not, of course, to discount the importance of revising for familiar words and shorter sentences, but to suggest a companion principle that does what readability formulas can't do.

PRACTICAL REVISION STRATEGIES

A principle for revising functional documents is only as good as it is useful. Although the notion of a scenario principle obviously needs further and more detailed linguistic analysis, the overriding purpose of this study was to look for a *practical principle* by which people could make reader-based revisions. Such a principle needs to be flexible (unlike the rule "Always avoid the passive voice," which is not always appropriate). And it needs to draw on the intuitions of practicing writers in business and government and to lead to revision of all levels, i.e., not only phrases and sentences, but the overall organization of the document.

We believe that we have found such a principle in the scenario principle, which states that revisers should structure information around *human agents* performing *actions* in particularized *situations*. In the following paragraphs, we will explain some of the specific ways in which revisers can apply the scenario principle at three different levels in functional documents: the top level, the local level, and the grammatical level.

Top Level

Organize around action, not terms — Because such functional documents allow people to make decisions and take actions, they should be organized where possible around the actions people take rather than around key terms. For example, a discussion organized around the decision, "How to decide if you are eligible," will be more understandable than a definitional discussion of eligibility. The information would remain the same, but its comprehensibility would increase.

Organize around the reader's questions — The top-level structure should in many cases be designed to answer the reader's questions. Good writing creates a context for its information, introducing new facts in light of old, answering questions, and fulfilling expectations. With functional documents this is particularly important since readers normally come to them with a purpose; they read to find answers to their own questions. We could imagine that there is a general set of questions people bring to most documents, such as: What is this about? To whom does it apply? What do I have to do? However, elementary research into the needs of actual users can often reveal many questions which are specific to a particular document. For example, Siegel and Gale, a firm which specializes in writing and designing commercial documents, conducts such research prior to revision. On one loan agreement, they discovered that one of the questions borrowers most frequently asked was, "Can I repay the loan early?" Yet this information was buried in the previous loan form because it was not critical to the writer, the bank.

Use headings with a human focus — Headings should accommodate the reader's search for needed information. They can do that if they 1) contain an agent or action, or 2) state or answer a question the reader will have. The headings in many current functional documents are meaningful to an agency reader, but not to a user reader. Or, they contain "miscues" which actually mislead the reader about the kind of information provided in the sections that the headings label [9].

Local Level

Give examples and cases — Giving examples and cases is a simple but space-consuming way to apply the scenario principle. In revising an insurance policy, Siegel and Gale drew the following case from the company's files to vividly illustrate the notion of "Broader Coverage" offered by the policy:

> You've boarded your neighbors' poodle while they're away on vacation. You're careless and the poodle runs away and gets lost. Your neighbors insist on your paying for the loss. If he was an ordinary poodle worth say $400, you pay $200 and we pay $200. But if he was a prize-winning show dog worth $4,000, you pay $250 and we pay $3,750.

Another, briefer version of this would be a short example interpolated into the prose, as in, "In addition, certain non-students (such as doctors serving as interns or residents) . . . "

There are, however, problems in using extended examples since some researchers have suggested that given the opportunity, readers prefer the example to the discussion and mistakenly assume that the example represents the range of the given term's meaning. In their income tax forms, Sweden has dealt with this problem by using elaborate scenarios and examples which cover the major typical categories of people who fill out income tax forms. Due in part to the clearly dramatized style of the instructions which accompany the tax forms (they look like the Sunday comics), a large percentage of Swedish taxpayers are able to fill out their own forms. The minority who don't fit in the typical cases must then turn to more complex instructions [Anna-Lena Ericsson, personal communication, 1979].

Use condition/action statements — Here is an example from the HEAL regulation which defines the "borrower's obligations" in terms of a concrete situation and the subsequent actions people take: "If the lender agrees to make the loan and if the Commissioner of Education approves the loan for HEAL insurance, the applicant must then sign a promissory note."

Use operational definitions — When possible, writers should use operational definitions which describe the meaning of a concept in practical, operational terms. Such definitions, much like a recipe, spell out the procedures for creating or attaining the thing defined. For example, HEAL defines eligibility in such a way that the reader can clearly determine whether he or she is eligible, and if not eligible, see the steps one would have to take to become so: "Eligibility: He or she must be carrying or plan to carry, during the period for which the loan is intended, the normal workload of a full-time student as determined by the school."

Grammatical Level

Write sentences with agents and actions in the subject and verb positions –
Our research indicates the importance of using agents and actions at all levels of
a functional document, including the individual sentences. In an important
article on the revision of functional documents in general, Williams has argued
for the value of making agents and grammatical subjects coincide [10].

Make the agents human agents – We feel it is particularly important to use
human agents, especially in regulations. Generally such documents are designed
to regulate the actions of the reader, but it is difficult for the reader to identify
his or her own role as agent when the prose doesn't. For example, one section
of the SBA regulation was organized around a long list of failures (such as
"failure to reasonably pursue commercial and competitive business in accordance
with the business plan projection"), when the real purpose was to threaten dire
consequences "if you [the reader] fail to pursue commercial, competitive
business according to the business plan you projected." On this count the
HEAL regulation set a fine precedent by setting up in the prose a Commissioner
who "approves" loans, "signs" documents, and "must be satisfied" at various
times. The SBA's constant reference to "an applicant concern" and "a section
8(a) business concern" was a step in the right direction, but one which many of
our readers found confusing and only on the borderline of "human."

AN UNANSWERED QUESTION

This study raises a provocative question: how far should we generalize the
value of the scenario principle? A working hypothesis that emerges from the
studies we describe in this essay is that scenarios are particularly appropriate for
functional documents, such as regulations, which people need to read in order to
act. As one way of testing this hypothesis we collected more reading protocols
from twenty subjects who read a passage of difficult prose under two conditions.
In the first condition the readers were instructed to verbalize their thoughts as
they tried to read and understand a passage *from a textbook*. In the second
condition the subjects were again instructed to verbalize their thoughts, but
were told that the passage (same passage) was one which they would have to
explain to someone else. One hypothesis in this experiment was that the
readers with the prospect of explaining these rules would behave like regulation
readers and resort to more scenarios than the textbook readers. However, in
fact, both groups behaved much like the first group of regulation readers, using
scenarios in about 40 per cent to 50 per cent of their clauses. Perhaps scenarios
are simply a way people translate any sort of difficult prose in an attempt to
make it comprehensible.

Support for this notion and for the general importance of scenarios comes
from an unexpected source. According to many rhetoric and composition
handbooks, for example those by Hairston [11] and McCrimmon [12],

scenarios are a pervasive feature of English prose, although from the handbook point of view they are a fault and are labeled as a "faulty complement" or "faulty predicate." An example would be, "Subversive propaganda is *when* someone tries to turn people against their country." Propaganda cannot technically be a "when," but perhaps the persistence of this fault of style is simply an indication of the importance of scenarios as a pattern with which people think.

CONCLUSION

This study had two goals. The first was to explore the kinds of "revision" readers make in their attempt to understand a difficult functional document. One of these revision strategies — the scenario principle — appears to have both theoretical interest and practical value for document writers. Our second, broader goal was to suggest that readability alone is an inadequate way to measure the effectiveness of much technical writing. The focus of new research, we believe, should be on the overall comprehensibility of the document, or on what Wright has called its usability [13]. This means that writers and revisers must find ways to create a reader-based structure of information in a text designed around its function, and around the comprehension strategies readers bring to it.

REFERENCES

1. L. S. Flower and J. R. Hayes, A Process Model of Composition, Document Design Project Technical Report No. 1, American Institutes for Research, Washington, D.C., 1979. (Also in *Cognitive Processes in Writing,* L. W. Gregg and E. R. Steinberg (eds.), Lawrence Erlbaum, Hillsdale, New Jersey, 1980.)
2. Y. Waern, *Thinking Aloud During Reading: A Descriptive Model and its Application,* Department of Psychology Report No. 546, University of Stockholm, Stockholm, Sweden, 1979.
3. R. J. Bobrow and J. S. Brown, Systematic Understanding: Synthesis, Analysis, and Contingent Knowledge in Specialized Understanding Systems, *Prepresentation and Understanding: Studies in Cognitive Science,* D. G. Bobrow and A. Collins (eds.), Academic Press, New York, pp. 103-129, 1975.
4. P. Wright, Feeding the Information Eaters: Suggestions for Integrating Pure and Applied Research on Language Comprehension, *Instructional Science,* 7, pp. 249-312, 1978.
5. D. G. Bobrow and D. A. Norman, Some Principles of Memory Schemata, *Representation and Understanding: Studies in Cognitive Science,* D. G. Bobrow and A. Collins (eds.), Academic Press, New York, pp. 131-149, 1975.
6. L. Flower, Writer-Based Prose: A Cognitive Basis for Problems in Writing, *College English, 41,* pp. 19-37, 1979.

7. R. P. Kern, T. G. Sticht, D. Welty, and R. N. Hauke, *Guidebook for the Development of Army Training Literature*, U. S. Army Institute for the Behavioral and Social Sciences, Human Resources Research Organization, Washington, D.C., November 1976.
8. H. H. Clark and E. V. Clark, *Psychology and Language: An Introduction to Psycholinguistics*, Harcourt Brace Jovanovich, Inc., New York, 1977.
9. H. Swarts, L. S. Flower, and J. R. Hayes, How to Misread a Federal Regulation, paper presented at the meeting of the American Educational Research Association, Boston, Massachusetts, 1980.
10. J. M. Williams, Defining Complexity, *College English, 40,* pp. 595-609, 1979.
11. M. Hairston, *A Contemporary Rhetoric*, Houghton Mifflin, Boston, Massachusetts, 1974.
12. J. M. McCrimmon, *Writing with a Purpose*, Houghton Mifflin, Boston, Massachusetts, 1963.
13. P. Wright, Usability: The Criterion for Designing Written Information, paper presented at the NATO Conference on Visible Language, Toronto, 1979.

CHAPTER 3

Topical Focus in Technical Writing

LESTER FAIGLEY
STEPHEN P. WITTE

While teachers of technical writing have long been concerned with the efficient transmission of information, little research has addressed what particular discourse features influence efficient communication. By and large, analyses of discourse features in technical writing have been informed by linguistic theory aimed at describing sentences, not whole pieces of discourse. Gopnik, for example, based her linguistic study of scientific texts on transformational grammar, providing extensive data on the types of syntactic structures in scientific writing but offering little explanation of why particular structures are used [1]. As a consequence, such studies have not had much impact on teaching students which discourse strategies to use.

In contrast to the predominant sentence-level orientation of American linguistics (in both its structural and transformational phases), European linguists have studied for many years linguistic phenomena beyond sentence boundaries. Especially important has been the work of Mathesius and his followers in the Prague School [2]. Mathesius was among the first to show that the surface structure of individual sentences in a text cannot be fully explained without reference to their textual setting. Among other things, Mathesius demonstrated that the variation among four Slavic passives is conditioned by the topic the speaker wishes to emphasize. Members of the Prague School such as Daneš [3], Sgall, Hajičová, and Benešová [4], and other linguists [5, 6], have pointed out that in addition to having syntactic structures, texts have a topical structure that carries the theme or topic through the text and that controls the placement of information relevant to the topic.

One way in which the topic of a written text is carried through that text is by means of topical subjects, which may or may not correspond to the grammatical subjects of sentences. Consider the following short text.

1. The Tupolev TU-144 was first seen by the Western World at the Paris Air Show in 1971.
2. The TU-144 was demonstrated during the show in 1973.
3. The TU-144 met with disaster during the demonstration.
4. It crashed, killing its crew of six and several people on the ground.

There can be no doubt that the main topic of this short text is the TU-144; neither can there be much doubt that the topical subject of each sentence is "TU-144" (or "It"), which corresponds to the grammatical subjects of the sentences. Now consider another short text. This text delivers essentially the same content as the text represented by 1 through 4 but differs from it in important ways.

5. The Western World first saw the Tupolev TU-144 at the Paris Air Show in 1971.
6. In 1973, the Show featured a demonstration of the TU-144.
7. The demonstration of the TU-144 met with disaster.
8. When the TU-144 crashed, its crew of six and several people on the ground were killed.

In this short text, the grammatical subjects are, respectively, "The Western World," "the Show," "The demonstration of the TU-144," and "crew . . . people." As with 1 through 4, the main topic of this text is again the TU-144. However, the grammatical subjects of 5 through 8 cannot be said to carry this main topic through the text in exactly the same way as the grammatical subjects of 1 through 4 carry the topic through that text. The topical focus, as well as the grammatical subjects, of the two texts differs. Even the grammatical subject of 7 — "The demonstration of the TU-144" — differs in important ways from the grammatical subjects of 1 through 4. Given the textual context of the other three sentences, the topical subject of 5 seems to be "the Tupolev TU-144," of 6 "a demonstration of the TU-144," of 7. "The demonstration of the TU-144," and of 8 "the TU-144." These topics seem to represent the most important elements in the respective sentences, but only one corresponds to a grammatical subject of a main clause. If our intuitive response to the sentences in these two texts can be trusted, then the topic of a sentence can be different from its grammatical subject.

Recently, another line of research has begun to explore whether there are surface features that cue readers to the topic of the text as a whole. Such features become important if the reader is unfamiliar with the concepts in a text. David Kieras has conducted a series of experiments in which readers were asked to name the "main idea" of a passage they had just read [7–9]. Kieras used macrostructure theory developed by Kintsch and van Dijk to represent the main idea or "topic" of test passages [10]. Macrostructure theory describes a set of processes which reduce the content of a text to a small number of macropropositions which express the main idea or topic of the passage. Kieras found that readers make use of surface signals to identify the main idea in passages with unfamiliar content. Readers were much more likely to identify the main idea when it was verbalized in the initial sentence than when it appeared in a non-initial sentence. Kieras also demonstrated that the structure of a passage affects how much readers remember about it [8].

The present study sought to bring together these two lines of research. We wanted to know if consistent assignment of a particular topic to grammatical subject positions would affect what readers consider as the topic of the passage. Second, we wanted to find out if assignment of a particular topic to grammatical subject positions would affect how much readers recall about the passage.

METHOD

Subjects

Fifty-one students enrolled in sophomore-level technical writing classes at the University of Texas participated in the experiment. All the students were native speakers of English, and all had previously completed two college-level writing courses.

Materials

Three passages, differing primarily in the topical focus of individual sentences, were written for the experiment. The passages were developed to control for content, high-level organization, and other variables. The information in the three passages was adapted from a popular history of aircraft [11]. All three passages had the same first paragraph, which provided a general introduction. One passage (which we will refer to as "Airliners") places the names of airliners in the grammatical subject slots in all the sentences (except those in the first paragraph). The grammatical subject was either the first sentence element or the first element after an adverbial phrase that provided a transition.

AIRLINERS

Immediately after the end of World War II, the American aviation industry began making the transition from military to civilian aircraft. Airlines needed planes for a new generation of passengers who had become accustomed to fast transportation during the war. The major

aircraft manufacturers — Douglas, Lockheed, and Boeing — were ready
with airliner designs the moment the war ended.

The DC-3, a symbol of American commercial aircraft before, during,
and after the war, was built by Douglas. Thousands of these airliners were
manufactured by them for wartime transport and cargo use. Wartime
surplus C-47's (peacetime's DC-3's) were sold cheaply to the new airlines
that sprang up after the war ended.

The C-54 Skymaster was another plane which Douglas had intended for
commercial airline use but was snatched up by the Air Force in 1942
instead. The C-54 was designed by Douglas to be three times the size of
the DC-3. The Skymaster returned to its original civilian dress in 1945 as
the Douglas DC-4.

The C-69, a plane even more advanced than the DC-4, became the
Constellation when Lockheed put the plane into commercial service. The
Constellation flew the first scheduled round-the-world flight in 1949,
carrying Lockheed officials.

The 377 Stratocruiser was first sold to commercial airlines by Boeing
in 1949. The 377 could accommodate sixty-one first-class passengers in
Boeing's original design, complete with private staterooms and sleeper
service on nonstop flights from New York to London and Paris. The 377
was eventually replaced with Boeing's first commercial jet aircraft.

In the second passage (which we will call "Manufacturers"), the names of the
airplane manufacturers occupy the grammatical subject slots in all but one
sentence after the first paragraph.

MANUFACTURERS

Immediately after the end of World War II, the American aviation
industry began making the transition from military to civilian aircraft.
Airlines needed planes for a new generation of passengers who had
become accustomed to fast transportation during the war. The major
aircraft manufacturers — Douglas, Lockheed, and Boeing — were ready
with airliner designs the moment the war ended.

Douglas built the DC-3, a plane which became the symbol of American
commercial aircraft before, during and after the war. They manufactured
thousands of these airliners for wartime transport and cargo use. The new
airlines that sprang up were able to purchase the wartime C-47's (peacetime's DC-3's) at low prices when the war ended.

Douglas also manufactured the C-54 Skymaster, which they had
intended for commercial airline use but was snatched up by the Air Force
in 1942 instead. Douglas designed the C-54 to be three times the size of
the DC-3. Douglas returned the plane to its original civilian dress as the
DC-4 in 1945.

Lockheed converted their C-69, a plane even more advanced than the
DC-4, to the Constellation when the plane went into commercial service.
Lockheed officials flew in a Constellation on the first scheduled round-the-
world flight in 1949.

Boeing first sold the 377 Stratocruiser to the commercial airlines in 1949. Boeing designed the 377 to accommodate sixty-one first-class passengers, complete with private staterooms and sleeper service on nonstop flights from New York to London and Paris. Boeing eventually replaced the 377 with its first commercial jet aircraft.

The third passage ("The Mixed Passage") incorporated sentences alternately from "Airliners" and "Manufacturers," giving both planes and manufacturers an equal share of the grammatical subject slots after the first paragraph. Just as in the "Airliners" passage, the grammatical subject was either the first sentence element or the first element after an adverbial phrase that provided a transition.

THE MIXED PASSAGE

Immediately after the end of World War II, the American aviation industry began making the transition from military to civilian aircraft. Airlines needed planes for a new generation of passengers who had become accustomed to fast transportation during the war. The major aircraft manufacturers – Douglas, Lockheed, and Boeing – were ready with airliner designs the moment the war ended.

Douglas built the DC-3, a plane which became the symbol of American commercial aircraft before, during and after the war. Thousands of these airliners were manufactured by them for wartime transport and cargo use. The new airlines that sprang up were able to purchase the wartime C-47's (peacetime's DC-3's) at low prices when the war ended.

The C-54 Skymaster was another plane which Douglas had intended for commercial airline use but was snatched up by the Air Force in 1942 instead. Douglas designed the C-54 to be three times the size of the DC-3. The Skymaster returned to its original civilian dress in 1945 as the Douglas DC-4.

Lockheed converted their C-69, a plane even more advanced than the DC-4, to the Constellation when the plane went into commercial service. The Constellation flew the first scheduled round-the-world flight in 1949, carrying Lockheed officials.

Boeing first sold the 377 Stratocruiser to the commercial airlines in 1949. The 377 could accommodate sixty-one first-class passengers in Boeing's original design, complete with private staterooms and sleeper service on nonstop flights from New York to London and Paris. Boeing eventually replaced the 377 with its first commercial jet aircraft.

Procedure

The experiment was conducted in three technical writing classes. Test booklets were randomly distributed to the fifty-one students. These booklets were identical except that a third contained "Airliners," a third contained "Manufacturers," and a third contained "The Mixed Passage." None of the passages had titles. The students were instructed to read carefully the passage they received and were informed that they would be asked questions about their passage later. They were told, however, not to read their passage more than once. After the students finished reading, they worked a word puzzle as an interruptive task prior to their being tested for specific knowledge of the passage. All students spent at least two minutes on the word puzzle.

The students were then asked to write a phrase that would serve as the title for the passage. This task has been used successfully by Kieras in experiments testing how the organization of a passage affects what readers perceive as the topic of that passage [7–9]. Next the students were asked to recall as much information as they could about the passage they read. Finally, they were asked to name the four planes and three manufacturers discussed in the passage. The latter two tasks tested for how much students remembered about the passage.

Scoring

We scored the protocols with the help of a student research assistant. Each protocol was independently scored two times, and the few discrepancies between raters were easily resolved. The protocols were analyzed in three steps. First, we devised a classification for the students' statements of the main idea in each passage. Three categories were defined. The first category included titles exclusively naming the planes, such as "A Brief History of Commercial Airliners" and "Commercial Aircraft after World War II." The second category included titles solely concerned with the manufacturers. Examples of the second category are "United States Aircraft Companies" and "Commercial Plane Manufacturers after World War II." The majority of titles fell into a third category. Those titles stated as the main idea the transition from military to civilian aircraft. All of these titles contained either a verb or a nominalized verb. Examples included "Conversion of Boeing, Lockheed and Douglas Planes to Commercial Airliners," "Aircraft Transformation from Wartime to Commercial," "The Development of War Planes into Commercial Planes after World War II," and "Converting Wartime Planes to Peacetime Use."

Second, we analyzed all three passages into propositions, following procedures employed in other discourse comprehension studies [12]. Propositions are semantic units which contain a relation and one or more arguments. Relations include predicates (verbs, set relations, and references), modifiers (qualifiers, quantifiers, partitives, and negations), and connections (conjunction, disjunction, causality, purpose, concession, contrast, condition, and circumstance). Arguments are analyzed using Fillmore's case grammar system [13]: agent (A), experiencer (E), instrument (I), object (O), source (S), and goal (G). Below is a propositional analysis for the first sentence in each passage. (Because propositions can be embedded within other propositions, the argument of a proposition is sometimes represented with the number of another proposition embedded within it.)

1. (MAKE: A: AVIATION INDUSTRY, G: TRANSITION)
2. (BEGAN: 1)
3. (QUALIFY: WWII, END)
4. (TIME: AFTER, 3)
5. (TIME: IMMEDIATELY, 4, 3)
6. (QUALITY OF: AVIATION INDUSTRY, AMERICAN)
7. (QUALITY OF: AIRCRAFT, MILITARY)
8. (QUALITY OF: AIRCRAFT, CIVILIAN)
9. (QUALIFY: FROM, 7, TO, 8)

The three test passages contain nearly the same number of propositions ("Airliners"=132, "Manufacturers"=127, "Mixed Passage"=132). We computed the number of correct propositions in the students' recall protocols. Incorrect or inferred propositions were not counted.

Third, we counted the number of correctly recalled airliners and manufacturers.

RESULTS

The title categories and the number of titles in each category are listed in Table 1. Eleven of the seventeen students who read the passage with the names of the airliners consistently in the grammatical subject position responded with a title in the "Airliners" category, such as "Commercial Airline History." Most students who read the "Manufacturers" passage and the "Mixed" passage supplied titles in the "Conversion" category, stressing the transformation of the airliners from military to civilian use. These differences are significant beyond the .0001 level in a Pearson chi-square analysis (43.06, 6 df) and a likelihood ratio chi-square analysis (44.93, 6 df).

Differences in propositions correctly recalled and names of airliners and manufacturers recalled did not prove to be significant in an analysis of variance. Means for the airliners and manufacturers correctly recalled are reported in Table 2. Only the difference in the number of manufacturers recalled approached significance ($F = 2.08$, $p = .136$).

Table 1. Distribution of Titles Given According to Passage Read

	Category of Title Given		
Passage Read	Airliners	Manufacturers	Conversion
Airliners	11	1	5
Manufacturers	2	3	12
Mixed	2	0	15

Table 2. Mean Number of Names Recalled According to Passage Read

	Mean Number of Names Recalled	
Passage Read	Airliners' Names	Manufacturers' Names
Airliners	2.4	2.2
Manufacturers	2.4	2.8
Mixed	1.8	2.8

DISCUSSION

The results strongly suggest that consistent assignment of a particular topic to the grammatical subject position does influence what readers perceive as the topic of a passage. The results presented in Table 1, however, at first seem anomalous. The names of the airliners appear to have had a strong effect when they occupied grammatical subject slots. On the other hand, the effect of the names of the manufacturers seems minimal. One possible explanation is that the airliners can be discussed as separate entities in the present context while the manufacturers are largely described in terms of what they did — convert wartime airplanes to peacetime airplanes. A more plausible explanation can be made by applying Kieras' findings to the present experiment. Kieras showed that most readers will select the first idea in a passage as the main idea unless that idea proves to be inconsistent with body of the passage [7—9]. All passages began with the same sentence: "Immediately after the end of World War II, the American aviation industry began making the transition from military to civilian aircraft." According to Kieras' theory and other recent theories of text processing, such as that of Kintsch and van Dijk [10], readers expect the first sentence in a passage to be thematic. "The American aviation industry" occupies the subject position in the first sentence; thus, subjects who read the "Manufacturers" passage or the "Mixed" passage by and large paraphrased the first sentence as the main idea of the passage. The consistent placement of the names of the airliners in grammatical subject slots, however, appears to have caused readers to reject the first sentence as the subject of the passage, replacing it instead with "airliners."

The data concerning facts recalled is more difficult to interpret because differences failed to reach significant levels. The greatest difference is in the number of manufacturers recalled. It may be that students given the "Manufacturers" passage better remembered the airliners because they most frequently appeared as direct objects (e.g., "Douglas built the DC-3"). In contrast, the "Airliners" passage included the manufacturers as modifiers or in passive constructions.

The implication for writers of complicated texts is clearly that the dominant subject matter should be kept in the topical focus as the grammatical subject of the main clause. Even in a text with a relatively clear overall organization, a reader may lose sight of topic if the topic is not kept in the grammatical subject position.

The present study also has several implications for further research in technical writing. As we have pointed out above, little research in technical communication has considered the effect on comprehension of discourse structures above the sentence level. Most of the research in technical communication related to comprehension centers on sentence length and level of vocabulary – ignoring relationships that span sentence boundaries. Popular indices of readability such as the Flesch measure [14], however, have not proven to be reliable measures of ease of comprehension, as Selzer points out in another essay in this volume. Indeed, a recent study aimed at simplifying instructions issued to jurors has found the Flesch measure inversely related to ease of comprehension [15]. The present study demonstrates the need for more research in how readers understand the topic of a given passage and how writers can signal readers about what information is important.

REFERENCES

1. M. Gopnik, *Linguistic Structures in Scientific Texts*, Mouton, The Hague, 1972.
2. J. Vachek, *The Linguistic School of Prague*, Indiana University Press, Bloomington, Indiana, 1966.
3. F. Daneš (ed.), *Papers on Functional Sentence Perspective*, Academia, Prague, 1974.
4. P. Sgall, E. Hajičová, and E. Benešová, *Topic, Focus, and Generative Semantics*, Sciptor, Kronberg, 1973.
5. M. A. K. Halliday, Notes on Transitivity and Theme in English, Part 2, *Journal of Linguistics, 3*, pp. 199-244, 1967.
6. W. Chafe, Givenness, Contrastiveness, Definiteness, Subject, Topic, and Point of View, in *Subject and Topic*, C. Li (ed.), Academic Press, New York, 1976.
7. D. E. Kieras, Initial Mention as a Signal to Thematic Content in Technical Passages, *Memory & Cognition, 8*, pp. 345-353, 1980.
8. D. E. Kieras, Good and Bad Structure in Simple Paragraphs: Effects on Apparent Theme, Reading Time, and Recall, *Journal of Verbal Learning and Verbal Behavior, 17*, pp. 13-28, 1978.
9. D. E. Kieras, The Role of Major Referents and Sentence Topics in the Construction of Passage Macrostructure, *Discourse Processes, 4*, pp. 1-15, 1981.
10. W. Kintsch and T. A. van Dijk, Toward a Model of Discourse Comprehension and Production, *Psychological Review, 85*, pp. 363-394, 1978.
11. E. Jablonski, *Man with Wings*, Doubleday, Garden City, New York, 1980.

12. A. Turner and E. Greene, *The Construction and Use of a Propositional Text Base,* Technical Report No. 63, Institute for the Study of Intellectual Behavior, University of Colorado, Boulder, Colorado, 1977.
13. C. Fillmore, The Case for Case, in *Universals in Linguistic Theory,* E. Bach and R. Harms (eds.), Holt, Rinehart, & Winston, New York, pp. 1-88, 1968.
14. R. Flesch, A New Readability Yardstick, *Journal of Applied Psychology, 32,* pp. 221-233, 1948.
15. R. P. Charrow and V. R. Charrow, Making Legal Language Understandable: A Psycholinguistic Study of Jury Instructions, *Columbia Law Review, 79,* pp. 1306-1374, 1979.

PART TWO

Reassessing Readability

CHAPTER 4

What Constitutes a "Readable" Technical Style?

JACK SELZER

Advice about style in technical writing derives ultimately from two sources. One — the long tradition of the plain style — has influenced the style of technical writing since Bacon and the birth of the scientific revolution [1]. The second — readability formulas — has influenced technical writing much more recently. Invented after World War I and designed to help elementary school teachers estimate the difficulty of reading materials intended for their students, readability formulas became very popular in the early 1950's after Rudolph Flesch and Robert Gunning developed and popularized formulas that could easily and inexpensively gauge the difficulty of written prose (see Figure 1). Like other readability researchers before them, Flesch and Gunning suggested that the difficulty of a text depends upon two variables: sentence length and word length. Unlike other readability experts, though, Flesch and Gunning were enormously influential. Their formulas, their extensive consulting work, their impact on other readability popularizers, and Flesch's best-selling book, *The Art of Readable Writing* [4], together changed the face of educational and business materials, journalism — and technical writing.

Many of the handbooks, textbooks, and journal articles on technical writing link their advice about style to readability formulas. For instance, Houp and Pearsall's popular *Reporting Technical Information* [5], like many other texts that it helped inspire, cites Flesch and other work in readability at length to

---

FLESCH'S READING EASE SCALE [2]

Reading Ease = 206.835 - .846 wl - 1.015 sl

where wl = number of syllables per 100 words
sl = average number of words per sentence

(Reading Ease corresponds to a number between 0 and 100, with 100
representing the easiest reading.)

GUNNING'S FOG INDEX [3]

Reading Grade Level = .4 (ASL + %PW)

where ASL = average sentence length
%PW = percentage of polysyllabic words

Figure 1. Two popular readability formulas.

justify its adages about style. Steven Pauley's *Technical Report Writing Today*
discusses in depth Gunning's Fog Index in its very first chapter [6]. An industry
writing manual on my desk — and a good one — punctuates its entire discussion
of style with approving references to readability research; in fact, it devotes one
entire chapter (out of nine) to a review of the work of Flesch, Gunning, and
other researchers [7]. George Klare, one of the most familiar names in
readability research, has published an article in *Technical Communication* on
readability and style [8]. And in *The Technical Writing Teacher,* David L.
Carson asserts that "readability formulas are still important adjuncts to the
writer in assessing the aptness of a prose style for the reading level of its
intended audience." [9, p. 9, 10]

In short, readability has become the criterion for judging style in technical
writing. That much does not concern me because reading comprehensibility and
reader efficiency seem to me particularly defensible goals for technical writing,
especially in light of E. D. Hirsch's advocacy of "relative readability" as a
criterion for assessing the quality of *all* writing [11]. What does concern me is
that, in giving advice to writers about style, we have often misused some
readability studies and overlooked others. Indeed, a close review of the recent
literature on readability reveals several important things: that we have jumped to

some hasty conclusions about what constitutes a readable technical style, especially conclusions about sentence length and word length; that we need to consider other factors besides sentence and word length when we give advice about style; and that there are promising new opportunities for research into the factors that make writing more or less readable. In the following pages, after I define readability, I want to defend in detail each of those propositions.

DEFINING READABILITY

Before turning to specific issues in readability, let me define my use of the term, for "readability" has been used in several different senses. As George Klare established in the "Introduction" to his important 1963 review of early research on readability, "the term *readability* has come to be used in three ways:

1. To indicate legibility of either handwriting or typography;
2. To indicate ease of reading due to either the interest-value or the pleasantness of writing;
3. To indicate ease of understanding or comprehension due to the style of writing." [12, p. 1]

Thomas Curran has suggested a fourth definition, one that distinguishes readability from comprehensibility. To Curran, readability is a text-based notion that denotes what is measured by readability formulas; comprehensibility, a reader-based concept that includes elements not considered by the formulas, refers to how efficiently a passage is understood by readers [13]. But the vast majority of researchers have followed Klare's lead: they have identified readability with comprehensibility. Thus, you will find Klare's third definition followed throughout this essay: "ease of understanding or comprehension due to the style of writing." In other words, readability is simply the efficiency with which a text can be comprehended by a reader, as measured by reading time, amount recalled, questions answered, or some other quantifiable measure of a reader's ability to process a text (such measures change from study to study).

SENTENCE LENGTH AND WORD LENGTH

Several traditional notions about technical style have recently come under fire. Where once the use of the passive voice was defended as "objective" and impersonal, nearly every style guide now allows, if not encourages, the use of the active voice. Similarly, Paul Anderson [14] and Merrill Whitburn [15] have worked to end the fictions surrounding the "impersonal" style. Personal pronouns once *verboten* now find their way routinely into scientific journals, research reports, and procedures manuals.

But at least one traditional notion remains unchallenged: we still advise writers that, other things being equal, a piece of technical writing will be better if its sentences and words are short. Encouraged by readability formulas like Flesch's, which correlate sentence length, word length, and reading difficulty, we continue to advise writers, "to communicate the most, use small words and short sentences" — as the readability-inspired industry writing manual I cited earlier puts it [7, pp. 3-7]. In the same way, Houp and Pearsall — using readability research as their authority — encourage writers to "hold your sentence length down" [5, p. 168], and inform them that "excessive word length is a significant factor in reducing reader understanding." [5, p. 177] Mills and Walter's influential and respected textbook, *Technical Writing*, in arguing that "you should . . . be careful about the length of your sentences," alludes directly to Flesch's work when it asserts that "the amount of difficulty a person experiences in reading a given text is positively correlated with sentence length and number of syllables per word. Research indicates that the average sentence length should probably not exceed twenty words." [16, p. 45] Andrew K. Clark agreed in a 1975 IEEE presentation: "Readability research tells us . . . that when we use longer sentences, . . . our writing becomes increasingly difficult to understand." [17, p. 69] George Klare's 1977 essay in *Technical Communication* advises us that "shorter words (versus longer) tend to make reading easier and faster" and that "shortened sentences . . . contribute to more readable writing." [8, p. 3] David L. Carson has recently summarized the situation succinctly: technical writing teachers have "accept[ed] the two most useful bits of information the [readability] tests have produced. For better reader comprehension, use short sentences and short words." [9, p. 9, 10]

However, such unqualified suggestions that technical writers should use short sentences are misguided, I contend. Contrary to oft-quoted opinion, there is no evidence that shortening sentences will make writing more comprehensible. And there are good reasons to amend the advice about short words, as well.

The belief that long sentences and words produce difficult writing arose out of a confusion between correlation and causation, between the *prediction* of readable writing and the *production* of it. Researchers and educators are divided on the question of whether the formulas reliably *predict* readable writing, especially writing intended for adults. On the one hand, George Klare is convinced that "as far as most kinds of prediction studies go, . . . readability formulas stand up very well." [18, p. 131] He points out that the Army and other government agencies have required — presumably on the basis of satisfactory results — that documents pass readability tests [8]. Indeed, the proceedings of a 1976 conference on readability research in the armed services demonstrate the government's longstanding and firm confidence in the predictive value of readability formulas [19]. On the other hand, Klare also acknowledges (with some understatement) that "reading is too complex for any formula to predict readability with perfect accuracy." [8, p. 2] Walter Kintsch and Douglas Vipond also assert that the formulas measure too few factors to be very accurate [20]. Jeanne S. Chall has made a strong case that validity correlations are too low (they range from .5 to .7) to warrant the use of the formulas [21]. And several studies have shown how the readability of certain texts has been unreliably predicted by formulas. The most famous is Wilson Taylor's demonstration that according to formulas, Erskine Caldwell's *Georgia Boy* is more difficult than Gertrude Stein's *Geography and Plays* – and not easier than *Finnegans Wake* [22] ! More recently, in 1970 Deborah Schwartz, John Sparkman, and James Deese found that "the Flesch count produce[s] some unsatisfactory results, showing, for example, sentences sampled from [James Gould] Cozzens to be more readable than those from popular magazines . . . , [even though] Cozzens is notorious for having a turgid prose style often characterized by tangled syntax. . . . The casual reader can probably make a judgment that has a higher validity (and reliability) than can be achieved by resorting to a clumsy, statistical word count." [23, p. 91] In 1979, R. P. Charrow and J. R. Charrow found that Flesch scores correlated *inversely* with the comprehensibility of jury instructions [24]. However, it is probably still too early to assess the value of formulas for technical documents, since surprisingly little work has been done to test the validity of formulas when they are used to rate technical materials intended for adults.

But whether readability formulas reliably *predict* the readability of technical documents after they are written is really beside the point of this essay. What is important to note is that readability formulas certainly cannot be used to guide the *production* of readable technical documents. Because readability formulas are often based on sentence length and word length, because sentence length and word length may *correlate* with readability, some people have mistakenly assumed that longer sentences and words cause reading difficulty. Flesch himself was one who confused correlation and causation. "If readability measurement is worth anything at all," he wrote, "then the formulas must be usable as tools in preparing readable materials." [25, p. 334]

However, nothing could be further from the truth. Though there may be a correlation between readability and sentence or word length that enables the formulas to be used as indicators, there is no causal relation between them. George Klare stresses that "formulas provide good *indices* of difficulty, but do not indicate causes of difficulty or say how to write readably." [26, p. 62] Thomas Curran emphasizes the same point: "Predicting the difficulty of written material 'after the fact' is a major problem, but equally or more important is the problem of producing 'readable writing' in the first place. For this latter task there is no 'formula' which one can directly apply." [13, p. 194] Psychologist David Pearson also warns about the "common error in interpreting correlational data by assuming that correlation means causality. The fact that sentence length, sentence complexity, or any other factor correlates with . . . difficulty . . . does not imply that altering these correlates will reduce difficulty." [27, p. 160] In short, it makes no more sense to shorten words and sentences to improve readability than it does to hold a lighted match under a thermometer when your house gets cold [8, p. 2].

Short Sentences

Since readability formulas seem to combine the two variables of word difficulty and sentence difficulty, many researchers have hoped that if either sentence or word length alone were varied, comprehension would be affected. However, that hasn't happened, especially in the case of sentence length. In fact, the studies show convincingly that "mere changing of sentence length, a major factor in [the] formulas, does not produce an automatic increase in comprehension." [12, p. 122] For example, Hite's 1950 study concluded that reading "material with short sentences resulted in no increase [in test scores] over that with longer." [12, p. 126] More recently, I. M. Schlesinger prepared several versions of a text that differed only in sentence lengths, assessed their readability by giving subjects comprehension tests, and found that "sentence length seems to have little effect on readability"; in fact, he suggested that "attention should be paid to the possibility of sentences being too short," not just too long [28, pp. 79-80] In 1974, David Pearson reported on several experiments that revealed the same thing: "the data lend no support to the recommendation that the difficulty of written discourse can be reduced by . . . reducing sentence length." [27, p. 189] On the contrary, Pearson found that combining sentences and therefore increasing length can improve comprehension if the two sentences are causally related, a fact that will not surprise many writing teachers. Similarly, when Richard M. Davis lengthened the sentences of a technical passage, he learned to his surprise that subjects' scores on a comprehension test remained the same [29]. Marshall and Glock's 1978 study of the comprehension of connected discourse also showed that shortening sentences does not necessarily improve comprehension [30, p. 54]. Recent studies of legal prose "clearly illustrate that sentence length has virtually no effect on subjects' performance" on comprehension tests [24, p. 1320]. John R. Bormuth of the University of Chicago, perhaps the foremost student of the factors that influence readability (he has investigated over 150 such factors), argues that sentence length does not affect comprehension because it itself is an aggregate of other factors; he concludes that his "studies make it seem virtually certain that the previous practice of attributing grammatical difficulty to sentence length is not only illogical but contrary to fact." [31, p. 53] Finally, in summarizing four decades of readability study, George Klare shows that sentence length has a negligible impact on readability when reader interest is high [18] — as it is typically in technical writing, where documents are written on request and read for use, not entertainment.

One study has shown that lengthening sentences retards readability. E. B. Coleman shortened sentences in a passage according to Flesch's advice,

"Look for the joints where conjunctions are — *if, because, as, and,* and so on — and split your sentences up." [32, p. 131] One of Coleman's findings is often cited by those who advise short sentences: "passages divided into short sentences [fifteen words on the average] were significantly more comprehensible [statistically] than their long sentence [twenty-three words on the average] counterparts." But those same people usually omit Coleman's other findings: that "the magnitude of the improvement was small" (only a single point on the cloze tests used by Coleman to measure comprehension) [32, p. 131]; and that when average sentence length was reduced from thirty-nine to twenty-three words, no statistically significant differences in comprehension were found [32, p. 132].

Thus, while sentence *difficulty* undoubtedly affects readability, sentence *length* does not seem to be the cause of that difficulty. In the words of Marilyn Wang, "it is not length *per se* which makes a sentence difficult to comprehend." [33, p. 403] Or, in Bormuth's words,

> Two major objections can be raised to considering sentence length as the sole factor affecting grammatical complexity. First, it forces us to accept the dubious proposition that all sentences containing the same number of words possess the same degree of complexity. . . . Second, the number of words in a sentence does not measure a natural unit of language. . . . Making a sentence more complex may or may not increase the number of words it contains; and increasing the number of words it contains may or may not increase the complexity of a sentence [34, p. 842].

Should we not conclude from all of this evidence and all of this testimony that it is a mistake to believe that merely shortening sentences will make writing more readable?

Short Words

The question of word length is more complex than that of sentence length. Although "the word or semantic variable is consistently more highly predictive than the sentence or syntactic variable." [26, p. 96], there are very good arguments for rejecting the conventional wisdom that technical writers should simply "use short words."

All students of readability agree with one commonsense observation: if a reader is not familiar with a word, his or her comprehension of a passage will be impeded; conversely, the more familiar a reader is with the words in a passage, the more readable the passage will be. Those who recommend short words, therefore, argue that they are simply more familiar words, more frequently used words. Since words often get shorter as they become more familiar, in the way *examination* tends to get shortened to *exam* or *intercontinental ballistic missile* to *ICBM* (the argument continues), the shorter words are more familiar ones. And those who argue that short words are more familiar and therefore easier to

process can cite research to support their claim. For instance, Bormuth's
exhaustive 1969 study of the factors that affect readability suggests strongly
that word length affects comprehension [31]. That suggestion has been
supported by Ronald Carver [35] and by E. B. Coleman and G. R. Miller [36],
whose work turned up strong correlations between word length and reading
difficulty.

But there are also studies that come to opposite conclusions, studies that
suggest that familiarity is not really related to length at all. For instance,
Seigel, Lambert and Burkett feel strongly that technical writers should attend
to the number of morphemes in a word — and that "the length of the words
themselves does not matter too much." [37, p. 2] (A morpheme is the minimal
unit of sense and structure in language. For instance, *form* has one morpheme;
formal has two; *formalism,* three.) Because of his own study of morphemes and
word length, Coleman agrees: "it simply does not seem reasonable to assume
that reducing the number of letters [in a word] . . . would improve
comprehensibility as much as reducing the number of morphemes." [38, p. 177]
Perhaps more important, a recent experiment by David Doggett and Larry G.
Richards questioned whether word familiarity and comprehension were affected
by length. They concluded that "word length influences recognition thresholds
if the words are unfamiliar, but not if they are familiar" [39, p. 583]; in other
words, "if [a person] knows a word, . . . then length has no effect." [39, p. 592]
Finally, since 1931 many people have tried unsuccessfully to link word length
directly to reading difficulty. A summary of that research (through 1960) by
Klare recounts six studies that simplified vocabulary in an attempt to improve
reading comprehension. Only one succeeded [12, p. 133].

Moreover, there are other arguments against the proposition that technical
writers should always shorten their words. It is surely misguided, for instance,
to suggest that writers use the average length of words in a passage as a guide.
For the average word length of a passage is often affected much more by the
number of function words (prepositions, articles, conjunctions) and personal
pronouns in it than by the presence of long, difficult content words. That is, a
passage can easily have a low average word length and still be very difficult, if it
contains many prepositions and personal pronouns [40].

In addition, it is not always easy to "use short words." Changing *activate* to
begin, communicate to *write, demonstrate* to *show, in addition* to *too, proceed*
to *go* may involve subtle changes in meaning or tone or sound that a technical
writer may be justifiably reluctant to make — especially since the shorter
member of each pair is probably no more familiar or less difficult to understand.
Put more negatively, the real problem may be the inappropriate formality that
technical writers often strive for (sometimes in an attempt to sound more
"professional"), rather than word length *per se.* We can still object to barbarisms
like *utilize* and *administrate,* then, but not on the basis of their length.

Finally, of course, technical terms present a special case in terms of length
and familiarity that is often forgotten. Many times technical terms cannot be

substituted for, no matter what their length; after all, what else can you call a *transistor* or a *renin angiotensin system*? And just as often length is a clearly inappropriate index to difficulty. For instance, *erg* is likely to be a difficult term not because of its length but because of the concept involved; conversely, engineers may read a familiar term like *electrostatics* with perfect ease.

Until more conclusive research is completed on the impact of diction on readability, I suggest that we simply stick to the advice of that old adage, "Don't use words your audience won't understand." And in concluding this entire section on sentences and words, I suggest that we heed the words of George Klare: "Altering word or sentence length, of themselves, can provide no assurance of improving readability. How to achieve more readable writing is another and much more complex endeavor." [26, p. 98]

OTHER READABILITY FACTORS

If we cannot count on short sentences and short words to produce readable writing, what can we count on? Unfortunately, the answers to that question can only be tentative at present. Since achieving more readable writing is such a "complex endeavor" (as Klare says), and since there are special difficulties associated with applying readability research to technical documents (as the final section of this article will indicate), we should be careful about applying basic research on readability factors to the real world of on-the-job writing. Nevertheless, some significant progress has been made — on word factors, sentence factors, and factors beyond sentences — that is worth knowing about.

Word Factors

Although we cannot say with justification that technical writers should use short words, we can say — if tentatively — that certain word choices do affect readability. For instance, I have already cited research by Coleman and Seigel that indicates that writers should perhaps attend to the average number of morphemes per word in a passage — although more research is needed to confirm that suggestion. More reliable is a long history of work in readability that indicates that words are more readable if they are familiar to the audience, frequently used by the audience, and concrete, instead of less familiar, less common, and more abstract. Since this information has been incorporated by most technical writing teachers and textbooks, and since it has already been summarized efficiently by George Klare [8, 41] by Lois Van Rooy [42], and by Veda Charrow and Melissa Holland [43], I will concentrate here on sentences and paragraphs.

Sentence Factors

While sentence length is not important to the production of readable writing, sentence difficulty certainly is; the structure and complexity of a sentence often affect a reader's response to a text. Although the particular sentence structures that affect readers have not been discovered yet in any detailed way, certain promising developments are worth reporting on.

For instance, although *sentence* length does not affect readability, *clause* length may. At least that is what is suggested by a 1965 study by E. B. Coleman [44]. Coleman tested by means of recall procedures whether sentences with relatively short clauses (e.g., "When the investigator studied the incident, it involved hours of tracing down suspects.") would be easier to read than sentences with longer clauses (e.g., "The investigator's study of the incident involved hours of tracing down suspects."). Coleman learned that "apparently a person can process content morphemes packaged into two clauses more easily than he can process the identical morphemes packed into a single clause. Thus it seems that the advice to prefer short sentences might be better rephrased as a rule to prefer short clauses." [44, pp. 340-341] More research confirming these conclusions is needed, though, before we can recommend them to students.

While clause *length* may be important to readability, clause *order* apparently is not. When Robert Szabo investigated the impact of placing adverbial clauses first, last, and in the middle of sentences, he found no differences in reading comprehension, as measured by standardized tests [45]. V. M. Holmes [46] and Nancy Marshall and Marvin Glock [30] have confirmed Szabo's conclusions.

Unfortunately, however, no such consensus has been reached about the readability of passive and active transformations. Once out of favor in technical writing circles, the active voice is now receiving renewed support, so much so that Klare has been moved to state that "the active form of a statement leads to easier recall and verification than the passive." [8, p. 3, 41, p. 23] Several other studies have supported Klare's belief that active sentences are more comprehensible than passives [31, 47–50]. But other research indicates that the matter is not so simple, especially when the effects of actives and passives are evaluated in rhetorical contexts. Gough, for instance, studied only very simple sentences (like "The girl was hit by the boy," and "The boy hit the girl") and only active and passive sentences isolated from other sentences. Thus, he counseled restraint in drawing conclusions from his work [48]. Moreover, when Seigel and Burkett studied the effects of passives and actives in the context of real paragraphs, they could find no effect on comprehension [51]. Slobin's work offers a possible explanation: in his first experiment he found that passives do increase reading time – unless the sentences are "not reversible." In other words, if the agent is deleted from if a passive sentence (e.g., "A polio vaccine was discovered in the 1950's.") or a passive sentence cannot be logically reversed (e.g., "The bread was cut by the knife." "The knife was cut by the bread."), then a passive structure is no harder to read than a corresponding active one. In short, "it seems that nonreversibility eliminates the problem of passivity . . . ; in fact, the passive form generally tended to be somewhat easier (though not significantly so) than the active form." [50, p. 226] Similarly, in an important follow-up study published two years later, Slobin concluded from subjects' performances on recall tests that passives are no more difficult than actives, especially when the agents in passive sentences are deleted (according to one estimate, between 70% and 94% of passive sentences in English fall into this category). In addition, he found that passives can actually improve readability when they enable a writer either to emphasize something appropriately by placing it in the subject position, or to delete an unknown or unimportant agent [52]. Charrow and Charrow also concluded that passive verbs were as easy to understand as actives, especially if they appeared in main clauses or if agents were deleted (though passives in subordinate clauses did seem to impede comprehension) [24]. Finally, in 1972 Olson and Filby judged the readability of actives and passives in the context of paragraphs by recording the length of time it took subjects to process sentences correctly. They concluded that active sentences are easier to comprehend than passives only if the agent is more important than the receiver of the action. When the receiver is more important (in terms of a passage's content), passives are easier to comprehend [53]. These findings will not surprise teachers of writing who have counseled students to manipulate the passive and active to emphasize or de-emphasize information.

In addition to clause length and the active and passive voice, two other important sentence factors have been studied that may well affect readability. The first factor is negation; as we might expect, positive constructions seem to be more quickly and more accurately verified than negatives [48, 50]. The second factor is nominalization or "faulty predication" (like the difference between "They agreed" and "They reached an agreement"); most teachers' suspicions about nominalizations have been confirmed by Coleman [44, 47] and by Charrow and Charrow [24], who found that sentences with them were more difficult to comprehend and recall than sentences with comparable active verbs. Research on these two factors — and on a few other sentence factors like "word depth" (a measure of the density of prose) and "bound" vs. "free" modifiers — has been conveniently summarized by Van Rooy [42] and Klare [41].

Factors Beyond the Sentence

Until the last decade, studies of factors affecting readability limited themselves to sentences and words. As John Bormuth reported in 1969, "intersentence syntax or discourse organization variables [have been] almost totally ignored." [31, p. 51] Recently, however, cognitive psychologists, psycholinguists, and discourse analysts have begun to study factors that affect the readability of connected discourse. Thomas Huckin's article elsewhere in this book demonstrates the relevance of some of that research to technical writing. Here I want to point out the relevance of recent studies on three particular factors: topic sentences, the given-new contract, and proposition density.

Technical writing texts are nearly unanimous in their support of Alexander Bain's precept that paragraphs should have topic sentences. And while topic sentences have lately fallen into some disfavor (especially as a result of Richard Braddock's analysis of "The Frequency and Placement of Topic Sentences in Expository Prose" [54]), recent readability research supports their use. For example, R. M. Gagne and V. K. Wiegand gave subjects passages that differed only in that some contained a topic sentence and others didn't; when they tested the subjects' comprehension by means of recall procedures, they found that topic sentences had improved readability [55]. Similarly, David E. Kieras found in 1978 that paragraphs with topic sentences are read faster and are recalled better; conversely, "paragraphs that violate the . . . topicalization conventions yield longer reading times, poorer recall, and distortions." [56, p. 27] Mark Aulls also discovered that "if the main idea [of a paragraph] is presented, it may serve to enhance recall by making more explicit the referential connection between the subtopics and the main topic." [57, p. 392] A decade of important work on the impact of the structure of prose on readers has led Bonnie J. F. Meyer to state that "explicit statement of the rhetorical structure facilitate[s] recall." [58, p. 217] Studies by three other prominent cognitive psychologists, Richard Hurtig [59], Patricia Carpenter and Marcel Just [60], have supported Meyer's conclusion; so have studies by J. D. Bransford and Marcia K. Johnson [61].

Topic sentences are familiar to technical writers. A more novel hypothesis about what affects the comprehension of connected discourse is the given-new contract. Although research on the given-new contract has only begun, Robert de Beaugrande has already suggested its potential value for technical writing [62].

What is the given-new contract? Rooted ultimately in the Prague school of linguistics and described in the past decade by psychologists Wallace Chafe [63] and H. H. Clark and Susan Haviland [64, 65], the given-new contract governs the placement of information in paragraphs and longer texts. According to this implicit contract, writers communicate with readers by agreeing to present information according to a certain format — by attaching it to what has come previously. Thus, "new" or previously unknown information (which usually appears at the end of a sentence) is tied explicitly to "given" or previously presented or known information (which usually appears at the beginning of the sentence). If too much new information comes at once or if new information is improperly tied to what has been given, communication is impaired.

So far, the given-new contract has stood up to research scrutiny. When Haviland and Clark first put the theory to the test, they verified that new information in one sentence is indeed more quickly processed if it is tied to given information that has a direct antecedent in the previous sentence [65]. Since 1977, Kathryn Bock, David Irwin, and two French psychologists, Hupet and le Bouedec, have further supported the theory [66–68]. Much work remains to be done — the theory needs further validation, and the particular rhetorical implications of the theory need to be drawn, tested, and validated, so that the theory can have practical value for writers. Nevertheless, the potential value of the given-new contract to technical writing is intriguing.

Other possibilities are presented by Walter Kintsch's work with propositions. A proposition is roughly analogous to the "kernal sentence" of transformational grammar. Thus, a sentence like "A great rocket stood in the desert" contains three propositions: "The rocket was great," "The rocket stood somewhere," and "The somewhere was in the desert." (For a fuller description of propositions, see the essay by Lester Faigley and Stephen P. Witte elsewhere in this volume.) Kintsch believes (with ample research evidence supporting him) that propositions are basic building blocks for both writers and readers. That is, on the one hand, we write texts by combining and arranging propositions into sentences, paragraphs, and larger sequences; on the other hand, when we read, we do it by processing propositions, not sentences [20, 69].

How is all this relevant to readability? Kintsch has shown that reading time increases when the number of propositions in a sentence increases, even when the number of words and clauses remains the same [70]. Similarly, Kintsch and his colleagues have shown that the time needed to read a paragraph increases when the number of propositions in it increases, even if paragraph length, sentence length, and other variables remain constant [71]. Thus, it may well be that proposition density is an important determinant of a passage's difficulty. If further research confirms Kintsch's ideas, proposition density may become an important index for writers. Instead of using formulas, they may be able to use proposition counts to get a sense of the difficulty of their writing.

RESEARCH OPPORTUNITIES IN READABILITY

These accounts of work on proposition density and the given-new contract, like the other sections of this article, suggest some of the rich possibilities for research that lie in the broad landscape known as "readability research." There are opportunities to develop and verify research that has already begun — research into the word, sentence, and paragraph factors mentioned in this article. For without painstaking replication and verification, conclusions about factors affecting readability can only remain tentative. In addition, there are opportunities to investigate other sentence and word factors that have so far gone unexamined. Finally, the whole area beyond the sentence still remains virtually an "unmapped frontier," an "immense and disputed realm" (in Hirsch's words) [11, p. 120]. As E. B. Coleman has said, "Surely most of us believe that the major determiners of readability for adults lie at this level — lie in the associations between clauses and paragraphs, in the overall organization." [72, p. 177] Yet this frontier — everything from sentence order to the overall organization of discourse — remains largely untracked.

Perhaps even more interesting to technical writing researchers are opportunities to apply and test basic research in readability in the real world of on-the-job writing. We have not sufficiently appreciated just how basic and theoretical the research in readability has been; too quickly we have assumed that results obtained under highly controlled and artificial laboratory conditions will simply transfer directly to the real world. As Nancy Marshall and Marvin Glock have pointed out, studies of the kind described in this article "are considered to be basic research. Those involved in basic research are interested in gaining insights into human behavior. Thus they study specific behaviors in isolation. As a result, the applications of any single piece of basic research to the real world, a very complex place indeed, are very limited." [30, p. 54] Ernst Rothkopf has also been critical of how hastily basic research in readability has been applied to the real world [40]. Consequently, we can do much practical work to test the applicability of basic research to real technical writing.

For instance, we can see if sentence, word, and paragraph factors that affect comprehension when they are studied in isolation from other words, sentences, and paragraphs have the same effects in the context of real discourse. Hirsch has rightly complained that "the psychology of language reception is still very imperfectly understood, and the bulk of experimentation in the subject has been limited to words and sentences in isolation. Work on language reception in actual speech transactions and in the reading of actual texts has been rather rare, despite general agreement that actual language processing is different in several respects from the processing of isolated words and sentences in test situations." [11, p. 93] Therefore we badly need to observe the effects of readability factors in real writing. And fortunately, researchers have already developed and described several sophisticated techniques for determining the relative readability of various language choices — including one developed for technical writing [73].

But we can do several other things, too. First, we need to observe the effects of readability factors when the subject matter is technical and when the audiences are technically oriented. Research strongly implies that technical reading and writing may differ in important ways from other kinds: Thomas Sticht's research into the nature of reading on the job, for example, shows that technical writing is more often "consulted" than "learned" and that it is often read in connection with repeated tasks, not new ones [74]; George Klare has noticed that the reader's background knowledge and the text's interest-value affect readability as well [18]. But how much and in what ways do these elements affect the readability of technical writing? Second, we need to know whether readability factors that affect one age group affect others as well. Since readability research was initially directed toward matching educational materials to children of various grade levels, most laboratory work has been done on children. But do factors that help or hinder children affect adults as much or in the same way? Third, we can investigate factors whose effects are highly individual. Most obviously, we must consider the great differences in reading ability among people of the same age, occupation, and education. In addition, since it seems very likely that readability makes very little difference to adult readers who are highly motivated [41], and since we can certainly describe readers of many technical documents as "highly motivated," we need to consider the effects of an individual's motivation very carefully. How important is motivation? How motivated are technical readers? How can a technical writer feed a reader's motivations? It also seems that adult readers can adjust their reading speed and comprehension to fit the material before them [40, 75]; they can "handle a substantial variety of difficulty levels and reduces them to the same level of internal representation by appropriate processing activities." [40, p. 321] How should this affect a writer's stylistic choices?

In short, readability research has oversimplified. It has assumed that all readers will respond to a passage in the same way, when in fact a reader's response is modified by age, vocation, educational level, motivation, interest — and probably other considerations. Before it can be useful in the real world, readability research must find a way to assess and incorporate those individual reading differences. Just as obviously, deciding what constitutes a readable technical style is more complicated than we have acknowledged. We have learned quite a bit about what kinds of words, sentences, and paragraphs make writing more readable. But we obviously have a lot more to learn before we can reduce the complexities of technical writing to reliable maxims.

REFERENCES

1. M. D. Whitburn, M. Davis, S. Higgins, L. Oates, and K. Spurgeon, The Plain Style in Scientific and Technical Writing, *Journal of Technical Writing and Communication, 8,* pp. 349-358, 1978.
2. R. Flesch, A New Readability Yardstick, *Journal of Applied Psychology, 32,* pp. 221-233, 1948.
3. R. Gunning, *The Technique of Clear Writing,* McGraw-Hill Book Company, New York, 1952 (revised 1968).
4. R. Flesch, *The Art of Readable Writing,* Harper and Brothers Publishers, New York, 1949 (revised, Harper and Row, 1974).
5. K. Houp and T. E. Pearsall, *Reporting Technical Information,* Glencoe Press, Encino, California, 1980.
6. S. E. Pauley, *Technical Report Writing Today,* Houghton Mifflin Company, Boston, Massachusetts, 1979.
7. J. O'Rourke, *Writing for the Reader,* Digital Equipment Corporation, Maynard, Massachusetts, 1976.
8. G. R. Klare, Readable Technical Writing: Some Observations, *Technical Communication, 24:2,* pp. 1-5, 1977.
9. D. L. Carson, Audience in Technical Writing: The Need for Greater Realism in Identifying the Fictive Reader, *The Technical Writing Teacher, 7,* pp. 8-11, 1979.
10. *Teaching Technical Writing: Teaching Audience Analysis and Adaptation,* P. V. Anderson (ed.), Association of Teachers of Technical Writing, Morehead, Kentucky, pp. 24-31, 1980.
11. E. D. Hirsch, *The Philosophy of Composition,* University of Chicago Press, Chicago, Illinois, 1977.

12. G. R. Klare, *The Measurement of Readability*, Iowa State University Press, Ames, Iowa, 1963.
13. T. E. Curran, Readability Research in the Navy, in *Reading and Readability Research in the Armed Services*, T. G. Sticht and D. W. Zapf (eds.), Human Resources Research Organization Report, Alexandria, Virginia, pp. 177-201, 1976 (ERIC #ED 130242).
14. P. V. Anderson, Helping Students Develop Their Personal Styles in Technical Writing, paper delivered at the Conference on College Composition and Communication, Minneapolis, Minnesota, 1979.
15. M. Whitburn, Personality in Scientific and Technical Writing, *Journal of Technical Writing and Communication, 6,* pp. 299-306, 1976.
16. G. H. Mills and J. A. Walter, *Technical Writing,* Holt, Rinehart, and Winston, New York, 1978.
17. A. K. Clark, Readability in Technical Writing — Principles and Procedures, *IEEE Transactions on Professional Communication, PC-18:*2, pp. 67-70, 1975.
18. G. R. Klare, A Second Look at the Validity of Readability Formulas, *Journal of Reading Behavior, 8,* pp. 129-152, 1976.
19. T. G. Sticht and D. W. Zapf (eds.), *Reading and Readability Research in the Armed Services,* Human Resources Research Organization Report, Alexandria, Virginia, 1976 (ERIC #ED 130242).
20. W. Kintsch and D. Vipond, Reading Comprehension and Readability in Educational Practice and Psychological Theory, in *Perspectives on Memory Research,* L-G. Nilsson (ed.), Erlbaum Associates, Hillsdale, New Jersey, pp. 329-365, 1979.
21. J. S. Chall, *Readability: An Appraisal of Research and Application,* Ohio State University Press, Columbus, Ohio, 1958.
22. W. L. Taylor, "Cloze Procedure": A New Tool for Measuring Readability, *Journalism Quarterly, 30,* pp. 415-433, 1953.
23. D. Schwartz, J. P. Sparkman, and J. Deese, The Process of Understanding and Judgments of Comprehensibility, *Journal of Verbal Learning and Verbal Behavior, 9,* pp. 87-93, 1970.
24. R. P. Charrow and V. R. Charrow, Making Legal Language Understandable: A Psycholinguistic Study of Jury Instructions, *Columbia Law Review, 79,* pp. 1306-1374, 1979.
25. R. Flesch, A Dissenting Opinion on Readability, *Elementary English, 26,* pp. 332-334, 1949.
26. G. R. Klare, Assessing Readability, *Reading Research Quarterly, 10,* pp. 62-102, 1974.
27. P. D. Pearson, The Effects of Grammatical Complexity on Children's Comprehension, Recall, and Conception of Certain Semantic Relations, *Reading Research Quarterly, 10,* pp. 155-192, 1974.
28. I. M. Schlesinger, *Sentence Structure and the Reading Process,* Mouton, The Hague, 1968.
29. R. M. Davis, Does Expression Make a Difference?, *Technical Communication, 23,* pp. 6-9, 1976.

30. N. Marshall and M. D. Glock, Comprehension of Connected Discourse: A Study into the Relationships Between the Structure of Text and Information Recalled, *Reading Research Quarterly, 14,* pp. 10-56, 1978.
31. J. R. Bormuth, *Development of Readability Analysis: Final Report,* Project #7-0052, Contract #OEC-3-7-070052-0326, U. S. Department of Health, Education, and Welfare, Washington, D. C., 1969 (ERIC #ED 029166).
32. E. B. Coleman, Improving Comprehensibility by Shortening Sentences, *Journal of Applied Psychology, 46,* pp. 131-134, 1962.
33. M. D. Wang, The Role of Syntactic Complexity as a Determiner of Comprehensibility, *Journal of Verbal Learning and Verbal Behavior, 9,* pp. 398-404, 1970.
34. J. R. Bormuth, New Developments in Readability Research, *Elementary English, 44,* pp. 840-845, 1967.
35. R. P. Carver, Word Length, Prose Difficulty, and Reading Rate, *Journal of Reading Behavior, 8,* pp. 193-203, 1976.
36. E. B. Coleman and G. R. Miller, A Measure of Information Gained During Prose Learning, *Reading Research Quarterly, 3,* pp. 369-386, 1968.
37. A. I. Seigel, J. V. Lambert, and J. R. Burkett, Techniques for Making Written Material More Readable/Comprehensible, Air Force Human Resources Lab, Lowry Air Force Base, Colorado, 1974 (ERIC #ED 097629
38. E. B. Coleman, Developing a Technology of Written Instruction: Some Determiners of the Complexity of Prose, in *Verbal Learning Research and the Technology of Written Instruction,* E. Z. Rothkopf and P. E. Johnson (eds.), Columbia University Teachers College Press, New York, pp. 155-204, 1971.
39. D. Doggett and L. G. Richards, A Reexamination of the Effect of Word Length on Recognition Thresholds, *American Journal of Psychology, 88,* pp. 583-594, 1975.
40. E. Z. Rothkopf, Structural Text Features and the Control of Processes in Learning from Written Materials, in *Language Comprehension and the Acquisition of Knowledge,* R. O. Freedle and J. B. Carroll (eds.), V. H. Winston Publishing, Washington, D. C., pp. 315-335, 1972.
41. G. R. Klare, *A Manual for Readable Writing,* REM Company, Glen Burnie, Maryland, 1975.
42. L. Van Rooy, *Readability Studies and the Writer of Instructional Materials,* Career Development for Children Project, Carbondale, Illinois, 1973 (ERIC #ED 089245).
43. V. Charrow with M. Holland, Psycholinguistics, in *Document Design: A Review of the Relevant Research,* D. B. Felker (ed.), Document Design Project, American Institutes for Research, Washington, D. C., pp. 7-25, 1980.
44. E. B. Coleman, Learning of Prose Written in Four Grammatical Transformations, *Journal of Applied Psychology, 49,* pp. 332-341, 1965.
45. R. J. Szabo, The Effect of Adverbial Subordinate Clause Position on Reading Comprehension, *Journal of Educational Research, 69,* pp. 331-332, 1976.

46. V. M. Holmes, Order of Main and Subordinate Clauses in Sentence Perception, *Journal of Verbal Learning and Verbal Behavior, 12*, pp. 285-293, 1973.

47. E. B. Coleman, The Comprehensibility of Several Grammatical Transformations, *Journal of Applied Psychology, 48*, pp. 186-190, 1964.

48. P. E. Gough, Grammatical Transformations and Speed of Understanding, *Journal of Verbal Learning and Verbal Behavior, 4*, pp. 107-111, 1965.

49. H. P. Blount and R. E. Johnson, Grammatical Structure and the Recall of Sentences in Prose, *American Educational Research Journal, 10*, pp. 163-168, 1973.

50. D. I. Slobin, Grammatical Transformations and Sentence Comprehension in Childhood and Adulthood, *Journal of Verbal Learning and Verbal Behavior, 5*, pp. 219-227, 1966.

51. A. I. Seigel and J. R. Burkett, Application of Structure-of-Intellect and Psycholinguistic Concepts to Reading Comprehensibility Measurement, Air Force Human Resources Lab, Lowry Air Force Base, Colorado, 1974 (ERIC #ED 099817).

52. D. I. Slobin, Recall of Full and Truncated Passives in Connected Discourse, *Journal of Verbal Learning and Verbal Behavior, 7*, pp. 876-881, 1968.

53. D. R. Olson and N. Filby, On the Comprehension of Active and Passive Sentences, *Cognitive Psychology, 3*, pp. 361-381, 1972.

54. R. Braddock, The Frequency and Placement of Topic Sentences in Expository Prose, *Research in the Teaching of English, 8*, pp. 287-302, 1974.

55. R. M. Gagne and V. K. Wiegand, Effects of a Superordinate Context on Learning and Retention of Facts, *Journal of Educational Psychology, 61*, pp. 406-409, 1970.

56. D. E. Kieras, Good and Bad Structure in Simple Paragraphs: Effects on Apparent Theme, Reading Time, and Recall, *Journal of Verbal Learning and Verbal Behavior, 17*, pp. 13-28, 1978.

57. M. W. Aulls, Expository Paragraph Properties that Influence Literal Recall, *Journal of Reading Behavior, 7*, pp. 391-400, 1975.

58. B. J. F. Meyer, Organization in Prose and Memory: Research with Application to Reading Comprehension, in *Reading: Theory, Research, and Practice,* P. David Pearson (ed.), 26th Yearbook of the National Reading Conference, Clemson, South Carolina, pp. 214-220, 1977.

59. R. Hurtig, Toward a Functional Theory of Discourse, in *Discourse Production and Comprehension,* R. O. Freedle (ed.), Ablex Publishing Company, Norwood, New Jersey, pp. 89-102, 1977.

60. P. A. Carpenter and M. A. Just, Reading Comprehension as Eyes See It, in *Cognitive Processes in Comprehension,* P. A. Carpenter and M. A. Just (eds.), Erlbaum Associates, Hillsdale, New Jersey, pp. 109-139, 1977.

61. J. D. Bransford and M. K. Johnson, Contextual Prerequisites for Understanding: Some Investigations of Comprehension and Recall, *Journal of Verbal Learning and Verbal Behavior, 11*, pp. 717-726, 1972.

62. R. A. de Beaugrande, Communication in Technical Writing, *Journal of Technical Writing and Communication, 8*, pp. 5-15, 1978.

63. W. L. Chafe, *Meaning and the Structure of Language,* University of Chicago, Press, Chicago, Illinois, 1970.
64. H. H. Clark and S. E. Haviland, Comprehension and the Given-New Contract, in *Discourse Production and Comprehension,* R. O. Freedle (ed.), Ablex Publishing Company, Norwood, New Jersey, pp. 1-39, 1977.
65. S. E. Haviland and H. H. Clark, What's New? Acquiring New Information as a Process in Comprehension, *Journal of Verbal Learning and Verbal Behavior, 13,* pp. 512-521, 1974.
66. J. K. Bock, The Effect of a Pragmatic Presupposition on Syntactic Structure in Question Answering, *Journal of Verbal Learning and Verbal Behavior, 16,* pp. 723-734, 1977.
67. J. K. Bock and D. E. Irwin, Syntactic Effects of Information Availability in Sentence Production, *Journal of Verbal Learning and Verbal Behavior, 19,* pp. 467-484, 1980.
68. M. Hupet and B. le Bouedec, The Given-New Contract and the Constructive Aspect of Memory for Ideas, *Journal of Verbal Learning and Verbal Behavior, 16,* pp. 69-75, 1977.
69. W. Kintsch, *The Representation of Meaning in Memory,* Erlbaum Associates, Hillsdale, New Jersey, 1974.
70. W. Kintsch and J. Keenan, Reading Rate and Retention as a Function of the Number of Propositions in the Base Structure of Sentences, *Cognitive Psychology, 5,* pp. 257-274, 1973.
71. W. Kintsch, E. Kozminsky, W. J. Streby, G. McKoon, and J. M. Keenan, Comprehension and Recall of Text as a Function of Content Variables, *Journal of Verbal Learning and Verbal Behavior, 14,* pp. 196-214, 1975.
72. E. B. Coleman, Experimental Studies of Readability, *Elementary English, 45,* pp. 166-178, 1968.
73. R. M. Davis, Experimental Research in the Effectiveness of Technical Writing, in *The Teaching of Technical Writing,* D. H. Cunningham and H. A. Estrin (eds.), National Council of Teachers of English, Urbana, Illinois, pp. 109-122, 1975.
74. T. G. Sticht, Comprehending Reading at Work, in *Cognitive Processes in Comprehension,* P. A. Carpenter and M. A. Just (eds.), Erlbaum Associates, Hillsdale, New Jersey, pp. 221-246, 1977.
75. E. U. Coke, Reading Rate, Readability, and Variations in Task-Induced Processing, *Journal of Educational Psychology, 68,* pp. 167-173, 1976.

CHAPTER 5

A Cognitive Approach
to Readability

THOMAS N. HUCKIN

Readability has long been one of the most widely discussed issues in technical writing. It has been the subject of numerous journal articles, conference papers, doctoral dissertations, master's theses, style manuals, handbook chapters, and other professional and academic treatments. It has been converted into innumerable "formulas," which in turn have been imposed on countless writers working in industry, government, and the military. And it is routinely talked about in technical writing courses.

Despite all this attention, however, there is widespread dissatisfaction with our current state of knowledge about exactly what it is that makes writing readable. Much of this dissatisfaction, I believe, derives from the fact that most readability research has been tied to the development of readability formulas. For various practical reasons, readability formulas are designed to measure only superficial linguistic variables, in particular those variables which are claimed to have some correlation with readability; readability formulas do *not* take into account, or even purport to take into account, the actual underlying determinants of readability. Readability formulists themselves have repeatedly emphasized this point, saying that such formulas should be used only to assess the written product, not to guide the writing process. Consequently, research directed toward the development of such formulas has done little to help us understand what really makes one piece of writing more readable than another.

And, as a result, we are on very shaky ground whenever we try to give advice on readability to students or practicing professionals.

In recent years, fortunately, there has developed a considerable body of scientific knowledge to help us out, most of it based on experimental research in cognitive psychology. The purpose of this article is to describe some of this research and show how it pertains to technical writing pedagogy and practice. Instead of focusing on the written product, as traditional readability research has done, this newer approach takes its strength from the fact it focuses on the reading process. It investigates the mind of the reader, in the sense that it seeks to discover the various mental operations that are called into play when different kinds of readers are exposed to different kinds of texts under different kinds of circumstances. I believe that understanding how readers read is essential if we are to give writers sound advice about how to write.

Before proceeding further, I should perhaps define what I mean by the term "readability." Writing is "readable" to the extent that its meaning can be easily and quickly comprehended for an intended purpose by an intended reader operating under normal conditions of alertness, motivation, time-pressure, etc. This definition differs from E. D. Hirsch's celebrated concept of "relative readability" insofar as the latter disregards differences among readers and purposes for reading [1]. Although defined in terms of comprehension, readability is closely related to ease of recall; thus, in most cases, highly readable writing not only conveys its meaning efficiently but also facilitates recall of that meaning. (There are exceptions, of course, in technical writing especially, where comprehension may not *require* recall. For example, sets of instructions may need to be comprehended only well enough to perform certain tasks on the spot, not to be "recalled" in any sense.) Readers are not oblivious to these qualities. When they find it easy to read something, they tend to read on. Consequently, highly readable writing is not only more easily understood and remembered than less readable writing but is more likely to even be read in the first place.

This article is organized into three sections. The first and major section contains a sampling of recent research in cognitive psychology that is particularly relevant to the study of readability. The second section presents eight guidelines for writers derived from this research. The final section then briefly compares the cognitive-psychological approach with the readability-formula approach, and concludes that they can be integrated.

RELEVANT RESEARCH IN COGNITIVE PSYCHOLOGY

The studies described in this article are directly relevant to the study of the readability of technical writing because they have all investigated the cognitive processes of educated adults reading expository prose discourse. They represent original empirical research, with large numbers of test subjects, reasonable controls, and, most importantly, lengthy samples (full paragraphs or more) of prose discourse. Some of them have even simulated, to a certain extent at least, the kinds of reading tasks, time limitations, and other conditions that prevail in the real world of technical writing and reading. As a result of these studies, a number of theoretical concepts, textual features, and reader variables have been found to be particularly relevant to the readability of technical documents.

Theoretical Concepts

The theoretical concepts developed by cognitive psychologists that seem most useful to technical writers are: "schema theory," "activated semantic contexts," the "levels effect," and the "leading edge strategy."

Schema Theory — We are all aware that knowing something about a subject makes it easier to learn more about that subject: our prior knowledge serves as a framework which makes the new information more meaningful and easier to absorb. Indeed, we implicitly acknowledge this phenomenon when we tell writers that writing for a lay reader is more difficult than writing for a fellow specialist. Until the past ten years, however, no one had actually provided theory-driven empirical confirmation of this long-held intuition, at least not with regard to readability. Then Bransford and Johnson did a pioneering study [2], since followed by others: Greeno [3], Spilich, Vesonder, Chiesi, and Voss [4], Chiesi, Spilich, and Voss [5], Graesser, Hoffman, and Clark [6], and Clifton and Slowiaczek [7], to cite but a few. These studies show conclusively that readers who already know something about a subject do indeed find it easier to process new information about that subject than do readers without such prior familiarity: they comprehend the new information more quickly and thoroughly, and they recall more of it, in greater detail.

Probably the best way to explain this phenomenon in theoretical terms is by reference to what is called "schema theory." Following the lead of Head [8], Bartlett [9], and Piaget [10], modern cognitive psychologists have postulated that the human mind routinely constructs, on the basis of patterns of experience, abstract generic concepts or "schemata." These schemata are stored in long-term memory and thereafter guide the way we perceive and remember things. Every schema (or "frame" or "script," as they are sometimes called) is made up of certain constituent features depending on the individual's prior experience: someone who has had much experience with a concept will have an accordingly richer schema for that concept (i.e., one having more features) than will someone who has had less experience.

The power of schemata in the communication process resides largely in their ability to induce inferences from the reader (listener, viewer, etc.). This process of schema-based inferring works as follows. When the writer and reader share a schema, that is, when their respective schemata for a particular concept are essentially similar, the writer does not have to refer explicitly to all the details of that schema for those details to be conveyed to the reader: the reader will simply supply any missing details by inference. In other words, a schema is conceived of as a mental construct with fixed place-holders for its constituent features; when a schema is evoked but not all of its features are explicitly mentioned, the reader can simply "fill in the slots." In this way, a single word or phrase can actually call up an entire constellation of images in the reader's mind [11–14].

This process of schema-based inferring plays a crucial role in all forms of communication. For one thing, it enriches the imagery of concepts, making them easier to perceive and easier to remember. Secondly, it can increase the coherence of a message by giving the reader a means of filling in various missing links. Writers do not normally spell out everything they mean; they usually count on the reader's being able to infer unstated details, including the details that tie the different parts of a message together. And much of this inferring is based on shared schemata. This is why subject-matter familiarity is so advantageous to a reader trying to comprehend a message: it provides a set of schemata that help him or her integrate the various parts of the message and thus create a meaningful whole.

All this is not to imply, however, that schema-based inferring is restricted to communication between specialists. On the contrary, it can also be used successfully by specialists communicating with nonspecialists. Through the proper use of metaphor, analogy, example, operational definition, and so on [15, 16], the specialist simply selects alternative, more commonplace schemata on which to base the communication, instead of the more esoteric schemata associated with a particular specialty. The communication will still be based on shared schemata, but on ones that are available to the nonspecialist.

All of these benefits, of course, are possible only when writer and reader attribute similar features to the schema for a particular concept. In cases where the writer's schema differs substantially from that of the reader, the writer would be well advised not to evoke that concept without fully describing it; otherwise, the reader might infer details that are not intended. Probably the most glaring examples of such miscommunication occur in cross-cultural contexts. When I use the word "highway," for example, I think of a broad paved surface, signs, divider line or median strip, etc.; these are the defining features of my "highway-schema," conditioned by my experience in a Western industrialized country. But someone coming from an undeveloped country may have a different "highway-schema," with different defining features: dirt surface, single lane, no signs, etc. In communicating with such a person, it would therefore be a mistake for me to use the word "highway" and expect him or her to infer the same details I would infer.

Activated Semantic Contexts – In general, subject-matter familiarity enables a reader to draw on many highly detailed schemata and thus make more inferences and comprehend a text better than can a reader without such familiarity. This is not to say, however, that subject-matter familiarity *automatically* facilitates comprehension. As Bransford and Johnson showed in their study of ten years ago, "In order for prior knowledge to aid comprehension, it must become an activated semantic context." [2, p. 724] In other words, the prior knowledge must be consciously in the mind of the reader during the ongoing process of comprehension. To see why, consider one of the experimental passages they used:

> The procedure is actually quite simple. First you arrange things into different groups. Of course, one pile may be sufficient depending on how much there is to do. If you have to go somewhere else due to lack of facilities that is the next step, otherwise you are pretty well set. It is important not to overdo things. That is, it is better to do too few things at once than too many. In the short run this may not seem important but complications can easily arise. A mistake can be expensive as well. ...

When readers were told what the topic of the passage was ("Washing Clothes") *before* reading it, they performed much better in comprehension and recall tasks than those who were either given the topic *after* reading it or never given the topic at all. The "Topic After" group, interestingly enough, did no better than the "No Topic" group. Of course, all three groups had had some real-life familiarity with washing clothes before undergoing this experiment; they all had "prior knowledge" of the subject. But only the "Topic Before" group had this prior knowledge consciously in mind when reading the passage; thus, only they were able to utilize their prior knowledge effectively.

In the terminology of schema theory, this study showed that a schema will facilitate comprehension and recall only when it is consciously in the reader's mind. Other studies have reported similar findings [17–19]. This leads, of course, to the following crucial question: What is it that brings a schema to the reader's conscious attention? What is it that "activates" a "semantic context"?

A number of studies suggest that "semantic contexts" (i.e., schemata) are activated whenever they are perceived by the reader as being *important* to comprehension. It has long been known, for example, that explicitly stated material is better recalled when it is centrally important to the meaning of a passage than when it is only marginally important [20–22]. More recent investigations by Anderson and his colleagues at the University of Illinois have demonstrated this effect by having readers recall ideas from stories that could be interpreted from either of two entirely different perspectives [23, 24]; they found that readers who were oriented to one perspective recalled different ideas than readers who were oriented to the other perspective. The investigators concluded that "it was an idea's significance in terms of a given perspective that influenced whether it was learned and, independently, whether it was recalled." [24, p. 314] Goetz has pushed these investigations one step further by studying the same effect as it relates to the inferring process [25]. Here too it seems that the perceived importance of a semantic context is what causes it to be activated: in Goetz's words, "When people read a story in which an event is important, they are more likely to make inferences about that event than if the event were unimportant." [25, p. 191]

Of course, what's important to one reader may not be important to another. This is where subject-matter familiarity can make a crucial difference. The studies cited above show that a specialist reader will normally call upon his or her special knowledge to determine whether or not certain information is important to comprehending the text as a whole; the importance of the information, in other words, will be determined not only by its mode of presentation in the text but also by its status "outside" the text, in the field as a whole — and only the specialist, not the nonspecialist, has access to this field. The nonspecialist reader, not having such knowledge to draw on, must rely much more heavily on how the information is presented in the text. This dependency on the text means that if certain information is structurally buried in the text, the nonspecialist reader will probably not perceive it as being important; as a result, he or she will pay less attention to it, infer few if any details about it, comprehend it poorly, and recall it poorly.

The Levels Effect — A great deal of recent research in cognitive psychology has shown that readers generally tend to process a text *hierarchically,* attributing more importance to information high in the hierarchy than to information low in the hierarchy [17, 20–22, 26–29]. They pay more attention to high-level information than to low-level information, they take longer to absorb it, and they recall it better. As Walker and Meyer's study showed, readers also tend to make more inferences about high-level information and are better able to integrate such information into their conception of the text as a whole than they are with low-level information [28].

This "levels effect," as it is called, has far-reaching implications for how a written text should be structured. To put it simply, the important points of a text should be placed in superior positions hierarchically: in headings, in subheadings, in topic sentences at the beginning of paragraphs, etc. If certain details are also important, they can be listed instead of subordinated; this maneuver "flattens out" the hierarchy and thus, in effect, puts supporting details on a higher level. Experimental studies by Wright [30] and Tenenbaum [31] have provided supporting evidence for these hypotheses. Tenenbaum, for example, used 200 to 400 word expository passages written in either a predominantly hierarchical style or in a predominantly listing style, and tested for both recall and recognition of both main ideas and details. She found that "the hierarchical structure enhanced recognition of the main idea . . . and, to a lesser extent, of a factual detail," while "the list structure modestly increased the amount of factual details recalled." [31, p. 532]

The Leading-Edge Strategy — Kintsch and his colleagues have devised a theoretical model of text comprehension which accounts for the "levels effect" [20, 26, 32, 33]; it has probably received more independent support than any other such model. As do most other psychologists, they see the reading process as governed basically by two psychological constructs: long-term memory and short-term (or "working") memory. Long-term memory is the repository of schemata, which, as we have seen, promote comprehension in a number of ways; an enormous number of schemata can be stored there. Short-term memory comes into play during the relatively automatic, linear processing of words and phrases. Its most notable feature is the one made famous by George Miller: the fact that short-term memory can only store about seven "chunks" of information at a time before "memory decay" sets in. Thus, in order for information to remain in short-term memory, it must be "reinstated," usually by explicit repetition.

These facts are all incorporated into Kintsch et al.'s model of comprehension (called the "leading-edge strategy") as follows. Information is absorbed, stored, and later recalled as a joint function of

1. height in the text hierarchy; and
2. recency of presentation.

The first of these two parameters has already been discussed as the "levels effect"; it is governed largely by long-term memory. The second parameter reflects the effects of short-term memory decay: if two pieces of information are equally important, the more recently communicated one is more likely to be stored and later recalled than the earlier one. (This "recency" phenomenon can easily be experienced simply by looking at a long string of randomly-sequenced single digits or letters, one by one, and then trying to recall as many as possible; most people recall the one at the end of the string best.) According to the "leading-edge strategy," then, the reader processes the text from top to bottom, simultaneously attending to both the larger framework — as dictated by high-level schemata drawn from long-term memory — and the various low-level details as they stream through short-term memory. Text is *coherent* to the degree that these two parameters are well-integrated, that is, to the degree that schemata create certain expectations about the kinds of details to follow and then the actual details fulfill these expectations.

What implications does the leading-edge strategy hold for writers concerned with making their writing more readable? To the extent that such writing is intended for nonspecialist readers, who cannot be expected to make inferential leaps and jumps and who therefore must be led step-by-step through the text, it means making every effort to activate schemata at high levels of the processing hierarchy, and then explicitly connecting to them as many details as possible from lower levels of the hierarchy.

Textual Features

The theoretical concepts just described (schema theory, activated semantic context, the levels effect, and the leading edge strategy) provide a background against which to understand the role that is played in the reading process by three features of text: headings, topic sentences, and the grammatical subjects of sentences.

Headings — Research suggests that the most direct and effective way of activating relevant schemata is by referring to them in headings and subheadings. Headings and subheadings are positioned at the beginning of large discourse units and are thus assumed by most readers to indicate hierarchical importance and therefore guide them in their effort to activate relevant schemata. Furthermore, they are typically set off by white space and are thus visually prominent. Many psychological studies have demonstrated the powerful effect of headings and subheadings on comprehension. Some, such as those by Dooling and Lachman [34], Bransford and McCarrell [35], Bransford and Johnson [2], and Schwarz and Flammer [36], have been based on the straightforward method of comparing comprehension of a passage *without* a heading against comprehension of the same passage *with* a heading. In all of these investigations, the version with headings was more easily and more fully comprehended. Other experiments, such as those by Kozminsky [37] and M. Bock [38], have deliberately used headings designed to bias a reader's judgment away from the intended meaning of the passage, and indeed have found a "biasing effect." However, it may be that the power of headings to influence comprehension is not absolute: studies by Charrow and Redish [39] and Swarts, Flower, and Hayes [40] suggest that although non-standard headings may be useful, standardized headings have no effect on the comprehension of well-organized prose by readers familiar with standardized formats.

Topic Sentences — Another common way of activating high-level schemata is by referring to them in topic sentences, especially topic sentences that lead off a paragraph. Because of indentation and other formatting devices, sentences at the beginnings of paragraphs are usually more prominent visually than are other sentences in a paragraph. For this reason, readers seem to use them to activate the schemata they will use when reading the rest of the paragraph. A number of studies suggest that the content of the first sentence of a paragraph influences the way the reader processes the sentences that follow: Gagne and Wiegand [41], Carpenter and Just [42], Meyer [22], and especially Kieras [27, 43–45], to mention a few.

Sentence Subjects — Occupying a lower level in the text hierarchy is the ordinary sentence, which has its own hierarchical structure. With this structure, the subject and predicate form the highest level, with the subject normally leading off the sentence and presenting the sentence topic. In effect, this "topic-presenting" role played by the subject at the sentence level is analogous to the same role played by the topic sentence at the paragraph level and by headings and subheadings at various discourse levels. Research by Perfetti and Goldman [46], MacWhinney [47], Kieras [27, 43, 45, 48, 49], and Faigley and Witte (in this volume), among others, has demonstrated how sentence subjects draw the reader's attention and orient his or her perspective on the rest of the sentence.

Sentence subjects are especially important in light of short-term memory limitations. Short-term memory, it may be recalled, can only store about seven items at a time; this is the size of the span, in other words, within which the active processing of text takes place. For schemata to be kept activated in the reader's mind, they must be continuously referred to, either directly or indirectly, before short-term memory decay sets in. The research cited in the preceding paragraph indicates that this referring is best done by words placed in the grammatical subject position. The grammatical subject, in other words, should be linked to the schema already activated in the reader's mind: in one form or other, it should reinstate the schema in the reader's active consciousness. Studies by Hayes-Roth and Thorndyke [50], Clark and Haviland [51], and others have shown that this reinstatement process is facilitated by *explicit* reference, either by pronouns (when the referent is clear) or by lexical repetition: otherwise, "bridging inferences" are required to maintain coherence.

Reader Variables

So far I have described research into various theoretical concepts and textual features that relate to readability as if the results of that research applied in about the same way to all readers in all reading situations. However, there are also some very important differences among readers that affect the way they would interpret a communication and, consequently, affect the readability of that communication for them. Two of these reader variables are the reader's familiarity with the communication's subject matter, and the reading style adopted by the reader [52].

Familiarity with Subject Matter — Although all readers make use of schemata when reading a text, there are important differences between the ways that specialist and nonspecialist readers use a text to activate the schemata they will employ while reading it. The nonspecialist, who lacks familiarity with the subject matter, must often rely on structural features of the text (headings, subheadings, topic sentences, etc.) and on lengthy explications (analogies, examples, operational definitions, etc.) to activate relevant schemata. The specialist reader, by contrast, often does not need such aids, at least not to the same degree, and may even feel at times that they just get in the way. The studies by Swarts, Flower, and Hayes [40] and Charrow and Redish [39], cited earlier, suggest that knowledgeable readers derive little if any benefit from headings and subheadings. Similarly, research by information theorists suggests that the use of extended analogies, elaborate examples, and other lengthy explications of important concepts may do more harm than good, if the concepts being explained are already familiar to the reader or can be succinctly related to already-familiar concepts. Because successful communication seems to manifest, optimally, an approximate 50-50 balance between "new information" and "redundant information" [53, 54], explications that are unnecessarily long raise the proportion of redundant information and risk boring the reader to the point of inattention.

What the specialist *does* seem to need from a written document, among other things, is a well-written introduction and a proper use of standard terminology. Recent research in problem-solving has suggested that words occurring early in a text generally serve as cues to the reader, telling him or her how to process the text as a whole. These early verbal cues have such power that, when improperly worded, they can easily mislead even specialists who are familiar with the particular subject under discussion and thus should know better [55–57]. It seems that specialists have such rich repertoires of schemata that they need only a small data sample to activate one or more governing schemata for a given text [58]. If these happen not to be the same schemata the writer had in mind, they may lead the reader to interpret the text in a way not intended by the writer. A clear introduction by the writer should prevent such "wild goose chases" from even getting started.

Of perhaps even more importance to the specialist reader is the proper use of standard terminology. One of the hallmarks of being a specialist, of course, is having a highly-developed, detailed knowledge of the various concepts, objects, processes, writings, and other things associated with that particular specialty; in the language of schema theory, each such concept, object, process, etc. is represented by a unique schema in the specialist's mind. Having a standard linguistic term for each of these unique schemata quickly brings to mind, for the specialist, all of the features associated with the particular schema. What this means is that writers should make every effort to use the standard terminology of a field when writing about that field to specialists in that field. If this means using long strings of compound nouns like *gas ejection ship attitude control system,* a practice long denigrated in writer's handbooks, so be it: a study by McNeill of NASA engineering jargon found that specialists had no trouble understanding such compounds [59]. Indeed, McNeill concluded that compound nouns are an essential part of effective communication among specialists: "An established nominal compound . . . is understood as a unit (and) probably is produced as a unit as well. . . . The result is that the nominal compound is a device that mainly benefits the 'culture,' guaranteeing that new technical terms will be available when needed." [59, p. 877]

Reading Style — Reading theorists have identified at least five different "styles" of reading: *skimming,* or reading for the general drift of a passage; *scanning,* or reading quickly with the purpose of finding specific items of information; *search reading,* or scanning with attention to the meaning of specific items; *receptive reading,* or reading for thorough comprehension; and *critical reading,* or reading for evaluation [60]. As we all know, most readers can easily switch from one style to another, according to the particular purpose of their reading. And since different readers often have different purposes in reading a given document, it is not uncommon for a single technical document — or even a single section of a technical document — to be subjected to all of these different reading styles, especially if it is circulated to a fairly large number of readers.

Of course, reading styles vary in the speed at which they are generally performed. Skimming, for example, is normally done at a much faster rate than receptive reading. Experimental research suggests that this variation can best be explained in terms of two distinctly different types of text processing: macrostructural (conceptual) and microstructural (linguistic). Macrostructural processing can vary greatly in the rate at which it is performed, depending on what kind of reading style is involved. Microstructural processing, on the other hand, is generally performed at the same rate for any given reader, regardless of reading style. Thus, the speed associated with any particular reading style appears to derive from

1. the speed at which macrostructural processing is carried out; and
2. the degree to which microstructural processing is called into play.

Skimming is fast because it uses fast macrostructural processing and virtually no microstructural processing; receptive reading is slow because it requires slow macrostructural processing and considerable microstructural processing.

Coke, for example, divided a group of sixty-eight subjects into two subsets, one of which ("the memory group") was asked to read for thorough comprehension and recall, the other ("the search group") to read only for the purpose of identifying certain items of information [61]. Some of the passages were rated as "difficult," others as "easy" — the ratings being determined jointly by a traditional readability formula (Flesch), by cloze testing, and by comprehension testing. As might be expected, the memory group read difficult passages more slowly than easy passages. The search group, however, was completely unaffected by passage difficulty (in fact, they read the difficult passages slightly *faster* than the easy ones!). Coke concluded from these results that the linguistic variables associated with standard readability measures may have "no effect on processing when the reader has to remember only a limited amount of text in order to make semantic interpretations of individual words." [61, p. 172] Coke's conclusion is supported by another study, carried out independently by Graesser, Hoffman, and Clark [6], who suggest that "it may be natural to consider linguistic processing and extended conceptual analyses as separate reading skills." [6, p. 146] They note, in particular, that "variations in instructions and reading goals influence the rate of executing macrostructure analyses, but not microstructure analyses." [6, p. 146] Other research, ranging from Wright's studies of formatting [62] to Tenenbaum's studies of text organization [31], supports these findings.

READABILITY GUIDELINES BASED ON COGNITIVE PSYCHOLOGY

The research described in the preceding section cannot be considered definitive, and its application to technical communication is not always clear. Among other things, more research needs to be carried out with actual technical writers and readers performing typical technical tasks. Nevertheless, existing research does allow us to formulate the following tentative guidelines for the technical writer:

1. State your purpose explicitly, in such a way that your reader can anticipate the approach you are taking to the subject. Make it clear to the reader what issue or conflict you're addressing.
2. Make the topic of each section and paragraph *visually prominent* − by using headings and subheadings, and by placing topic sentences at the beginning of paragraphs.
3. Keep the topic in the reader's mind by referring to it frequently, preferably in the grammatical subject position of sentences.
4. Try to anticipate what reading style the reader is likely to use. If it's just skim-reading, concentrate on formatting, headings, topic sentences, visual aids, and other general guides to the informational hierarchy of the text. But if the reader will need to read for detailed comprehension or evaluation, employ techniques that help the reader in the step-by-step processing of information in short-term memory; the remaining guidelines describe some of these techniques.
5. Structure the text according to the nature of the information you want the reader to pay most attention to. If it's main ideas, use a hierarchical (general-to-particular) structure; if details, use a listing (coordinate) structure.
6. Once you've started referring to something by a particular name, *continue* referring to it that way. Don't vary your terminology just for the sake of variation.
7. When writing for nonspecialists, be sure to explicate the most important concepts in your text by using examples, operational definitions, analogies, or other forms of illustration. In other words, use familiar concepts to explain unfamiliar ones.
8. When writing for specialists, on the other hand, do not *over*explain. That is, do not use lengthy examples, operational definitions, analogies, and so on for concepts the reader is likely to already be familiar with. Instead, rely on the standard terminology of the field, even when such terminology is long and complicated.

These few suggestions do not exhaust the possibilities; rather, they are simply illustrative of the many implications that emerge from contemporary psychological research when one looks at it from the point of view of the technical writer or technical writing instructor. The suggestions themselves, taken as a whole, do not constitute any sort of radical change from current technical writing practice or pedagogy; if anything, they reinforce our increasing emphasis on audience analysis. What is different and, I believe, important about the approach taken here is that it is based on carefully controlled empirical investigation of factors that cause comprehension and recall to improve; thus, it allows us more confident and authoritative in prescribing guidelines for students and professionals.

Of course, the guidelines given above have been deliberately oversimplified for the sake of convenience. Guideline 4, for example, implies that there are only two styles of reading and that the reader will use either one or the other but not both — directly contrary to what I said earlier. Guideline 5 also misleadingly implies an either/or choice; there are situations, certainly, where important information is to be found in both the main ideas of a text *and* the details. Finally, the last two guidelines are addressed to only the two end-points of the specialist-nonspecialist spectrum. Anyone familiar with technical writing knows that its audiences are very often composed of a mixture of readers: experts, technically sophisticated non-experts, semi-experts, technicians, and lay readers of different types. Because the same features that make a text more readable for one type of reader can make it less readable for another, composing a piece of writing that will be optimally readable for such diverse audience is an extremely difficult task in which the guidelines suggested above can probably be of only limited use. This dilemma for the technical writer does not appear to be resolvable through the use of readability guidelines as such. In fact, the research cited above suggests that the only solution is, in effect, to write separate reports or parts of reports (as described, for example, in Mathes and Stevenson's *Designing Technical Reports* [63]) for the different types of readers with different kinds of purposes.

COGNITIVE PSYCHOLOGY VERSUS READABILITY FORMULAS

Cognitive psychology is, by definition, a *process-oriented* science. It seeks to understand how people interpret, store, retrieve, and otherwise manipulate highly abstract entities in their minds. Readability formulas, on the other hand, are inherently *product-oriented*. Developed largely because of the desire of large corporations and bureaucracies to have a single, uniformly applied, organization-wide standard of readability for all of their publications, readability formulas are used properly only when they are applied to finished products.

This basic difference between the two approaches to describing readability carries more detailed differences with it. For one thing, the cognitive-psychological approach attributes major importance to the reader's prior familiarity with the subject matter being discussed, claiming that such familiarity greatly facilitates reading comprehension and that this, in turn, calls for different tactics by the writer if readability is to be optimized. The readability formula approach, by contrast, pays little attention to whether or not the reader has prior familiarity with the subject matter. Thus, because they focus primarily on the written document, readability formulas are largely unable to take into consideration differences among readers.

A second difference between the cognitive-psychological approach and the readability-formula approach concerns reading styles. It is a well-established fact that any document can be read in many different ways. Cognitive psychologists are actively investigating reading styles and how they relate to readability; the research reported on so far (some of it cited above) indicates some significant effects. But the developers of readability formulas have shown no particular interest in this variable.

A final difference between the two approaches has to do with the kind of guidance each provides for writers. The cognitive-psychological approach is manifestly process-oriented: it tries to pin down exactly what it is that makes the reading process easy or difficult; that is, it searches for the factors that actually cause readability to increase or decrease. As a result, the cognitive-psychological approach naturally leads to directly applicable advice, as exemplified by the guidelines given above. This advice can be utilized during the writing process to whatever degree the writer desires; even haphazard utilization would be of some help. For example, if you "keep the topic in the reader's mind by frequently referring to it, preferably in sentence-subject position" (Guideline 3), you will presumably enhance the readability of the text, even if you do not conscientiously follow the guideline throughout the text. The readability formula approach, by contrast, is concerned not with causal factors but with quantitative factors that are concerned with overall readability; this concern leads to its product orientation. As Bormuth, Klare, MacGinitie, and other readability formulists have often said, manipulating the surface variables that are used in the formulas will change the readability score but will probably *not* change the comprehensibility of a text. Therefore, it is a mistake to base writer's guidelines on such variables, as some technical writing handbooks have done: "Avoid excessive sentence length" [64], "Hold your sentence length down . . . We suggest a twenty-one word average to aim for in most situations" [65], and "Sentence length should average between seventeen and twenty words." [66] Consciously following such advice during the writing process will probably have little effect on overall comprehensibility, as the research cited in Jack Selzer's article (in this volume) makes quite clear. This point is even more vividly illustrated by a story recounted by Charles Sides at the 1981 International Technical Communication Conference [67]. Sides once had a student whose writing was "incontrovertibly soporific." It turned out that the student had once been told by his eighth-grade English teacher that "the average American English sentence contained eighteen words," and he thereafter had devoted his writing life to producing eighteen-word sentences! Indeed, Sides counted words and sentences in one of his papers and found that of the thirty-eight sentences in it, thirty-six were eighteen words long (the other two were seventeen and nineteen words long)!

All this is not to say, however, that the cognitive-psychological approach to readability is incompatible with the readability-formula approach or that readability formulas are useless in general. Far from it. When used properly — as a rough gauge of the likely readability of a finished text — readability formulas often seem to have a certain predictive validity. It may be that when writers take certain measures to make things easier for a reader — such as using examples, operational definitions, analogies, etc., when writing for a nonspecialist — they often use simpler vocabulary, shorter clauses, and other readability-formula variables in the process, as Bormuth has suggested [68]. If so, the variables that are measured by readability formulas would in fact be correlated with the features that contribute to reading comprehension.

If readability formulas do have the kind of limited but nonetheless useful scope of application just described (and claimed for them by many researchers down through the years), there is no reason why they could not be used along with cognitive-psychological guidelines as part of an integrated approach to readability. Cognitive guidelines like those suggested above could guide the writer during the composing process (in conjunction perhaps with other process-oriented guidelines resulting from psycholinguistic investigations; see, for example, Hirsch [1] and Robbins [69]). Readability formulas could then be used as an "early warning check" of the complete draft, as Brendel puts it [70], followed by cloze testing with the intended audience (every nth word of the text is left blank, and the intended user tries to guess what words have been deleted), opinion surveys, and on-site observation: "The cloze procedure and readability formulas are general indices of a document's suitability; opinion surveys and discussions with users can identify specific problems." [70, p. E-9] It is important to emphasize, though, that testing alone will not solve the readability problem: the text must first be written before it can be tested. When writing, writers need to understand how a text communicates — how readers process it and learn from it. This is precisely the domain of cognitive psychology. And this is why, in my opinion, we should turn to cognitive psychology if we want to truly understand the phenomenon of readability.

REFERENCES

1. E. D. Hirsch, Jr., *The Philosophy of Composition,* The University of Chicago Press, Chicago, Illinois, 1977.
2. J. D. Bransford and M. K. Johnson, Contextual Prerequisites for Understanding: Some Investigations of Comprehension and Recall, *Journal of Verbal Learning and Verbal Behavior, 11,* pp. 717-726, 1972.
3. J. J. Greeno, Cognitive Objectives of Instructions: Theory of Knowledge for Solving Problems and Answering Questions, in *Cognition and Instruction,* D. Klahr (ed.), Lawrence Erlbaum Associates, Hillsdale, New Jersey, pp. 123-159, 1976.
4. G. J. Spilich, G. T. Vesonder, H. L. Chiesi, and J. F. Voss, Text Processing of Domain-Related Information for Individuals with High and Low Domain

Knowledge, *Journal of Verbal Learning and Verbal Behavior, 18*, pp. 275-290, 1979.

5. H. L. Chiesi, G. J. Spilich, and J. F. Voss, Acquisition of Domain-Related Information in Relation to High and Low Domain Knowledge, *Journal of Verbal Learning and Verbal Behavior, 18*, pp. 257-273, 1979.

6. A. C. Graesser, N. L. Hoffman, and L. F. Clark, Structural Components of Reading Time, *Journal of Verbal Learning and Verbal Behavior, 19*, pp. 135-151, 1980.

7. C. Clifton, Jr. and M. L. Slowiaczek, Integrating New Information with Old Knowledge, *Memory and Cognition, 9*, pp. 142-148, 1981.

8. H. Head, *Studies in Neurology*, Oxford University Press, New York, 1920.

9. F. C. Bartlett, *Remembering*, Cambridge University Press, London, 1932.

10. J. Piaget, *The Origins of Intelligence in Children*, International Universities Press, New York, 1936.

11. D. Norman and D. Bobrow, On the Role of Active Memory Processes in Perception and Cognition, in *The Structure of Human Memory*, C. Cofer (ed.), Freeman, San Francisco, California, pp. 114-132, 1975.

12. T. Winograd, A Framework for Understanding Discourse, in *Cognitive Processes in Comprehension*, P. A. Carpenter and M. A. Just (eds.), Lawrence Erlbaum, Hillsdale, New Jersey, pp. 63-88, 1977.

13. D. E. Rumelhart and A. Ortony, The Representation of Knowledge in Memory, in *Schooling and the Acquisition of Knowledge*, R. C. Anderson, R. J. Spiro, and W. E. Montague (eds.), Lawrence Erlbaum, Hillsdale, New Jersey, pp. 99-135, 1977.

14. P. W. Thorndyke and B. Hayes-Roth, The Use of Schemata in the Acquisition and Transfer of Knowledge, *Cognitive Psychology, 11*, pp. 82-106, 1979.

15. J. M. Royer and G. W. Cable, Facilitated Learning in Connected Discourse, *Journal of Educational Psychology, 67*, pp. 116-123, 1975.

16. J. M. Royer and G. W. Cable, Illustrations, Analogies, and Facilitative Transfer in Prose Learning, *Journal of Educational Psychology, 68*, pp. 205-209, 1976.

17. P. W. Thorndyke, Cognitive Structures in Comprehension and Memory of Narrative Discourse, *Cognitive Psychology, 9*, pp. 77-110, 1977.

18. D. Schallert, Improving Memory for Prose: The Relationship between Depth of Processing and Context, *Journal of Verbal Learning and Verbal Behavior, 15*, pp. 621-632, 1976.

19. A. M. Lesgold, S. F. Roth, and M. E. Curtis, Foregrounding Effects in Discourse Comprehension, *Journal of Verbal Learning and Verbal Behavior, 18*, pp. 291-308, 1979.

20. W. Kintsch and J. Keenan, Reading Rate and Retention as a Function of the Number of Propositions in the Base Structure of Sentences, *Cognitive Psychology, 5*, pp. 257-274, 1973.

21. B. J. F. Meyer and G. McConkie, What is Recalled after Hearing a Passage?, *Journal of Educational Psychology, 65*, pp. 109-117, 1973.

22. B. J. F. Meyer, *The Organization of Prose and its Effects on Memory*, North-Holland Publishing Company, Amsterdam, 1975.

23. J. W. Pichert and R. C. Anderson, Taking Different Perspectives on a Story, *Journal of Educational Psychology, 69,* pp. 307-315, 1977.
24. R. C. Anderson, R. E. Reynolds, D. L. Schallert, and E. T. Goetz, Frameworks for Comprehending Discourse, *American Educational Research Journal, 14,* pp. 367-381, 1977.
25. E. T. Goetz, Infering from Text: Some Factors Influencing Which Inferences Will Be Made, *Discourse Processes, 2,* pp. 179-195, 1979.
26. W. Kintsch, E. Kozminsky, W. J. Streby, G. McKoon, and J. M. Keenan, Comprehension and Recall of Text as a Function of Content Variables, *Journal of Verbal Learning and Verbal Behavior, 14,* pp. 196-214, 1975.
27. D. Kieras, Initial Mention as a Signal to Thematic Content in Technical Passages, *Memory and Cognition, 8,* pp. 345-353, 1980.
28. C. H. Walker and B. J. F. Meyer, Integrating Different Types of Information in Text, *Journal of Verbal Learning and Verbal Behavior, 19,* pp. 263-275, 1980.
29. R. K. Cirilo and D. J. Foss, Text Structure and Reading Time for Sentences, *Journal of Verbal Learning and Verbal Behavior, 19,* pp. 96-109, 1980.
30. P. Wright, Writing to be Understood: Why Use Sentences?, *Applied Ergonomics, 2,* pp. 207-209, 1971.
31. A. B. Tenenbaum, Task-Dependent Effects of Organization and Context upon Comprehension of Prose, *Journal of Educational Psychology, 69,* pp. 528-536, 1977.
32. W. Kintsch and D. Vipond, Reading Comprehension and Readability in Educational Practice and Psychological Theory, in *Proceedings of the Conference on Memory,* L-G. Nilsson (ed.), Lawrence Erlbaum, Hillsdale, New Jersey, pp. 329-365, 1978.
33. W. Kintsch and T. A. van Dijk, Toward a Model of Text Comprehension and Production, *Psychological Review, 85,* pp. 363-394, 1978.
34. D. J. Dooling and R. Lachman, Effects of Comprehension on Retention of Prose, *Journal of Experimental Psychology, 88,* pp. 216-222, 1971.
35. J. D. Bransford and N. S. McCarrell, A Sketch of a Cognitive Approach to Comprehension, in *Cognition and the Symbolic Processes,* W. B. Weimer and D. S. Palermo (eds.), Lawrence Erlbaum, Hillsdale, New Jersey, pp. 189-229, 1981.
36. M. N. K. Schwarz and A. Flammer, Text Structure and Title — Effects on Comprehension and Recall, *Journal of Verbal Learning and Verbal Behavior, 20,* pp. 61-66, 1981.
37. E. Kozminsky, Altering Comprehension: The Effect of Biasing Titles on Text Comprehension, *Memory and Cognition, 5,* pp. 482-490, 1977.
38. M. Bock, Some Effects of Titles on Building and Recalling Text Structures, *Discourse Processes, 3,* pp. 301-311, 1980.
39. V. R. Charrow and J. C. Redish, *A Study of Standardized Headings for Warranties,* Document Design Project Technical Report No. 6, American Institutes for Research, Washington, D.C., 1980.
40. H. Swarts, L. S. Flower, and J. R. Hayes, *How Headings in Documents Can Mislead Readers,* Document Design Project Technical Report No. 9, American Institutes for Research, Washington, D.C., 1980.

41. R. M. Gagne and V. K. Wiegand, Effects of a Superordinate Context on Learning and Retention of Facts, *Journal of Educational Psychology, 61,* pp. 406-409, 1970.

42. P. A. Carpenter and M. A. Just, Reading Comprehension as Eyes See It, in *Cognitive Processes in Comprehension,* P. A. Carpenter and M. A. Just (eds.), Lawrence Erlbaum, Hillsdale, New Jersey, pp. 109-139, 1977.

43. D. Kieras, *Initial Mention as a Cue to the Main Idea and Main Item of a Technical Passage,* Technical Report No. 3, University of Arizona Psychology Department, Tucson, Arizona, July 1979.

44. D. Kieras, *Abstracting Main Ideas from Technical Prose: A Preliminary Study of Six Passages,* Technical Report No. 5, University of Arizona Psychology Department, Tucson, Arizona, July 1980.

45. D. Kieras, *Topicalization Effects in Memory for Technical Prose,* Technical Report No. 6, University of Arizona Psychology Department, Tucson, Arizona, August 1980.

46. C. A. Perfetti and S. R. Goldman, Thematization and Sentence Retrieval, *Journal of Verbal Learning and Verbal Behavior, 13,* pp. 70-79, 1974.

47. B. MacWhinney, Starting Points, *Language, 53,* pp. 152-168, 1977.

48. D. Kieras, *The Relation of Topics and Themes in Naturally Occurring Technical Paragraphs,* Technical Report No. 1, University of Arizona Psychology Department, Tucson, Arizona, January 1979.

49. D. Kieras, The Role of Major Referents and Sentence Topics in the Construction of Passage Macrostructure, *Discourse Processes, 4,* pp. 1-15, 1981.

50. B. Hayes-Roth and P. W. Thorndyke, Integration of Knowledge from Text, *Journal of Verbal Learning and Verbal Behavior, 18,* pp. 91-108, 1979.

51. H. H. Clark and S. E. Haviland, Comprehension and the Given-New Contract, in *Discourse Production and Comprehension,* R. O. Freedle (ed.), Ablex, Norwood, New Jersey, pp. 1-40, 1977.

52. T. G. Sticht, Comprehending Reading at Work, in *Cognitive Processes in Comprehension,* P. A. Carpenter and M. A. Just (eds.), Lawrence Erlbaum, Hillsdale, New Jersey, pp. 221-246, 1977.

53. W. R. Garner, *Uncertainty and Structure as Psychological Concepts,* Wiley, New York, 1962.

54. S. Darian, The Role of Redundancy in Language and Language Teaching, *System, 7,* pp. 47-59, 1979.

55. D. A. Hinsley, J. R. Hayes, and H. A. Simon, From Words to Equations: Meaning and Representation in Algebra Word Problems, in *Cognitive Processes in Comprehension,* P. A. Carpenter and M. A. Just (eds.), Lawrence Erlbaum, Hillsdale, New Jersey, pp. 89-106, 1977.

56. J. Larkin, *Teaching Problem Solving in Physics: The Psychological Laboratory and the Practical Classroom,* Technical Report, Group in Science and Mathematical Education, University of California, Berkeley, 1978.

57. D. P. Simon and H. A. Simon, A Tale of Two Protocols, in *Cognitive Process Instruction,* J. Lockhead and J. Clement (eds.), The Franklin Institute Press, Philadelphia, Pennsylvania, pp. 119-132, 1979.

58. B. J. Grosz, *Focusing and Description in Natural Language Dialogues,* Technical Note 185, SRI International, Menlo Park, California, 1979.
59. D. McNeill, Speaking of Space, *Science, 152,* pp. 875-880, 1966.
60. A. K. Pugh, *Silent Reading: An Introduction to Its Study and Teaching,* Heinemann, London, 1978.
61. E. U. Coke, Reading Rate, Readability, and Variations in Task-Induced Processing, *Journal of Educational Psychology, 68,* pp. 167-173, 1976.
62. P. Wright, Behavioral Research and the Technical Communicator, *The Communicator of Scientific and Technical Information,* pp. 3-13, July 1977.
63. J. C. Mathes and D. W. Stevenson, *Designing Technical Reports: Writing for Audiences in Organizations,* Bobbs-Merrill, Indianapolis, Indiana, 1976.
64. T. Sherman and S. Johnson, *Modern Technical Writing,* 3rd Edition, Prentice-Hall, Englewood Cliffs, New Jersey, 1975.
65. K. W. Houp and T. E. Pearsall, *Reporting Technical Information,* 3rd Edition, Glencoe Press, Beverly Hills, California, 1977.
66. T. L. Warren, *Technical Communication,* Littlefield, Adams & Co., Totowa, New Jersey, 1978.
67. C. H. Sides, Syntax, Comprehension, and Believability: Implications for Technical Writers, *Proceedings of the 28th International Technical Communication Conference,* Society for Technical Communication, Washington, D.C., pp. E95-E98, 1981.
68. J. R. Bormuth, Readability: A New Approach, *Reading Research Quarterly, 1,* pp. 79-132, 1966.
69. J. Robbins, Improving the Understandability of Technical Text: Some Practical Implications of Recent Psycholinguistic Research, *Proceedings of the 27th International Technical Communication Conference,* Society for Technical Communication, Washington, D.C., pp. R241-R245, 1980.
70. S. E. Brendel, Field Evaluating Documents: What Can We Really Expect?, *Proceedings of the 28th International Technical Communication Conference,* Society for Technical Communication, Washington, D.C., pp. E7-E10, 1981.

PART THREE

Approaches from Rhetoric, Discourse Theory, and Sociology

CHAPTER 6

The Role of Models in Technical and Scientific Writing

VICTORIA M. WINKLER

A good theory is eminently practical. The challenge facing teachers of technical and scientific writing in the eighties is to develop an interdisciplinary problem-solving rhetorical theory to improve the teaching of technical, scientific, and professional writing while also guiding research in communication theory. In this effort, we can draw upon the assistance of composition theorists, who have argued that the process approach to teaching writing is more effective and more comprehensive than the product approach. The publication in 1970 of Young, Becker, and Pike's *Rhetoric: Discovery and Change* [1] and Janice Lauer's bibliography, "Heuristics and Composition" [2] marked the beginning of a gradual shift from the product approach to the process approach in the teaching of writing. The product approach is characterized, in freshman composition, by concern for Standard Edited English, and, in technical writing, by an additional adherence to prescribed organizational patterns. The process approach to teaching writing is characterized by expanding the scope of composition theory to include rhetorical invention, which introduces procedures for discovering the substance of discourse.

When we compare technical communication theory in the 1970's to composition theory during that time, we discover a curious disjunction: although all but one of the technical writing texts published before and during that period clearly reflect a product approach to writing [3], they all include sections

on audience and purpose, which are prewriting or inventional considerations
associated with the process-oriented approach to writing. Thus, insofar as the
technical communication discipline has long been concerned with audience
and purpose, we were ahead of modern composition theorists; however, we were
prevented from leading the way to a process approach by our positivist
epistemology, manifested in our preoccupation with structural models and
"objective" style and in our assumption that the content of technical discourse
is given.

More recently, however, Dwight W. Stevenson and Dennis Hall have been
urging technical writing teachers not only to include invention in their courses
but to emphasize it [4, 5]. Hall encourages us to move technical writing from
"competence in a form" to "competence in a method" by including invention.
J. W. Allen even provides us with a practical exercise for introducing technical
students to inventional heuristics [6]. The changes being urged would
ultimately require the field of technical communication to give up its product
orientation and adopt a process-oriented approach to writing.

The purpose of this article is to examine the real differences between the
product and process pedagogies by exploring the different types of theoretical
models that inform the two approaches. An examination of how these models
function will provide us with an understanding of the basic assumptions
underlying our theories of composing.

MODELS AND WRITING PEDAGOGY

The product approach to teaching writing which we see reflected in so many
technical writing texts is the natural consequence of the assumption made by the
authors of these texts that "the writer is teeming with information and that the
writer's principal, if not exclusive, problems are matters of clear and concise
statement and of ordering statements in one of several appropriate forms . . . . "
[5, p. 19] As teachers of technical writing, we have concerned ourselves with
teaching formal or *structural models,* which describe completed texts. These
models help writers arrange information in acceptable formats for proposals,
progress reports, physical science reports, feasibility studies, technical articles,
and so on. The use of these models, which is the dominant characteristic of the
product approach to writing, leads to an emphasis on style and correctness of
the finished product.

The process approach to writing, on the other hand, assumes that we must
help writers discover the subject matter before concentrating on arrangement or
editing. The underlying assumption in the process approach is that the subject
matter is not "given"; it must be invented. The process approach provides
writers with systematic procedures — heuristics, if you will — to help generate
the content of discourse. These systematic procedures are really *inventional
models,* which describe ways in which the mind can organize experience. These

models can guide the writer's exploration of a problem or topic and enable him or her to systematically discover the substance of discourse. To better understand the function of structural and inventional models, we must examine how each model operates.

Although structural models are typically associated with generating the form of discourse and inventional models with generating its substance, the two basic types of models cannot be entirely distinguished in terms of their functions. In his introduction to *Contemporary Rhetoric,* W. Ross Winterowd calls inventional models "conceptual frameworks" and indiscriminately assigns to them not only the purposes I ascribe to inventional models, but also the purposes I ascribe to structural models: "A conceptual framework . . . allows one to organize a subject, and it automatically becomes an inventive heuristic for the discovery of subject matter." [7] Similarly, Young, Becker, and Pike do not clearly distinguish between the inventional and arrangement functions served by the tagmemic heuristic they propose. Although the primary function of invention is to generate the substance of discourse, the authors present several arrangement patterns which they imply are also generated in some way by their inventional model. We could argue, therefore, that although inventional models are concerned primarily with generating substance, they also serve an arrangement function. Likewise, the structural models serve more than an arrangement function since they name categories of information that might be included, thereby aiding the writer in discovering substance. For the purposes of this article, however, I will label models "structural" or "inventional" based on the approaches to writing they presuppose: structural models presuppose a product approach while inventional models presuppose a process approach.

Structural Models as Manifest Analogies

Teachers of scientific and technical writing recognize that reliance on structural models stems from their usefulness as pedagogical tools for identifying the parts of a discourse and indicating how to sequence information. Different structural models are used for generating the arrangement patterns for different types of discourse, such as the causal analysis format for trouble-shooting reports and the intellectual problem-solving structure for the discussion of experimental research results. Other structural models would include formats for proposals, progress reports, and various types of business correspondence.

When writers employ these structural models as conceptual frameworks to assist them in processing information, they are modifying their existing knowledge in response to the limits and constraints imposed by the model itself. These limits and constraints help the writer to control the subject matter by providing a flexible framework to suggest possible arrangement patterns and by serving as a checklist for ensuring that he or she has not overlooked something. To demonstrate how structural models guide the writer in making rhetorical choices, let us examine the "purpose statement" model from Mathes and

STRUCTURAL MODEL FOR A PURPOSE STATEMENT	DISCOURSE
Problem and Context	The accounting department is currently computerizing many of its functions. One of the functions to be computerized is the pricing of the international order-to-ship (OTS). Each OTS can contain equipment and/ or miscellaneous components (MC's). Two different methods of computer- ization have been discussed: one using MAPPER, and one using structured
Assignment or Technical Task	IS&C programming. I have been asked to create a computerized method using MAPPER to price MC's on the international OTS. This report
Rhetorical Purpose	explains how the MAPPER computerized method works and recommends that it be adopted for use within the accounting department.

Figure 1. The purpose statement as structural model.

Stevenson's *Designing Technical Reports* [8] and a discourse sample generated from this model, shown in Figure 1.

When we compare the model for an effective purpose statement with the discourse sample, we find that the structural model is not identical with but *analogous* to the discourse. The model itself is an abstraction and the thing modeled is a specific discourse unit. The model indicates to the writer what *kinds* of information should be included in the purpose statement and describes a preferred arrangement of its contents. In this way, the model sets up a direct, almost proportional, relationship with the discourse (A : B). It can also be used as a checklist to keep the writer from omitting any essential information, but as a checklist, the model is transcendent and not data-conditioned [9]. In other words, its operations transcend the subject matter of this or any particular discourse, permitting writers to use it in a variety of situations calling for a purpose statement. The relationship of analogy between a structural model and the discourse modeled will become clearer if we examine the relationship between the model and the discourse as shown in Figure 2.

Whenever we analyze a standard technical article and identify its parts (i.e., introduction, statement of the problem, survey of the literature, experimental procedures, discussion of results, conclusions), we are identifying the structural

TOPIC OR PROBLEM + STRUCTURAL MODEL → DISCOURSE		
	(used to select	
	and arrange data)	
Example: information concerning	structural outline	the actual
a technical investigation $+$	for a technical article $→$	technical article

Figure 2. The structural model: a product approach to writing.

model which has been used to organize the information. With slight variations, this model could be used to arrange the information for nearly any formal technical article or laboratory report. When we teach report writing, we begin by teaching the model. We show examples of how the model has been successfully used and how its structure may be varied in specimen reports. Finally, we instruct our students to use the model as a guide for organizing information from a technical investigation to produce their own technical articles or laboratory reports.

All models operate via analogy. In the case of structural models, the analogic form they take is what W. H. Leatherdale calls a "manifest analogy," that is, a direct, proportional analogy which identifies and explains the formal (structural) and functional similarities between the model and the thing modeled [10]. Since these similarities (properties, qualities, relations) can be inferred from normal sense experience or from ordinary perception, the structural model is based on an inductive generalization. In other words, the structural model is on a higher level of generality than the instance, like the particular purpose statement or article being written. If we compared the arrangement patterns of a number of technical articles or laboratory reports, we could infer a structural model from specific instances. The kinds of analogic relations it has with the discourse unit are manifest. Manifest analogies, which we use as writing models, differ from mathematical ratios (2 : 4 :: 8 : 16) because they deal with structural and functional similarities of a kind which go beyond mathematical proportions.

Although the structural models for teaching writing suggest the *kinds* of information writers need for a particular discourse type, they do not provide writers with the means for generating that information. It seems apparent that a more appropriate "place" for structural models and the product approach to writing that they presuppose is as a sub-process in a process theory of writing. Composing does not begin with the process of arranging data into specific patterns; it begins with a felt difficulty, an anomaly, or the recognition of a problem to be solved. The content is not "given"; it is the result of an investigation and is shaped by rhetorical considerations. A more practical and comprehensive theory of composing should begin at the beginning with the formulation and exploration of the problem and rhetorical situation, rather than *in medias res* with the application of structural models.

Inventional Models as Imported Analogies

Leatherdale provides a basis for this more comprehensive theory in his discussion of a second type of model, which operates by means of *imported analogy*. The imported analogy employs an analogue drawn from a totally different domain from that of the subject under consideration. Consider, for example, the use of hydraulics as an imported analogy to explain electricity. The imported analogy (hydraulics) is both better known and easier to understand than the subject under investigation (electricity). By comparing the properties, similarities, and relations in the imported analogy (pressure and flow) with those of the lesser known topic (voltage and amperage), we are able to explore the latter systematically. The imported analogy also serves as an important pedagogical tool for discovering what we can about a topic under investigation by helping us describe and explain the unfamiliar in terms of the familiar.

Leatherdale tells us that unlike manifest analogy, which is based on properties "given in immediate sense experience or in ordinary perception," [10, p. 4] imported analogies are based on the formulation of novel, more esoteric relations between two analogues, called the topic analogue and the imported analogue. The topic analogue is the field of phenomena that requires ordering or explanation. The imported analogue, brought into the mind either spontaneously or by an effort, gives order or explanation. Figure 3 illustrates the use of these terms by showing how they operate in Bohr's analogy between the structure of the atom (topic analogue) and the planetary system (imported analogue).

In formulating the Bohr-Rutherford model of atomic structure, Bohr noticed a vague similarity between planetary systems and atomic structure. When he began to explore the similarity, he discovered that since the properties of planetary systems were directly observable, well worked out, and easy to extend and generalize about, he could use the planetary system as an imported analogue to make the strange and unknown familiar. In working out the implications of these similarities, Bohr identified and analyzed the positive, negative, and neutral (or questionable) analogues generated by his analogical act. When he compared, for example, the solar system's large central sun orbited by planets with the atom's nucleus orbited by electrons, he identified a positive analogue. The discrepancies in size and physical composition between planetary systems and atoms were identified as negative analogues (or areas where the analogy breaks down). The positive and negative analogues extend the investigator's knowledge of the topic analogue and they guide his or her investigation systematically yet flexibly.

Useful imported analogues should enable an investigator to discover properties or relations in the topic analogue that are suggested by the analogic act. The prediction of new relations suggested by the imported analogue attests to the heuristic value of the imported analogy. It is precisely this suggestive power that manifest analogies lack. For example, since Bohr knew that there is a force called gravity holding the planets in their orbits around the sun, he was

TOPIC ANALOGUE	+	IMPORTED ANALOGUE	=	ANALOGICAL ACT
Topic or problem under investigation	+	Inventional model or creative analogue	=	Raw data; novel insights; unique perspectives leading to positive, negative, and neutral analogous relations
Example:				
atomic structure	+	planetary system model	=	novel act of recognition
nucleus of atom	+	sun in center of solar system	=	positive analogue
minute size	+	gargantuan size	=	negative analogue
electromagnetic charges	+	gravity	=	neutral analogue, later confirmed as part of positive analogue

Figure 3. The analogical act.

led to postulate an analogous force (electromagnetic charges) holding electrons in their orbits around the nucleus. Such novel predictions based on known properties of the imported analogue guide research and induce intuition systematically rather than haphazardly. The initial illuminating perception of similarity between the imported analogue and the topic analogue and the prediction of novel relations based on neutral analogues help the investigator to generate preliminary hypotheses which guide his or her research efforts.

Leatherdale says that imported analogies lead to scientific discovery and progress because they make room for imagination, intuition, and scientific innovation. Imported analogies serve as fruitful methods of discovery in science because they admit of some special relations and insights "going beyond routine method." These special relations involve "novel perceptions" and these novel perceptions are "instantaneous and comprehensive." [10, p. 12] However, their full implementation, elaboration, and qualification may take a long time:

> It is true that the analogical act in so far as it is an illuminating perception of resemblance is momentary and instantaneous. However, considered in all its fullness, it should be connected with a whole complex of antecedent behavior and knowledge and a similar complex of consequent implication and association. Before the illuminating perception occurs, the topic analogue is ranged over, and sometimes one, sometimes another, part is brought into focus or juxtaposed with this or that other part. The topic analogue is itself an amorphous entity, ever growing and changing, sometimes crystallizing out only to dissolve again under the pressure of discordant facts drawn from other areas of the topic analogue. Imported analogies breed and interbreed with each other [10, pp. 16-17].

If imported analogies lead to scientific discovery, similarly they can be the basis for new ideas in writing. Although Leatherdale describes the analogical act as "momentary and instantaneous" in the mind, it would be more useful for us to think of the analogical act as both the "illuminating perception of resemblance" and the working out of its consequent implications and associations. This extension of Leatherdale's definition of an analogical act is remarkably similar to Young, Becker, and Pike's account of the process of inquiry that the writer engages in to solve rhetorical problems. The process consists of four stages: preparation, incubation, illumination, and verification — paralleling what Leatherdale describes as occurring in our extended definition of an analogical act. The similarities between analogical acts in scientific discovery and in rhetoric would lead us to believe that analogical acts provide us with an interdisciplinary explanation of creative thinking.

In rhetoric this process of discovery is called invention. Traditionally, invention is seen as the creation or discovery of the substance of discourse, as distinct from subsequent considerations of organization and style. Rhetorical theorists have devised many systematic heuristics to assist in the invention of discourse substance. Each system presupposes its own model of concept-formation that I will call an inventional model. The inventional model described by Young, Becker, and Pike, for example, assumes that people organize experience into concepts by comprehending the static, dynamic, and relational aspects of that experience. Burke's Pentad, on the other hand, assumes that people organize their experience in dramatistic terms: that is, we seek to understand what action is taking place, who or what is the agent, what agency was used, what was the scene, and what was the purpose. These models, therefore, may be thought of as imported analogies.

The application of an inventional model to explore a problem involves an analogical act in which we look at chaotic experience *as though it were* organized according to the systematic terms of the inventional model. We do this by looking at experience first from the perspective of one of the terms of the model (agent) and then from another (scene). This systematic shifting of perspectives, looking at the subject under investigation *as if* it were something else, proceeds by means of foregrounding and backgrounding. The writer cannot keep all of the associations generated by the analogical act in the mind's eye at once, but rather " . . . the spotlight of attention ranges discursively over an area any part of which can be brought into focus at will while the rest of the field remains constantly accessible — a sort of hinterland from which one can readily import perceptions and judgements." [10, p. 15]

The inventional models guide the writer's exploration of a problem by leading him or her through a set of cumulative procedures which are flexible and recursive — allowing "a return to previous operations or a leap to subsequent ones if an evolving insight prompts such recursiveness." [11] Therefore, the writer is neither trapped in a set of mechanical lock-step procedures nor is he or she abandoned to trial-and-error meanderings. As Robert de Beaugrande points out, "the act of invention is situated within the broad range between ungoverned associating (e.g., daydreaming) and mechanical reproduction of conventional knowledge (e. g., dictionary entries). . . . Hence, the freedom of the inventive writer to produce new associations . . . is constantly balanced against the responsibility to provide new perspectives on common knowledge and experience. Invention is not the mere creation of novelties, but rather the modification of existing knowledge in response to a specific intention and goal." [12] De Beaugrande's definition of invention seems particularly apposite for technical writers because so much of what they write modifies existing knowledge or opinion in response to audience and purpose.

Although the inventional models guide our exploration of a topic or problem, they are not subject-matter models because they are transcendent and not data-conditioned. In other words, the same inventional model may be used repeatedly from one topic to another. What these models describe is a *process* for generating substance rather than a product (the discourse itself). Inventional models describe a theory of concept formation; and they thereby provide us with a set of operations for investigating problematic situations in preparation for communicating about them.

Thus, inventional models serve a much different function from the one that structural models serve. The relationships between structural and inventional models in a process approach to writing is shown in Figure 4. Inventional models are creative analogies that guide and direct the writer's cognitive processes in generating the substance of discourse. They serve as cognitive maps to an unknown territory—guiding the writer's perceptual processes, problem-solving processes, learning processes, and verbal skills to explore the subject. Structural models assist the writer in giving form to that substance. The inventional model describes a way in which the mind orders experience; it can, therefore, be used as an imported analogue in an analogical act, whose purpose is to order a problematic realm of experience, the topic analogue. Used in this way, it enables writers to generate the substance of discourse. The structural model provides rhetorical form such that the resulting discourse is related to the model through a manifest analogy.

THE PROCESS APPROACH TO
TEACHING TECHNICAL WRITING

As the previous discussion explains, all models — including structural models — operate as analogues. Consequently, these models by their very nature are not prescriptive. Writing teachers who are unaware of the analogical nature of product and process models might be tempted to teach them prescriptively, but both structural and inventional models should serve as heuristics, rather than algorithms. These models do not guarantee success; they simply increase the writer's chances of consistently producing more effective discourse. As William Irmscher points out, the use of inventional models and the process approach brings us closer to a humanistic rationale for teaching writing:

> If we think of education as concerned with learning to know, finding meaning by association, organizing knowledge, and, finally, developing our capacity to use that knowledge in new situations, then certainly writing serves us all as a way of learning and developing. I would like to suggest that our integrity as teachers of writing lies not solely in being the best possible skills-technicians but in promoting composition as a way of learning and developing, basic to all disciplines [13, p. 244].

We could summarize the role of analogical thinking in concept formation and, correspondingly, in the use of inventional models in the composing process, by noting that analogical thinking involves the perception of novel insights and resemblances as well as the modification of existing knowledge. The systematic exploration of these insights, guided by the structure of the imported analogue, brings our problem-solving skills to bear on the data. As we compare the topic and imported analogues, we generate the substance of discourse and we learn. When we attempt to communicate what we have learned in the process, besides

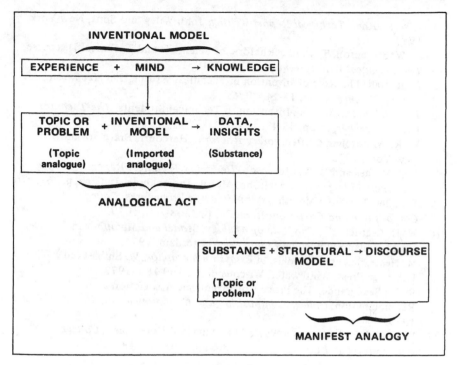

Figure 4. The inventional model: a process approach to writing.

involving our synthetic and analytic skills, we also involve our verbal skills. To communicate our perceptions, we sometimes even borrow the language of the imported analogue (such as hydraulics) to talk about the topic analogue (electricity) until we either extend the meaning of the old terms (pressure and flow) or until we create a new set of terms and concepts (like voltage and amperage) to represent our new knowledge. Therefore, by teaching inventional models as conceptual strategies in the technical writing classroom, we are forging another link between learning strategies and writing strategies. The analogical acts we perform in applying inventional models to generate the substance of discourse provide us with a more comprehensive approach to teaching writing which complements, without denigrating, the earlier structural models.

REFERENCES

1. R. E. Young, A. L. Becker, and K. L. Pike, *Rhetoric: Discovery and Change*, Harcourt, Brace and World, New York, 1970.
2. J. Lauer, Heuristics and Composition, *College Composition and Communication, 21*, pp. 396-404, 1970.

3. J. W. Souther, *Technical Report Writing*, John Wiley and Sons, New York, 1957.
4. D. W. Stevenson, Toward a Rhetoric of Scientific and Technical Discourse, *The Technical Writing Teacher, 5*, pp. 4-10, 1977.
5. D. R. Hall, The Role of Invention in Technical Writing, *The Technical Writing Teacher, 4*, pp. 13-24, 1976.
6. J. W. Allen, Introducing Invention to Technical Students, *The Technical Writing Teacher, 5*, pp. 45-49, 1978.
7. W. R. Winterowd, *Contemporary Rhetoric*, Harcourt, Brace Jovanovich, New York, 1975.
8. J. C. Mathes and D. W. Stevenson, *Designing Technical Reports: Writing for Audiences in Organizations*, Bobbs-Merrill, Indianapolis, Indiana, p. 26, 1976.
9. J. Lauer, Toward a Metatheory of Heuristic Procedures, *College Composition and Communication, 30*, pp. 268-269, 1979.
10. W. H. Leatherdale, *The Role of Analogy, Model and Metaphor in Science*, North-Holland Publishing Company, Amsterdam, 1974.
11. M. Hesse, Scientific Models, in *Essays on Metaphor*, W. Shibles (ed.), The Language Press, Whitewater, Wisconsin, pp. 169-180, 1972.
12. R. De Beaugrande, The Process of Invention: Association and Recombination, *College Composition and Communication, 30*, pp. 260-267, 1979.
13. W. Irmscher, Writing as a Way of Learning and Developing, *College Composition and Communication, 30*, pp. 240-244, 1979.

CHAPTER 7

A Rhetoric for Research in Sciences and Technologies

JAMES P. ZAPPEN

Current theories of rhetoric for science and technology [1–7] are based primarily upon studies in the history and philosophy of science and technology that emphasize their communal character [8–16]. According to this tradition, the scientific community has developed a rhetoric suited to the goals of science, which are epistemic, and the technological community has developed a rhetoric suited to the goals of technology, which are productive. This line of reasoning is misleading, however, since it assumes that all of the goals of science are epistemic and all of the goals of technology are productive. That is, it infers from the activities of science and technology the goals proper to each. It fails to notice that the activities of both science and technology actually serve several different communities, each with its own goals.

For these reasons, I want to press current theories of rhetoric for science and technology in another direction. From the perspective of rhetoric, the important distinction has to do not with any differences between activities in sciences and in technologies but with differences among the various contexts of these activities. Toulmin's theory of the development of sciences and technologies provides a frame of reference for distinguishing and characterizing these contexts and the documents proper to each. In this article I show why Toulmin's theory can be interpreted as a rhetoric for science and technology and how that rhetoric can be adapted and applied to the relatively narrow area of research in both the sciences and technologies.

A CONTEMPORARY DEFINITION OF RHETORIC

Rhetoric in its contemporary sense may be defined as collective, cooperative inquiry. This definition of rhetoric departs from the traditional definition of rhetoric in at least two important respects. First, contemporary rhetoric departs from the traditional identification of rhetoric with persuasion. Aristotle may be taken to represent traditional rhetoric. Aristotle defines rhetoric as "the faculty of discovering the possible means of persuasion in reference to any subject whatever" [17, p. 15], and he goes on to provide a complete catalogue of those possible means of persuasion. In contrast, Booth may be taken to represent contemporary rhetoric. Booth defines rhetoric as "the art of discovering warrantable beliefs and improving those beliefs in shared discourse." [18, p. xiii] If contemporary rhetoric is in any sense persuasion, then it is collective, cooperative persuasion: "The supreme purpose of persuasion in this view could not be to talk someone else into a preconceived view; rather it must be to engage in mutual inquiry or exploration." [18, p. 137]

Second, contemporary rhetoric departs from the traditional association of rhetoric with an established community of belief. Aristotle is able to catalogue the possible means of persuasion both because he is able to appeal to such a community of belief [19, 20] and because his ethical and political theory provides for a community of belief. Aristotle's ethical and political theory governs rhetoric and the other faculties:

> . . . the most authoritative of the sciences . . . is manifestly the science of Politics; for it is this that ordains which of the sciences are to exist in states, and what branches of knowledge the different classes of the citizens are to learn, and up to what point; and we observe that even the most highly esteemed of the faculties, such as strategy, domestic economy, oratory, are subordinate to the political science [21, pp. 5-7].

The possible means of persuasion are the reasons, virtues, emotions, and characters accredited by an actual community of believers or, at the least, mandated by Aristotle's own ethical and political theory. Like Aristotle, Booth provides a catalogue of good reasons that reasonable persons ought to accept. Unlike Aristotle, he is unable to assume the existence of an established community of belief. The only reason that Booth gives to accept his good reasons is "Why not?" [18, p. 201]. Booth's good reasons derive from no established community of belief but serve merely as a basis for mutual inquiry or exploration. Such is the modern predicament, and it has had no small influence upon the efforts of contemporary historians and philosophers of science and technology to determine criteria of evaluation in science and technology and, in turn, to determine general standards of judgment for accepting some criteria of evaluation rather than others. The theory of the development of sciences and technologies that best resolves these difficulties will provide the best basis for a rhetoric as well.

THEORIES OF RHETORIC FOR
SCIENCE AND TECHNOLOGY

Conventional language theory provides a means of classifying theories of rhetoric for science and technology. Ogden and Richards use a triangle to represent three components of meaning in language: thought or reference, symbol, and referent [22]. Subsequently, this representation has been used in several language disciplines. Hörmann uses the Ogden-and-Richards triangle in psycholinguistics [23]. Abrams and Kinneavy add a fourth component in literary theory and discourse theory, respectively, when they divide thought or reference into speaker or writer, on the one hand, and listener or reader, on the other [24, 25]. These four components provide a means of classifying theories of rhetoric for science and technology. In Kinneavy's discourse theory, all scientific, informative, and exploratory discourse is referential, or object-oriented, with respect to other forms of discourse. By analogy, I suggest that all theories of rhetoric for science and technology are more or less object-oriented with respect to other theories of rhetoric. However, they are not equally object-oriented with respect to each other. Each reconstructs the objective world, but each attempts to validate its reconstruction by different means. Thus while all theories of rhetoric for science and technology may be classified as object-oriented rhetorics, each may be further classified as a symbol-oriented (language-oriented), speaker- or writer-oriented, or listener- or reader-oriented (audience-oriented) rhetoric.

Korzybski may be taken to represent language-oriented rhetoric. Working under the influence of the new mathematical physics of Einstein, Minkowski, and others, Korzybski seeks to establish a universal mathematical language for science and society. The purpose of such a language "is to match our verbal structures, often called theories, with empirical structures, and see if our verbal predictions are fulfilled empirically or not, thus indicating that the two structures are either similar or dissimilar." [8, p. 63] Unfortunately, it is not always possible to know whether or not a new theory is valid. One can assert, but not prove, the validity of the Einstein theory, for example. How, then, does one establish its validity? By what criteria does one judge the similarity of a theory to the empirical world? Is accuracy of representation the only criterion? By what standards does one judge the merit or relevance of various criteria? The problem is twofold. What, in Booth's terms, constitute good reasons (criteria of evaluation) for accepting a new theory, and what reasons (general standards of judgment) can one give for accepting some good reasons rather than others? Korzybski's language-oriented rhetoric does not resolve these difficulties, nor does it even address them explicitly, and they remain problems for later theories.

Polanyi may be taken to represent speaker- or writer-oriented rhetoric. Protesting against the dominant strain of objectivism in philosophy from Kant to the logical positivists, Polanyi seeks to establish a personal standard of judgment

in science and, by extension, in society at large. Thus Polanyi expressly
addresses the twofold problem of criteria of evaluation and standards of
judgment in sciences. Scientific values or criteria include accuracy, systematic
relevance, and intrinsic interest. These criteria compete with each other. Thus,
for example, a deficiency in accuracy may be outweighed by excellence in
systematic relevance or intrinsic interest: "Take for example the evolution of
species. Neo-Darwinism is firmly accredited and highly regarded by science,
though there is little direct evidence for it, because it beautifully fits into a
mechanistic system of the universe and bears on a subject — the origin of man —
which is of the utmost intrinsic interest." [9, p. 136] In weighing the relative
importance of competing criteria, Polanyi insists upon a personal standard of
judgment: "Unless ye believe, ye shall not understand." [9, p. 266] This
personal standard of judgment is not a retreat from objectivism to subjectivism
but a personal commitment to "universal intellectual standards" regarding facts,
knowledge, proof, reality, and the like [9, p. 303]. These standards are
impersonally established by consensus among scientists but exist for the
individual scientist only as the object of personal commitment. Knowledge is
neither objective nor subjective, but personal. The difficulty with such a theory,
as Polanyi readily acknowledges, is the inevitable controversy that it engenders
and the difficulty of resolving such controversy except by recourse to the
persuasive power of the individual scientist, a questionable tactic in the absence
of an established community of belief.

Audience-oriented rhetorics seek to resolve such controversy by denying the
personal standard of judgment. Popper, Kuhn, and Toulmin may be taken to
represent audience-oriented or, more properly, context-oriented rhetoric. The
phrase context-oriented rhetoric reflects the fact that, in these rhetorics, the
audience includes not only actual audiences (immediate listeners or readers) but
the collective audience of science or technology, or of a particular science or
technology. Context-oriented rhetorics best serve the purpose of collective,
cooperative inquiry since they place criteria of evaluation and standards of
judgment within the collective audience, or context, of science or technology.

Popper represents an early version of context-oriented rhetoric. Popper raises
the issue of criteria of evaluation when he argues that *"the criterion of the
scientific status of a theory is its falsifiability, or refutability, or testability."* [11],
p. 37] He raises the issue of standards of judgment when he characterizes
scientific method as a succession of conjectures and attempts at refutations
through which scientific theories are subjected to judgment by a scientific
community. A theory is scientific only if and when it is put forward in the
community in a form that permits testing and possible refutation. Popper's
rudimentary notion of context — the scientific community — as the locus of a
standard of judgment applicable to scientific theories is further developed by
Kuhn and Toulmin.

Kuhn represents a later version of context-oriented rhetoric. Based upon his
notion of a paradigm, or disciplinary matrix, Kuhn's theory is context-oriented

in the sense that a paradigm implies, by definition, acceptance by a scientific community. Paradigms are "accepted examples of actual scientific practice — examples which . . . provide models from which spring particular coherent traditions of scientific research." [14, p. 10] Accepted paradigms admit of what Kuhn calls normal science since they both define the problems that science can address and also provide the criteria of evaluation applicable to preferred solutions. However, Kuhn points out, the problem-solving activity of normal science often produces anomalies — phenomena that cannot be accounted for by the prevailing paradigms. Crisis, the proliferation of alternative theories and the development of competing paradigms, may follow and may necessitate what Kuhn calls a paradigm shift, or scientific revolution. The possibility of competition between paradigms raises the fundamental problem in Kuhn's theory, that is, "the incommensurability of standards" of competing paradigms [14, p. 149]. Individual scientists may be persuaded by reasons or considerations — criteria of evaluation — such as the potential problem-solving ability of a paradigm or the individual scientist's sense of the appropriate or the aesthetic. But reasons are not proofs, as Kuhn acknowledges. Given the incommensurability of standards of competing paradigms, there is no general standard by which competing paradigms, or the reasons or considerations or criteria of evaluation applicable to competing paradigms, may be subjected to judgment: "As in political revolutions, so in paradigm choice — there is no standard higher than the assent of the relevant community." [14, p. 94] There are only the separate standards of competing scientific communities, or collective audiences, or contexts — the advocates of competing paradigms.

Toulmin represents a more recent version of context-oriented rhetoric. In contrast to Kuhn, who allows for no continuous general standard of judgment applicable to competing paradigms, Toulmin argues that general standards of judgment applicable to scientific concepts are located within each of the particular intellectual disciplines that constitute science and technology. The members of any particular intellectual discipline are and remain members of that discipline precisely because they share common ideals or goals, current capacities, and problems. The activities of members of intellectual disciplines generate various ways of achieving these goals, increasing these current capacities, and solving these problems. According to Toulmin, disciplines select among these ways by a process that is essentially evolutionary. Toulmin's evolutionary view addresses the twofold problem of criteria of evaluation and general standards of judgment in sciences and technologies. Just as organic evolution is the result of a reciprocal relationship between the genetic potential of a given organic population and the ecological demands of a given niche, so also intellectual evolution is the result of a reciprocal relationship between available populations of scientific concepts and the goals, current capacities, and problems that provide the general standard of judgment within any given intellectual discipline. Moreover, just as any particular organic change is not best according to any given criterion of evaluation but simply better than some other change, so any particular intellectual change, a particular scientific concept, is not best according to any given criterion of evaluation but simply better than some other available scientific concept at achieving the goals, increasing the current capacities, and solving some outstanding problem of the given intellectual discipline. Thus the goals, current capacities, problems, and criteria of evaluation upheld within particular intellectual disciplines constitute "forums of competition" within which new concepts are appraised and subsequently accepted or abandoned [16, p. 140]. Toulmin's evolutionary account of intellectual disciplines has its strength as a rhetoric precisely in its concern for audiences, whose collective goals, current capacities, problems, and criteria of evaluation provide a general standard of judgment applicable to scientific concepts. This account of the development of sciences and technologies is especially compatible with the contemporary definition of rhetoric as collective, cooperative inquiry since it identifies a continuous general standard of judgment within individual communities of belief, particular intellectual disciplines.

A RHETORIC FOR RESEARCH IN SCIENCES AND TECHNOLOGIES: THEORY AND APPLICATION

Toulmin's theory, interpreted as a context-oriented rhetoric, lends itself to a rhetorical distinction among the collective audiences, or contexts, of sciences and technologies. However, Toulmin's context-oriented rhetoric, like other current theories of rhetoric for science and technology, suffers the limitation that it rests upon a philosophical distinction between sciences and technologies, from which it infers a corresponding distinction between their respective contexts. Toulmin's philosophical distinction derives ultimately from Aristotle's distinction among three kinds of science, theoretic, practical, and productive, or sciences of knowing, doing, and making [26]. To the sciences of knowing Aristotle assigns metaphysics, mathematics, and physics; to the sciences of doing he assigns politics and ethics; and to the sciences of making he assigns medicine, architecture, cobbling, and rhetoric, among others. Similarly, Bacon distinguishes speculative and operative sciences: physics, metaphysics, and mathematics as speculative sciences, on the one hand, and experimentation, philosophy, and magic, on the other [27]. So also Skolimowski distinguishes between knowing in science and producing in technology [28]. And Toulmin distinguishes between the explanatory goals of sciences and the practical, by which he means productive, goals of technologies. As a result of this philosophical orientation, Toulmin infers from the distinction between science and technology a corresponding distinction between the collective audiences, or contexts, of sciences and technologies. Thus the forum of competition (and standard of judgment) in sciences is the intellectual discipline while the forum of competition in technologies is at once the intellectual discipline (the laboratory or test bench) and, inevitably, a variety of extradisciplinary concerns as well (the patent office, the marketplace, and the forum of public debate). However, both the sciences and technologies actually address any one or several such contexts.

extradisciplinary concerns as well (the patent office, the marketplace, and the forum of public debate). However, both the sciences and technologies actually address any one or several such contexts.

A rhetorical distinction among the collective audiences, or contexts, of sciences and technologies may be made on the basis of the contexts actually addressed by practicing scientists and technologists. Research provides a case in point. One need only peruse the publications of a professional association such as The Institute of Electrical and Electronics Engineers, for example, to observe that research in technologies is sometimes addressed solely to the goals, current capacities, problems, and criteria of evaluation upheld within an intellectual discipline. Conversely, one need only peruse the publications of a government regulatory agency such as the U. S. Environmental Protection Agency, for example, to observe that research in sciences is sometimes addressed solely to the goals, current capacities, problems, and criteria of evaluation upheld within a government regulatory agency and by the public it represents. Research in both the sciences and technologies is routinely addressed to a variety of contexts in documents proper to each context. These documents reflect the goals, current capacities, problems, and criteria of evaluation upheld within each context.

In the rest of this article I show how Toulmin's context-oriented rhetoric may be adapted and applied to the relatively narrow area of research in both the sciences and technologies. Research scientists and technologists address several distinct contexts, including the intellectual discipline; the business, industrial, or military organization; the government regulatory agency; and the private or government funding agency. To the context of the intellectual discipline is addressed basic research, both explanatory, as in sciences, and practical, as in technologies. To the context of the business, industrial, or military organization and the context of the government regulatory agency is addressed applied research in both the sciences and technologies. The use of applied research reveals the complex relationship between these two contexts: government regulatory agencies use applied research to regulate, among other things, the use of applied research by business, industrial, or military organizations. Finally, to the context of the private or government funding agency are addressed both basic and applied research in both the sciences and technologies.

An individual scientist or technologist may address any one or several of these contexts. A research scientist employed by a university, for example, may report research to an intellectual discipline on one occasion and demonstrate how that research may be applied in a business or industrial organization on another. Similarly, a technologist employed in business or industry may most often be engaged in research and may report research directed to the problems of business or industry. But that same technologist may on another occasion demonstrate to the appropriate intellectual discipline that that same research solves a problem of the intellectual discipline.

In addition, the individual scientist or technologist may address more than one context at the same time. For example, the technologist who addresses a problem in business or industry or in government must take into account the goals, current capacities, problems, and criteria of evaluation upheld within the appropriate intellectual discipline in order to produce a solution that is satisfactory, even from the point of view of business or industry or government. Similarly, the research scientist or technologist who addresses the private or government funding agency must address other contexts represented by the funding agency, including the intellectual discipline; the business, industrial or military organization; and/or the government regulatory agency. The illustrations that follow show how an adaptation of Toulmin's rhetoric may be applied to each of several contexts of research in both the sciences and technologies and to the documents proper to each context. These documents are the research article, addressed to the intellectual discipline; the applied research article, addressed to the business, industrial, or military organization; the government research report, addressed to the government regulatory agency; and the research proposal, addressed to the private or government funding agency.

The Intellectual Discipline

One context of research in sciences and technologies is the intellectual discipline or subdiscipline. Toulmin's rhetoric can be adapted to this context, with the qualification that the individual researcher not only in sciences but also in technologies may at some time address the context of the intellectual discipline. In such an instance the researcher addresses the goals, current capacities, problems, and criteria of evaluation that derive from and operate within the discipline. According to Toulmin, the goals of sciences are explanatory, those of technologies, practical. Criteria of evaluation applicable to a scientific explanation include its power, relevance, or applicability; those applicable to a technological solution to a practical problem include its feasibility, efficiency, or ease of manufacture (the last, I suggest, actually derives from the business, industrial, or military organization). Despite such differences, the sciences and technologies are similar insofar as they address the goals, current capacities, problems, and criteria of evaluation upheld within their respective intellectual disciplines.

The passage shown in Figure 1 is from a research article addressed to an intellectual discipline, in this instance a subdiscipline of electrical and electronics engineering [29]; numerous instances could be drawn from other technologies or from sciences. The article was co-authored by researchers at University Science Malaysia and published by The Institute of Electrical and Electronics Engineers. Consistent with Toulmin's rhetoric, the authors of the article address a goal (paragraph 1), a current capacity ("When compared . . . "), a problem ("However, . . . "), a solution ("In the present work, . . . "), and criteria of evaluation ("This enables . . . " and "Further, . . . ") of their subdiscipline. The research is basic research, albeit of a practical kind. Thus the authors address

GOAL	In the recent past, Neelakantaswamy *et al.* [1, 4] developed a class of microwave radiators termed as "Gaussian-beam launchers", to produce a focused exposure field in biological experiments for partial-body irradiations. These compact and simple structures with their ability to focus the microwave energy in a very small region indicate their practical utility, in the areas of biological researches and medical applications of microwaves, such as for selective heating of diseased/cancerous tissues. These launchers can also be used in noninvasive beam-wave reflectometric and spectrometric instrumentations for measuring complex permittivity of biological material at microwave frequencies, as indicated by Neelakantaswamy elsewhere [5, 7].
CURRENT CAPACITY	When compared to the microwave beam-launching system described in [8], which consists of a plane-wave irradiated dielectric sphere (lens), the launcher formed by combining a scalar horn and a dielectric sphere [1] is a more practical source of microwave Gaussian beam. However, the use of a dielectric sphere as the focusing lens results in significant amount of spherical aberrations in the focal field, as indicated by Neelakantaswamy *et al.* in [9] ....
PROBLEM	
SOLUTION	In the present work, a Gaussian-beam launcher is formed by placing a dielectric hemisphere (instead of a full sphere) at the aperture end of corrugated circular waveguide (scalar horn). This enables a reduction in the path length of the ray in the lens-medium, and hence the spherical aberration effects are relatively minimized. Further, by using a hemisphere in the place of a full sphere, the launcher structure becomes less massive and smaller.
CRITERIA OF EVALUATION	

SOURCE: P. S. Neelakantaswamy and F. C. Hong, Dielectric Hemisphere-Loaded Scalar Horn as a Gaussian-Beam Launcher for Microwave Exposure Studies, *IEEE Transactions on Microwave Theory and Techniques, MTT-27*, p. 797, 1979.

Figure 1. Passage from an introduction to a research article.

only those criteria of evaluation upheld within the subdiscipline, that is, the minimization of the spherical aberration effects and the reduction in weight and size of the launcher structure (paragraph 3). They do not address the criteria of evaluation that would be introduced in biological research or in medical applications, for example, the safety of a subject or patient. The potential applications of the proposed Gaussian-beam launcher are identified (paragraph 1) but are not taken into account in the article. This article is one of numerous instances of research in both the sciences and technologies addressed directly to the goals, current capacities, problems, and criteria of evaluation upheld within intellectual disciplines.

The Business, Industrial, or Military Organization

A second context of research in sciences and technologies is the business, industrial, or military organization. Toulmin's rhetoric can be adapted to this

GOALS	Robot technology has advanced to the point that it will soon be ready for many applications. Thousands of industrial robots are now in service and have proved their economic value. For example, the Ford Motor Co. had 150 industrial robots in service in November 1977 and planned to put 400 more in service by 1980 [15].
CURRENT CAPACITY	However, industrial robots have a very limited capacity for intelligent behavior. The success of industrial robots proves that the cost of manipulator hardware is now *low* enough to compare favorably with the cost of men in a limited number of tasks.
PROBLEM and CRITERIA OF EVALUATION	More intelligent controls are needed to expand the range of practical robot applications.
PROBLEM and CRITERIA OF EVALUATION	We must also remember that development of computer technology is proceeding at so rapid a pace that applications which are economically marginal today may be quite practical within *five* years. PERLIS [18] projects a decline in cost per operation of a factor of 20 per decade. Computers are getting smaller, faster, cheaper, and are consuming less power. Thus, we can develop elaborate robot programs in a large computer with reasonable assurance that an equivalent small and cheap computer will be available by the time our robot is ready to go to sea.

SOURCE: J. K. Dixon, H. A. Johnson, and J. R. Slagle, The Prospect of an Underwater Naval Robot, *Naval Engineers Journal, 92,* p. 66, 1980.

Figure 2. Passage from an introduction to an applied research article.

context, with the qualification that the individual researcher in either the sciences or the technologies may at some time address the context of the business, industrial, or military organization. In such an instance the researcher addresses the goals, current capacities, problems, and criteria of evaluation that derive from and operate within the organization. These may include reasonable cost and ease of manufacture, marketability, limits of liability, employee safety and satisfaction, public health and safety, and protection of the environment.

The passage shown in Figure 2 is from an applied research article on robot technology addressed to business, industrial, and military organizations [30]; numerous instances could be drawn from other technologies, fewer from sciences. The article was co-authored by researchers at the Naval Research Laboratory and published by the American Society of Naval Engineers. Consistent with Toulmin's rhetoric, the authors of the article identify goals of business, industrial, military, and other potential users (paragraph 1), current capacities ("However, . . . " and "The success . . . "), and remaining problems and criteria of evaluation, in particular the need for increased intelligence ("More intelligent controls . . . ") and lower cost (paragraph 3). The authors address the goals, current capacities, problems, and criteria of evaluation upheld by potential users of the research, not those upheld within intellectual disciplines. Thus the goals of the research are expressed entirely in terms of applications (paragraph 1). Accordingly, the authors reflect the characteristic concern of potential users with the balance of efficiency, in this instance higher intelligence, and cost (paragraphs 2 and 3). The concern with applications illustrates an important distinction between the basic research article and the applied research article. In the basic research article, potential applications are ignored or mentioned only in passing; in the applied research article, they are addressed directly. For example, in the article about the Gaussian-beam launcher, the authors mention potential applications only in passing and only in the opening paragraph; in the article on robot technology, the authors conceive the entire research project entirely in terms of its applications. The article on robot technology is one of numerous instances of research in technologies — there are fewer in sciences — addressed directly to the goals, current capacities, problems, and criteria of evaluation upheld within business, industrial, or military organizations.

The Government Regulatory Agency

A third context of research in sciences and technologies is the government regulatory agency. Toulmin's rhetoric can be adapted to this context, again with the qualification that the individual researcher in either the sciences or the technologies may at some time address the context of the government regulatory agency. In such an instance the researcher addresses the goals, current capacities, problems, and criteria of evaluation that derive from and operate within the regulatory agency. These may be the same as those of related intellectual disciplines or of business, industrial, or military organizations. However, they usually emphasize, in general, the quality of human life and, in particular, such public concerns as employee safety and satisfaction, public health and safety, and protection of the environment.

The passage shown in Figure 3 is from a government research report based upon research in a composite of biological sciences and addressed to a government regulatory agency [31]; numerous instances could be drawn from other sciences or from technologies. The report was co-authored by researchers at The Midwest Research Institute for review by the Corvallis Environmental Research Laboratory, U. S. Environmental Protection Agency, and used by the Agency as a data base for regulatory and enforcement actions. Consistent with Toulmin's rhetoric, the authors of the report identify a goal (paragraphs 1 and 2), a current capacity ("Most toxicity testing . . . "), a problem ("however, while these results . . . "), criteria of evaluation ("Thus, for more reliable comparison . . . "), and a solution ("As an approach to some aspects of this problem, . . . "). The goal, current capacity, problem, and criteria of evaluation are those of the research institute, the regulatory agency, and the public they both represent. Like most reports addressed to government regulatory agencies, this one emphasizes the implications of the research for the quality of human life. Thus the authors emphasize the relationship between their research program and the

GOAL	The large scale, worldwide use of insecticides, herbicides, and defoliants has prompted the U. S. Environmental Protection Agency to undertake studies to evaluate the global implications of general pesticide use.
GOAL	As particularly toxic or persistent pesticides are identified, efforts are made to find replacements for them. Not wishing to allow equally hazardous chemicals to be used as replacements for condemned pesticides, the U. S. Legislature passed Public Law 93-135 on October 24, 1973. This law established the Substitute Chemicals Program which is directed at testing new pesticides before they are adopted for wide usage.
CURRENT CAPACITY	Most toxicity testing is done with laboratory animals; however, while these results can be used to compare the toxicity of different chemicals, as determined in laboratories anywhere,
PROBLEM	the animal models cannot be directly applied to the actual native fauna at risk. Thus, for more reliable comparison with the
CRITERIA OF EVALUATION	results in laboratory animals, it would be advantageous to test pesticides in representative native species.
SOLUTION	As an approach to some aspects of this problem, this study subjected four species of vole (*Microtus* spp.) to toxicologic evaluation . . . .

SOURCE: J. M. Cholakis, L. C. K. Wong, and C. C. Lee, *Study of the Chemical and Behavioral Toxicology of Substitute Chemicals in Microtine Rodents,* EPA-600/3-78-082, Corvallis Environmental Research Laboratory, Office of Research and Development, U. S. Environmental Protection Agency, Corvallis, Orgeon, p. 1, 1978.

Figure 3. Passage from an introduction to a government research report.

Substitute Chemicals Program mandated by law and directed at protecting the public against new pesticides unsuited for wide usage (paragraph 2). Similarly, they emphasize the larger governmental and public concern for the global implications of general pesticide use (paragraph 1). Like the authors of the article on robot technology, these authors are concerned with the direct applications of basic research, in this instance, the application of laboratory test results to actual environmental conditions (paragraph 3). The report is one of numerous instances of research in both the sciences and technologies addressed directly to the goals, current capacities, problems, and criteria of evaluation upheld within government regulatory agencies.

The Private or Government Funding Agency

A fourth context of research in sciences and technologies is the private or government funding agency. Toulmin's rhetoric can be adapted to this context, with two qualifications. First, an individual researcher in either the sciences or the technologies may at some time address the context of the private or government funding agency. Second, the researcher proposes rather than reports

GOALS

AGENCY OBJECTIVES AND METHODS

The Foundation thus has been charged with advancing several different but interrelated major objectives:
* **Accomplishment of basic research.**
* **Accomplishment of applied research in selected areas.**
* **Long-term maintenance and strengthening of potential to accomplish both basic and applied research in the future.**

SOURCE: National Science Foundation, *Guide to Programs: Fiscal Year 1980,* U.S. Government Printing Office, Washington, D.C., p. viii, 1980.

Figure 4. Passage from a statement on goals in an announcement of research programs.

completed research. Still Toulmin's rhetoric applies. In this instance the researcher at once addresses the goals, current capacities, problems, and criteria of evaluation upheld within several different and potentially competing contexts, including necessarily the intellectual discipline (through reviewers of the research proposal), possibly the business, industrial, or military organization (potential users of the research) or the government regulatory agency (other potential users), and necessarily the private or government funding agency and the private or public interests it represents.

The passages shown in Figures 4 and 5 are from an announcement of research programs of a government funding agency [32]. The announcement was issued by the National Science Foundation (NSF) and is addressed to science disciplines, which, as NSF defines them, include also technological disciplines. The purpose of the announcement is to assist both scientists and technologists in preparing research proposals for submission to NSF. Among other things, the announcement identifies what NSF considers to be appropriate goals of both basic and applied research (Figure 4). These goals apply to both the sciences and the technologies since both sciences and technologies engage in both basic and applied research, as the NSF announcement indicates in its description of particular research programs. The announcement also identifies four categories of criteria of evaluation that NSF applies to research proposals (Figure 5). Two categories, A and D (not shown in Figure 5), relate to the performer, the performer's institutional base, and the long-term scientific potential of the United States. The two other categories, B and C (shown in Figure 5), relate to the internal structure of science and to national objectives, respectively. Within these categories, Criteria 4 and 5 reflect the concerns of intellectual disciplines in both the sciences and technologies. Criteria 6 through 8 reflect the concerns of, among others, potential users in business, industry, the military, or the government. Criterion 9 reflects the concerns of, among others, the

CATEGORY B

Criteria relating to the internal structure of science itself:

    4. Probability that the research will lead to important discoveries or significant conceptual generalizations within its field of science and, in most favorable cases, extending to other fields as well.

    5. Probability that the research will lead to significant improvements or innovations in investigative methods within its own field and possibly in other fields of science.

CATEGORY C

CRITERIA OF
EVALUATION

Criteria relating to utility or relevance to national objectives:

    6. Probability that the research can serve as the basis for new inventions or improved technology.

    7. Probability that the research will contribute substantially to technology assessment — i.e., to assessing or predicting the direct and indirect, intended and unintended, effects of existing or proposed technologies.

    8. Identification of an immediate programmatic context for, and user(s) of, the anticipated research results.

    9. Probability that the research will assist in solving societal problems, in improving the knowledge base for national policies requiring science and technology, or in furthering the interests of international cooperation in science.

SOURCE: National Science Foundation, *Guide to Programs: Fiscal Year 1980,* U. S. Government Printing Office, Washington, D.C., pp. ix-x, 1980.

Figure 5. Passage from a statement on criteria of evaluation in an announcement of research programs.

government funding agency itself and the public interests it represents. Although NSF does not apply all of these criteria of evaluation in precisely the same manner to all kinds of research, its announcement does introduce the possibility that authors of research proposals may have to address at least some of a wide range of criteria of evaluation that reflect the concerns of several different contexts. Reviewers of research proposals are recruited from one or, more probably, several of these contexts. The NSF announcement is one of several such announcements in both the sciences and technologies that bring together several different and potentially competing contexts within the larger context of the private or government funding agency.

CONCLUSION

A context-oriented rhetoric for research in sciences and technologies is by no means a complete theory of rhetoric for science and technology. A language-oriented rhetoric such as Korzybski's can insure accuracy of representation while a speaker- or writer-oriented rhetoric such as Polanyi's can insure personal commitment. But context-oriented rhetoric, especially as represented by Toulmin, best serves the contemporary ideal of rhetoric as collective, cooperative inquiry since it identifies, within individual communities of belief, both criteria of evaluation and a general standard of judgment applicable to new theories or concepts in sciences and technologies. Adapted to the relatively narrow area of research in sciences and technologies, Toulmin's rhetoric provides a means of distinguishing and characterizing the several contexts of research common to both the sciences and technologies and the documents proper to each context. Extended to other areas of activity in sciences and technologies, Toulmin's or other versions of context-oriented rhetoric might provide a means of distinguishing and characterizing the various contexts of these activities — from research, on the one hand, to such complex activities as technology assessment and environmental impact assessment, on the other. Such a rhetorical analysis of sciences and technologies can contribute to both a general theory and a practical art of rhetoric for science and technology.

REFERENCES

1. P. N. Campbell, Poetic-Rhetorical, Philosophical, and Scientific Discourse, *Philosophy and Rhetoric, 6,* pp. 1-29, 1973.
2. P. N. Campbell, The *Personae* of Scientific Discourse, *The Quarterly Journal of Speech, 61,* pp. 391-405, 1975.
3. W. B. Weimer, Science as a Rhetorical Transaction: Toward a Nonjustificational Conception of Rhetoric, *Philosophy and Rhetoric, 10,* pp. 1-29, 1977.
4. M. A. Overington, The Scientific Community as Audience: Toward a Rhetorical Analysis of Science, *Philosophy and Rhetoric, 10,* pp. 143-164, 1977.
5. S. M. Halloran, Technical Writing and the Rhetoric of Science, *Journal of Technical Writing and Communication, 8,* pp. 77-88, 1978.
6. C. R. Miller, Technology as a Form of Consciousness: A Study of Contemporary Ethos, *Central States Speech Journal, 29,* pp. 228-236, 1978.
7. C. R. Miller, A Humanistic Rationale for Technical Writing, *College English, 40,* pp. 610-617, 1979.
8. A. Korzybski, *Science and Sanity: An Introduction to Non-Aristotelian Systems and General Semantics,* 4th ed., Institute of General Semantics, Lakeville, Connecticut, 1958.
9. M. Polanyi, *Personal Knowledge: Towards a Post-Critical Philosophy,* corrected ed., University of Chicago Press, Chicago, Illinois, 1962.
10. M. Polanyi, *The Tacit Dimension,* Doubleday, Garden City, New York, 1966.
11. K. R. Popper, *Conjectures and Refutations: The Growth of Scientific Knowledge,* Harper & Row, New York, 1962.
12. K. R. Popper, *The Logic of Scientific Discovery,* rev. ed., Harper & Row, New York, 1968.

13. J. M. Ziman, *Public Knowledge: An Essay Concerning the Social Dimension of Science*, Cambridge University Press, London, 1968.
14. T. S. Kuhn, *The Structure of Scientific Revolutions*, 2nd ed., International Encyclopedia of Unified Science, Vol. 2, No. 2, University of Chicago Press, Chicago, Illinois, 1970.
15. *Criticism and the Growth of Knowledge*, I. Lakatos and A. Musgrave (eds.), Cambridge University Press, London, 1970.
16. S. Toulmin, *Human Understanding: The Collective Use and Evolution of Concepts*, Princeton University Press, Princeton, New Jersey, 1972.
17. Aristotle, *The "Art" of Rhetoric*, J. H. Freese (trans.), Loeb Classical Library, Harvard University Press, Cambridge, Massachusetts, 1967.
18. W. C. Booth, *Modern Dogma and the Rhetoric of Assent*, University of Chicago Press, Chicago, Illinois, 1974.
19. S. M. Halloran, On the End of Rhetoric, Classical and Modern, *College English, 36*, pp. 621-631, 1975.
20. D. S. Kaufer, Point of View in Rhetorical Situations: Classical and Romantic Contrasts and Contemporary Implications, *The Quarterly Journal of Speech, 65*, pp. 171-186, 1979.
21. Aristotle, *The Nicomachean Ethics*, H. Rackham (trans.), Loeb Classical Library, Harvard University Press, Cambridge, Massachusetts, 1975.
22. C. K. Ogden and I. A. Richards, *The Meaning of Meaning: A Study of the Influence of Language upon Thought and of the Science of Symbolism*, Harcourt, Brace & World, New York, 1923.
23. H. Hörmann, *Psycholinguistics: An Introduction to Research and Theory*, H. H. Stern (trans.), Springer, New York, 1971.
24. M. H. Abrams, *The Mirror and the Lamp: Romantic Theory and the Critical Tradition*, W. W. Norton, New York, 1953.
25. J. L. Kinneavy, *A Theory of Discourse: The Aims of Discourse*, Prentice-Hall, Englewood Cliffs, New Jersey, 1971.
26. R. McKeon, General Introduction, *Introduction to Aristotle*, R. McKeon (ed.), 2nd ed., University of Chicago Press, Chicago, Illinois, 1973.
27. F. Bacon, Advancement of Learning, *The Works of Francis Bacon*, J. Spedding, R. L. Ellis, and D. D. Heath (eds.), Vol. 3, Friedrich Frommann Günther Holzboog, Stuttgart-Bad Cannstatt, 1963.
28. H. Skolimowski, The Structure of Thinking in Technology, *Technology and Culture, 7*, pp. 371-383, 1966.
29. P. S. Neelakantaswamy and F. C. Hong, Dielectric Hemisphere-Loaded Scalar Horn as a Gaussian-Beam Launcher for Microwave Exposure Studies, *IEEE Transactions on Microwave Theory and Techniques, MTT-27*, pp. 797-799, 1979.
30. J. K. Dixon, H. A. Johnson, and J. R. Slagle, The Prospect of an Underwater Naval Robot, *Naval Engineers Journal, 92*, pp. 65-72, 1980.
31. J. M. Cholakis, L. C. K. Wong, and C. C. Lee, *Study of the Chemical and Behavioral Toxicology of Substitute Chemicals in Microtine Rodents*, EPA-600/3-78-082, Corvallis Environmental Research Laboratory, Office of Research and Development, U. S. Environmental Protection Agency, Corvallis, Oregon, 1978.
32. National Science Foundation, *Guide to Programs: Fiscal Year 1980*, U. S. Government Printing Office, Washington, D. C., 1980.

CHAPTER 8

A Theoretical Perspective On "How To" Discourse

ELIZABETH HARRIS

"How to" discourse is fundamentally important. By "how to" discourse, I mean whole pieces of writing that exist to instruct their readers in the performance of some physical or intellectual task. Although titles do not always distinguish the kinds of writing I am talking about from simply informative discourse, "how to" discourse appears under titles such as: *Architectural Graphic Standards; Crude Oil Tanks; DEC-10 User's Pocket Reference List; How to Get Good Medical Care; How to Make American Historical Costumes; How to Prepare Your 1980 Income Tax Return;* "How to Use Your Kodak Instamatic X-35F Camera"; *Learning to Look; Metalsmithing; Modern Carpentry; The Organic Way to Plant Protection; Service Manual, Volvo 164, 1970; Understanding Poetry;* and *Writing a Technical Paper.* From aesthetic and scholarly perspectives, such writing may seem dull and humble, its interest residing in what it is "about," rather than what it is. It is not literary art. Though it may be exceedingly artful and in certain respects beautiful, it does not exist for those purposes. It is work with words, not play. Sometimes, especially when such writing is about intellectual tasks, it may be the instrument of new discovery. More often it conserves and disseminates knowledge, rather than extending it in any absolute sense. "How to" writing, as my list of titles suggests, is not specific to high technology, bureaucracy, or consumer society, although it has important applications for all of these. The kind of writing I am talking about, however, instructs much of

Western society in the performance of basic tasks. In literate cultures where many people perform tasks besides the ones their parents performed, "how to" writing has replaced oral traditions about how to plant potatoes, stanch bleeding, and drive mules. It has also manifested and promoted the rationalization and democratization of Western cultures. Such writing exposes customary practice to reasoned criticism and opens new areas of experience to literate people. The importance of this kind of writing invites and justifies our asking what, exactly, it is. What generalizations can we make about it, as language in relation to other language?

A THEORETICAL APPROACH

Implicit in this question is the more elementary one of how we can generalize about language, and specifically about whole pieces of writing, at all. Persuasively rigorous answers to these elementary questions are provided by semiotic, the study of sign-systems, and by semiotically-based discourse theory. Semiotic is concerned with the common features of systems as apparently diverse as Boolean algebra, the symptoms of diseases, insect communications, and what are called natural languages, of which English, Hopi, Swahili, and Japanese are all examples. In *Foundations of the Theory of Signs* (1938), Charles Morris, one of the founders of American semiotic, posits that every act of sign-communication involves three components. There must be something that acts as a sign, something the sign refers to, and some effect on an interpreter "in virtue of which the thing in question is a sign." [1, p. 19] Thus, Morris says, when we study sign-communication we can study three aspects of it: the signs themselves, their relations to their referents, and their effects on, or uses by, interpreters. (In the case of natural-language signs, which are intentionally produced, we can also study their uses by producers.) The study of the signs themselves — their constitution as signs and their formal relations to each other — Morris calls *syntactics*. The study of signs' relations to referents he calls *semantics*. And the study of signs' uses by interpreters (and producers) he calls *pragmatics* [1, pp. 21-22]. All sign-communications, then, can be studied syntactically, semantically, and pragmatically.

James Kinneavy, a more recent theorist of discourse who uses a semiotic model, observes that we can identify syntactic, semantic, and pragmatic aspects of natural language on more than one level [2]. Relevant to this discussion are the potential and the actual, which are, respectively, the linguistic and the discourse levels. Since "how to" writing is an actual use of language occurring in real situations, this discussion will focus on the discourse level. At the discourse level, we can discuss "how to" writing in the three main ways described by Morris. First, we can examine it from the perspective of *discourse semantics*, which considers the epistemology of whole utterances, how they "know" or "perceive" the world. (The phrasing which asserts that discourses "know" is important, for it deliberately conflates epistemology and language. Semiotic, along with much contemporary philosophy, takes the position that we know only in terms of symbolic systems — that even sensory perceptions depend on symbolic systems. Thus, we cannot speak of knowing the world and then somehow translating our knowledge into discourse. We must speak of knowing *in* discourse — or of discourse's "knowing.") A second perspective from which we can examine "how to" writing is that of *discourse syntactics,* which takes up topics in the constitution and formal relations of the signs that uniquely make up whole utterances. These topics include the nature of the discourse "signal," as speech or writing or display, the channel, or medium, through which the signal is conveyed, and how "parts" of the signal are put together into the whole. "Parts" can be defined variously: in conventional terms as sentences, paragraphs, arguments, examples, and the like, or in structural terms as any functional units of the whole in which its formal structure can be understood. One study of discourse syntactics is how sentences are put together into paragraphs. A third perspective from which we can examine "how to" writing is that of *discourse pragmatics,* which studies how a particular utterance is used by writers or speakers and readers or listeners, and what they are actually aiming to do when they are using it. Of course, these three main areas for study are merely different ways of looking at the same object, "how to" writing. They are by no means independent of each other. Discourse is the actual realization of language potentials, and writers and readers realize the potentials of language purposively. Language use is purposive behavior. Thus, pragmatics usually tends to determine syntactics and semantics.

THE SEMANTICS OF "HOW TO" DISCOURSE

I will begin with the semantics of "how to" discourse, its relations to the world that its signs "stand for." The semantics of "how to" discourse has been dealt with in a very general way, though not under that rubric, by textbooks in technical writing. There, "how to" writing is usually identified with the rhetorical mode *process*, sometimes with *narration.* These terms describe the epistemology of the simplest instances of "how to" discourse: such discourse knows the world temporally, as change (by contrast, for instance, with purely descriptive discourse, which knows the world spatially, as stasis). An example of the simplest "how to" discourse is the instructions for applying my parking sticker to my windshield:

> Peel protective backing from permit. Make sure glass is clean and dry. Apply permit to windshield smoothly, pressing firmly.

The discourse as a whole refers to an action, applying the permit, which extends over time. Objects, apprehended as extending in space, are referred to only insofar as the action requires.

Besides perceiving the world temporally, even simple "how to" discourse about concrete physical tasks perceives the world relatively abstractly. The ideas of two rhetorical theorists who are concerned with epistemology make this clear. The term *narration* is sometimes used to mean any discourse which knows its referent temporally. But Leo Rockas, in *Modes of Rhetoric,* distinguishes two temporal modes of knowing, a concrete and an abstract, and calls narration — which he defines as concerned with unique, unrepeatable events — the concrete mode. The abstract mode — concerned with repeatable, duplicable events — is *process* [3]. "How to" discourse, *prima facie* concerned with repeatable events, would be, in Rockas's definition, *process.* James Moffett also distinguishes modes of knowing reality on the basis of their relative abstraction, and his model, too, exposes the relative abstraction of "how to" discourse. In Moffett's conception, discourse such as "how to" writing, which tells "what does happen," is called *generalization.* By contrast, Moffett's *narration,* less abstractly, tells "what has happened." [4] The simplest "how to" discourse, therefore, knows the world not only temporally, as change, but fairly abstractly, as repeatable change, or generalization about change.

Only a small proportion of "how to" discourse, however, is as simple as the parking-sticker instructions above. More complex instances know the world in other modes in addition to process, and sometimes these other modes even replace process entirely. A common textbook paradigm analyzes "how to" discourse into an introductory description of tools and materials followed by the main process. Sometimes the paradigm allows for the alternation of description and process. In either case, such discourse knows the world as a composite of space and time, stasis and change.

Under some circumstances, however, description may come to overshadow or replace process entirely. Consider a chapter titled "Control Insect Pests with Correct Plant Feeding," in *The Organic Way to Plant Protection.* Most of the chapter is given over to the description of organic means to improving soil. Subheadings include "Blood Meal and Dried Blood," "Bone Meal," "Compost," "Cottonseed Meal," "Grass Clippings," and so on. The actual process itself, of making and applying fertilizer mixtures, is so simple and familiar to the established gardener for whom the book is written as to be represented in a few sentences. Another chapter, titled "Insect Friends of Man," is given over entirely to the description of helpful insects. The process, of sparing these natural enemies of garden pests, is implied but never related at all.

Just as description can accompany or displace process in "how to" discourse, so also can other modes of perceiving reality in language. One of these is *classification.* Kinneavy, Cope, and Campbell regard *classification* as the second of two spatial modes, in which things, apprehended statically, are grouped with other things on the basis of some similarity [5]. Classification, like description, knows the world statically, as groups arrayed in space, and often appears with description. In "how to" writing, processes themselves may be classified, steps in a process may be classified, tools and materials may be classified, and so forth. For instance, a manual titled *Crude Oil Tanks: Construction, Strapping, Gauging, and Maintenance,* gives instruction in a number of processes. A few examples are "Erection of Riveted Tanks," "Strapping Wooden Taper-Type Production Tanks," "Checking for Free Water," "Inspection of Ship's Tanks," "Cleaning Methods and Procedures," and "Preparing Surfaces for Painting," The various processes are classified into four groups, as the manual's subtitle indicates, and the manual is divided into four chapters. In the first of these, "Tank Construction," there is further classification (of tanks into types) and extensive description — more of these two modes than of process.

Classification by itself rarely displaces process entirely, though it may, for instance, in laboratory handbooks which simply classify, without describing, substances or organisms on the basis of results from tests whose processes are elementary and universally understood by practitioners in the field. More often, classification and description together will replace process. This happens in the chapter mentioned above from *The Organic Way to Plant Protection,* where insects are classified and described, but the process they are to be subjected to is only implicit, because obvious.

Another mode which may accompany process or may displace it entirely is *definition.* Rockas regards definition as a mode in itself, the more abstract of his two static modes, with description being the more concrete. Whenever things are regarded statically and as types, rather than unique individuals, Rockas says, they are being defined. (Kinneavy, Cope, and Campbell would regard definition as an instance of classification, in which a thing is first placed in a group and then differentiated from other members of the group.) However we understand definition, we can see that in "how to" writing, processes are often defined before being related, and instrumental concepts, the tools of intellectual processes, are often defined in lieu of being described. Furthermore, if we think of definition as Rockas does, as description of things regarded as types, then the "descriptions" of insects and organic fertilizers in *The Organic Way to Plant Protection* are actually definition, and in the chapter on beneficial insects, process has been displaced entirely by definition.

A last mode I shall mention which sometimes appears with process or displaces it in "how to" writing is *evaluation.* Kinneavy, Cope, and Campbell define evaluation as a dynamic mode of perceiving reality. In evaluating, they say, we measure some achieved reality against some potential which we see it as having once had. Evaluation thus "knows" the world as fulfilled or unfulfilled potential. Evaluation is especially likely to appear in writing about intellectual tasks. For example, computer manuals typically instruct the user to evaluate the computer's response against a potential the manual says the computer has, and then to proceed according to the results of the evaluation: "If the terminal types double letters when you log in, type _____, then _____." In some "how to" discourses, evaluation, like description, definition, or even classification, may displace process entirely. Such is the case in a pamphlet titled *How to Get Good Medical Care,* which is about judging (and choosing) doctors and hospitals. The process of choosing, however, is merely implied. The pamphlet evaluates actual kinds of medical practice ("Solo Practice," "Group Practice," "Nonmedicine and Quackery," "Hospital Affiliation") against potentials it attributes to modern medicine.

For simplicity's sake I have examined how perceptions of reality other than process replace it singly in "how to" writing, and how classification and description do so in combination. But, of course, other combinations occur as well, often all simultaneously.

I have not yet considered the graphic displays of "how to" writing, which — in another kind of sign-communication — can be examined semantically also. Diagrams, pictures, tables, graphs, and so forth bear, like natural-language signs and discourses, relations to the world which are more or less literal (as with photographs) or metaphoric (as with diagrams, graphs, and charts). That is, the relations of graphic displays to reality, like the relations of single words and whole modes of discourse, may be more or less concrete or abstract. Graphic displays, as they appear in stationary media, are in themselves spatial, but they may be also thought of as representing reality temporally or spatially, and even in the same modes in which natural language does. Thus, a graph can narrate, relate process, describe, define, classify, and evaluate. A flow chart can narrate, relate process, describe, define, and classify. A photograph, drawing, or series of either, can narrate, relate process, describe, define, classify, and evaluate ("normal" vs. "deprived"). For example, consider a book titled *Architectural Graphic Standards,* which instructs architects, drafters, and builders how to produce designs that meet the standards required by common materials and municipal laws. This discourse exists entirely in extensively captioned drawings. It classifies reality primarily as types of constructions ("Retaining Walls," "Footings and Foundations," "Chimneys," "Masonry Arches"). Both in captions and in drawings, it describes, relates the process of designing, and evaluates designs.

"How to" discourse, then, may exist entirely in description, classification, definition, process, or evaluation, or in some combination of these. Readers familiar with epistemological theories of discourse will recognize that these include all four of the modes of knowing reality that Kinneavy, Cope, and Campbell posit (description, classification, narration, and evaluation), though not some that other theoreticians propose. Does this mean that we cannot distinguish "how to" discourse on the basis of its semantics alone? I think it does, that descriptions of the syntactics and, especially, the pragmatics of "how to" writing are also necessary to any theoretical characterization of it. Nevertheless, we can make certain generalizations about its semantics, as follows.

"How to" writing at its simplest knows the world as process. In more complex instances, it can be imagined as knowing the world in a full complement of additional modes and combinations of modes, any of which can displace process. But when process is displaced in the epistemology of the discourse, it is always implied or assumed in the discourse.

THE SYNTACTICS OF "HOW TO" DISCOURSE

In this section, I will consider first the constitution and second the internal relations of "how to" discourse. By defining "how to" discourse initially as *writing,* I have confined my discussion of syntactics to "signals" constituted in only one way. Discourse can be constituted in speech and visual display, as well as in writing, and can be conveyed in person, over the telephone, on television, and via other media. Instructions can be given in many media. And medium defines the limits of discourse in such a way as to determine ground rules for the relation of the whole discourse to its parts and its parts to each other. For example, oral media require more redundancy at certain points than written media, which can be reread at need. But, as Kinneavy observes, "the systematic study of media is presently in its infancy" [2, p. 35], and a full understanding of "how to" discourse, written, spoken, and displayed, must await the development of that study. Some of my discussion here applies to non-written media, but I will not address any of these directly except for graphics accompanying writing.

Confining myself to "how to" writing alone, with its accompanying graphics, I can make the following observations about its constitution as a signal. The signal is a written and displayed text which can be conveyed in a variety of media: handwriting, typing, print, drawing, still photography, the CRT screen of a computer terminal. The print media are probably the commonest and include manuals, pamphlets, brochures, instructional sheets, books, magazines, and newspapers. As the range of media for "how to" writing implies, its audience covers the full range of sizes and distances from the writer, that Moffett identifies [4, p. 33]. Some "how to" writing could be produced, in handwriting or typing, for oneself, one or two other individuals, or a small-to-medium sized group. More is undoubtedly produced in print, for the large, though not mass audience, of books, manuals, instructional sheets, and so forth. Some is produced in print for the mass audience of newspapers, government forms, and so forth.

The signal of most "how to" writing is what Moffett calls monologue, *apparently* the utterance of one person. This is true even when, in fact, several writers have produced the text, or when the rhetorical persona is an explicit corporate "we." In either case, the actual or allegedly plural sign-producers speak, as it were, with one voice. Some "how to" writing, however, is dialogue, *apparently* the utterance of two persons. The two "voices" may actually emanate from two persons or groups of persons, or may only appear to. Genuine written "how to" dialogue is probably commonest in non-print media such as handwriting or typing, which imply audiences smaller and closer to the writer, or on the screen of a computer terminal. But "how to" dialogue, both genuine and simulated, also appears in print: in the "Ask Mr. Fixit" newspaper column, or in instructions written in the question-and-answer format. Since dialogue presents special problems and is not central to "how to" writing, I shall further restrict my discussion of the internal relations of "how to" writing to signals constituted as monologues.

What generalizations can we make about the relations of parts of written "how to" monologues to each other and to the whole? Two kinds of organizing principles seem to operate: those drawn from discourse semantics and those drawn from discourse pragmatics. That is, discourses seem to be organized both by their relations to reality and by their uses. Semantic principles are those of time and space. Pragmatic principles include considerations of audiences' special needs or interests, and logical considerations. Although we may not ordinarily think of logic as pragmatically determined, in fact, what is logical for one purpose is not necessarily so for another. Kinneavy examines in some detail throughout *A Theory of Discourse* the different logics of discourses with different primary uses. Logical argument probably plays a smaller role in organizing the parts of "how to" discourse than other pragmatic considerations, or than semantic ones. There is, as I shall explain later, a sense in which all "how to" discourses make a logical argument: that the activities related will produce the result claimed. In this argument, each part of the discourse which relates an activity in the task becomes a piece of inductive evidence in the argument: "this is how to do it." Parts of the discourse are ordered so as to prove the hypothesis — but, as we shall see, they can be ordered in many different ways.

To see how semantic principles contribute to organizing "how to" discourse, consider, first, the simplest-case example I introduced in examining the semantics of "how to" writing, the instructions for applying the parking sticker. Suppose we take individual sentences as the "parts" of the discourse. Then we can say that each part corresponds roughly to an activity in the task. The parts of the parking-sticker discourse are ordered in a sequence that corresponds roughly to the temporal order of activities in the task. That is, the simplest "how to" discourse is ordered by the temporal aspect of its semantics.

When we turn to "how to" discourse that is even somewhat more elaborate, we find that pragmatic principles begin to contribute to organization. In the textbook paradigm of "how to" discourse, primary parts are the semantic units of description and process, and these are put together according to both semantic and pragmatic principles. The semantic principle of chronology still operates; units of process are arranged generally in the order in which tasks they relate are to be performed. But units of description are arranged in relation to units of process on the basis of pragmatic considerations. Tools and materials are always described before the activities using them. That is, the appearance of certain descriptions before certain narrations is pragmatically determined. Moreover, so is the proximity of certain descriptions to certain narrations. Textbooks usually explain that tools and materials can be described at the beginning of the discourse, immediately before the activities using them, or in both places. The grounds of choice are said to be the complexity of tools and materials, and since "complexity" is highly audience-relative, it is therefore primarily a pragmatic issue.

In the two kinds of examples we have considered so far, the semantic principle determining organization is temporal. But in discourses which are more elaborate combinations of modes, parts may be ordered, too, by the spatial dimension of their semantics — as well as by the temporal dimension and by pragmatic considerations. "Insect Friends of Man," discussed earlier, is ordered partly spatially. Its main sections (e.g., "Dragonflies and Damselflies," "Helpful Wasps") are spatially determined by the classification of beneficial insects into types. These parts are then further ordered spatially by a grouping into predators and parasites. Within the predator groups, types of insects are ordered alphabetically — that is, temporally, presumably for easy access by the audience. Within the parasite group pragmatic principles take over directly: types of insects are ordered by a logical progression from the general, "Parasitic Insects," to the particular, "Helpful Wasps." And the two main groups, predators and parasites, are ordered in relation to each other by pragmatic — specifically rhetorical — considerations, the second group, parasites, being, we are told explicitly, "less spectacular."

Especially in elaborate "how to" discourses, the pragmatic requirement of easy access often plays a major role in determining how the parts will be ordered. For example, consider the *DEC-20 User's Pocket Reference List,* a brochure giving basic instruction in using the DEC SYSTEM-20 computer. The discourse gives many small instructions such as "Type carriage returns <CR>." These individual instructions are ordered temporally into processes which give common commands to the computer. The commands themselves, however, are ordered in relation to each other in the whole discourse primarily for easy accessibility. The pocket list is, after all, a short reference work. Vestiges of temporal ordering appear in the arrangement of the commands. "Logging In" is the first one taken up by the discourse. But "Logging Out" appears halfway through the discourse, instead of at the end. With some exceptions, commands are taken up in the order of their probable usefulness to the reader. For instance, "Erasing" and "Changing Your Password" appear very early.

Directly pragmatic patterns, however, such as a hierarchy of assumed importance, are not the only ways to make accessible the parts of "how to" discourses likely to be used for reference. Patterns derived from discourse semantics are also useful. Spatialization, by classification, is one. For example, consider the highly spatialized *Architectural Graphic Standards,* which consists entirely of subtitles, captions, and drawings. Structures represented are grouped into types ("Retaining Walls," "Footings and Foundations") and types into larger categories on the bases of larger parts of buildings in which the structures appear and building materials. These spatializations make information accessible by creating parallel groups. Knowing that the text is organized to some degree on the basis of materials, I will know to look for information on fireplaces in the same general area as information on stonework, brick courses, and terra cotta.

Temporalizations, too, can contribute to accessibility. In the simplest "how to" discourse, the reader who wants to know only about, say, the final activity in the task, merely looks at the parts of the discourse near its end. More complicated discourses that are likely to be used as formal reference works are often given an artificial temporal order. That is, activities which are actually simultaneous or very complexly sequenced are represented by parts of the discourse which are ordered into a simple sequences. A book titled *Writing a Technical Paper* typifies this arrangement. Writing, like many intellectual tasks and some physical ones as well, is what is called *recursive.* That is, the writer continues to plan as he or she drafts and revises. But the book is organized into chapters beginning with "Evolution," "Revision," "Presenting the Data," proceeding through "Grammar," "Style," "Jargon," and concluding with "The Physical Manuscript." The order of the chapters, especially with "Evolution" at the beginning and "The Physical Manuscript" at the end, implies that, first, the writer evolves a plan and a first draft, then revises it, presents data, avoids grammatical errors, stylistic infelicities, and jargon, and finally produces a physical manuscript. Of course, this implication is nonsense, as every writer knows. Data is presented in notes and first drafts, stylistic revisions may be made continually, and a physical manuscript is produced from the moment the writer sets writing instrument to paper. The book is organized as it is, however, to simplify instruction in an intricate process. A largely artificial temporal order is imposed on parts of the discourse in order to abstract "single processes" from the chaotic phenomenal experience of the task of writing. If the writer wants to refer to the book to find out — at whatever stage of the writing task — how to revise, he or she has easy access to the right part of the book. A book organized with more semantic accuracy, that is, to follow the temporal order of the writing task more closely, could well be inaccessible for reference.

I have said that logical argument plays a smaller role than other pragmatic and semantic considerations in organizing "how to" discourse. Subsidiary logical arguments, however, can order parts of the discourse. For example, sections of *How to Get Good Medical Care,* a discourse whose semantics I mentioned earlier, are organized deductively by the syllogism:

> Modern medicine is a large field.
> No individual practitioner can know a large field fully.
> Therefore, no individual practitioner can know modern medicine fully.

Sentences in several paragraphs, too, are ordered by deductive and inductive patterns to argue for the specific evaluative standards the discourse applies.

Parts of "how to" discourses, then, are ordered into wholes in various ways, according to semantic and pragmatic principles. In the simplest discourses, parts are put together in a sequence that corresponds to the temporal order of activities in the task. In somewhat more elaborate discourses, parts are ordered by pragmatic considerations of logic and complexity — as complexity is likely to be perceived by the audience. In discourses which represent combinations of several modes, parts may be put together according to spatial principles, as well as according to temporal and pragmatic ones. The pragmatic consideration of easy reference often dominates the organization of relatively elaborate "how to" discourses, either directly, as in orderings by importance, or indirectly, by determining particular temporal or spatial orderings. Pragmatics is thus an important consideration in organizing all but the simplest "how to" discourses.

THE PRAGMATICS OF "HOW TO" DISCOURSE

In considering the pragmatics of "how to" discourse, I shall be, as I said, concerned with its special uses by writers and readers. Since language is purposive behavior, the pragmatics of "how to" discourse addresses what we recognize intuitively as its most distinctive characteristics. Two scholars, Roman Jakobson and James Kinneavy, using semiotic models of discourse, have classified the uses of language in a way that can help us understand the pragmatics of "how to" discourse. Both Jakobson's and Kinneavy's models are specially adapted to describe the intentional sign-communication that takes place in natural language. The basic model is as follows. Every act of language communication involves at least four entities. For our purposes, we can call these *writer, reader, message* (the discourse itself), and *referent* (whatever the discourse refers to, or is "about"). Jakobson adds two more entities. He observes that every message exists in a *code,* for our purposes the language itself; and every message requires some *contact,* "a physical channel and psychological connection" between the writer and reader "enabling both of them to enter and stay in communication." [6, p. 299] Some aspects of what Jakobson calls *contact* would appear to be of what I have already called medium. Thus, both theorists agree that all discourse involves writer, reader, message, and referent, and Jakobson adds code and contact. But, both theorists argue, any individual piece of discourse can be described as focused on one of the basic entities more than on the others.

The uses of discourse by writers and readers can thus be described in terms of the basic entity with which the discourse is most concerned. Discourse used primarily to express the writer, Jakobson calls *emotive,* Kinneavy *expressive.* Discourse used primarily to affect the reader, Jakobson calls *conative,* Kinneavy *persuasive.* Discourse used primarily to attract attention to its message, as

message, that is, as an artifact made out of language, Jakobson calls *poetic,*
Kinneavy *literary.* Discourse used primarily to refer to extra-linguistic reality
both theorists call *referential.* Jakobson distinguishes two additional types of
discourse, *metalingual,* used primarily to refer to the code itself, and *phatic,* used
primarily to establish and maintain contact between reader and writer.
Metalingual discourse is language about language, for example, definitions. And
phatic discourse includes, for example, all of those polite social rituals, such as
the "Dear Sir or Madam" and the "Yours sincerely" of business letters.
Jakobson's two categories of metalingual and phatic discourse, Kinneavy would
absorb into the broad categories of referential and persuasive discourse,
respectively.

All discourse, certainly, may be used to some degree for all of the above four
or six purposes, but both Jakobson and Kinneavy argue that for any discourse a
primary use can be distinguished. In Jakobson's words, "Although we
distinguish six basic aspects of language, we could, however, hardly find verbal
messages that would fulfill only one function." [6, p. 299] Jakobson argues
further that:

> The diversity lies not in a monopoly of some one of these several
> functions but in a different hierarchical order of functions. The verbal
> structure of a message depends primarily on the predominant function.
> But . . . the accessory participation of the other functions . . . must be
> taken into account . . . [6, p. 299] .

How, then, shall we describe the primary function of "how to" discourse —
its primary use by writers and readers? "How to" discourse does not seem to be
primarily emotive, poetic, or phatic, though it has important phatic, or contact-
maintaining, features. Some "how to" discourse is noticeably — if not
primarily — metalingual: the purpose of *Writing a Technical Paper* or
Understanding Poetry might be described as to give instruction about language.
But this expression "give instruction about" presents a problem, the same
problem presented by our choice between the remaining two categories,
referential and persuasive discourse. Shall we say that writers and readers use
"how to" discourse primarily to refer to the world (or, in the specialized case of
the books about writing and poetry, to refer to the language), that is, to refer to
whatever process the discourse is "about"? Or shall we say that writers and
readers use "how to" discourse primarily to affect readers, to enable them to
perform the task being referred to?

This is an interesting question, because its answer tells us whether, when we
are writing "how to" discourse, we should think more about the process we are
giving instructions in, or more about the reader we are giving instructions to. Of
course, we do not have to choose absolutely. Obviously, we must think about
both of them. But which is primary? In Jakobson's terminology, the question
is which function, reference or conation, heads the hierarchy of language
functions in "how to" discourse, and which comes second. Charles Morris, in

Signs, Language and Behavior, argues that what he calls "technological discourse," in which he includes "how to" discourse, is primarily "informative" (referential) rather than "incitive" (conative, or persuasive). Though, Morris says, such discourse does prescribe actions, it does not aim "to incite the actions it prescribes for reaching a goal. . . . A goal is taken for granted." [7, p. 221] The discourse tells only what the reader must do, in the world of the task, to reach the goal. Because the reader is being affected only in limited ways, Morris sees "how to" discourse as oriented towards the referent rather than towards the reader. And certainly, when we try to think of "how to" discourse as persuasion, we become aware of how different it is from the persuasion of advertising or political speeches. Obvious differences include the relative infrequence of emotional appeals in "how to" discourse, and the constraints on it to make accurate statements about the world its signs purport to represent. On the other hand, "how to" discourse also differs from referential writing. A book detailing *Architectural Graphic Standards* so they can be followed by certain readers is not the same as a discourse simply telling its readers about such standards for purposes of information. *Architectural Graphic Standards* does, like primarily referential discourse, make accurate statements about the world, but to do so is not its primary purpose. It makes accurate statements about the world in order to enable the reader to do something in the world being represented. How can we describe "how to" discourse so as to account for its focus on the reader's activity?

The best solution seems to be to think about "how to" discourse as a special kind of persuasion, one that employs the characteristic arguments of persuasive discourse in distinctive ways. Thinking about "how to" writing in this manner, we can account for both its reader-orientation and its difference from other persuasion. Persuasive discourse is used by writers and readers primarily to do things to readers. "How to" discourse is used only to do certain things — to enable readers to perform tasks they have already decided to perform. Dwight Stevenson makes, in another connection, a distinction between writing to affect and writing to effect [8]. In the classifications I have described, both kinds of writing are persuasive. "How to" discourse is writing to effect. We can extend our understanding of the kind of persuasion "how to" writing is by observing how it employs the characteristic arguments of persuasion. As Kinneavy observes, theoreticians beginning with Aristotle have identified three main techniques, or arguments, of persuasion. One is what we may call here the argument from character. This kind of argument derives its force from the character of the writer or speaker or the character of persons being otherwise associated with the discourse — as any of these characters is previously understood by the audience, or is explicitly represented or implicitly projected in the discourse. A second argument persuasion employs is emotional. And a third argument is logical, or apparently logical. The logical arguments of persuasion need not be valid nor offer true conclusions. In persuasion, generally regarded, such arguments need only appear valid and true to their audience.

To some degree, "how to" discourse may employ all three of these arguments, but it employs arguments from character and emotion least. Projections of the writer's youthfulness, health, handsomeness, or moral character — often central to the persuasions of advertising or politics — are of no concern in "how to" discourse. Explicit claims of his or her expert authority may play some part. A textbook or cookbook signed by a recognized authority may, other things being equal, command the reader's trust more fully than one signed by someone else. But the important arguments from character in "how to" discourse are projections in the discourse itself of the writer's knowledgeability about the task and empathy with the reader's problems in performing it. If the writer makes statements which the reader discovers to be false, then the writer appears imperfectly knowledgeable, and his or her character as writer of the discourse — i.e., as instructor competent in the task — suffers in the reader's estimation. Similarly, if the writer omits statements the reader discovers to be essential for his or her performance of the task, then the writer appears imperfectly empathic and, again, his or her character as writer — this time, as instructor empathic with the student — suffers in the reader's estimation. In either case, the reader may become suspicious of the writer's instructions and reluctant to follow them, and the discourse may fail in its primary purpose as a result. The important arguments from character in "how to" discourse are thus made by the accuracy and effective reader-orientation of the discourse. That is, these arguments from character actually seem to depend on other argument.

Emotional argument plays a relatively small part in "how to" discourse, but does appear. There are, for instance, reassurances, warnings, appeals to pride and ambition, and the like. The *DEC-20 User's Pocket Reference List* reassures the reader that the command character "?" will provide assistance. The list also warns the reader not to try to use the <Ctrl-H> command to erase, which works on the previous system, the DEC-10, but does not work on the DEC-20. More dramatically, *Crude Oil Tanks* warns the reader in capital letters that:

> A CONCENTRATION [of H_2S] AS SMALL AS 20 PARTS PER MILLION IS THE LIMIT FOR SAFE EXPOSURE FOR AN 8-HOUR WORKING DAY.

A book titled *The Technique of Stained Glass* appeals to the pride of craft and the ambition to work well, as follows:

> Craftsman's discipline and keeping the studio in order is sometimes thought of as a kind of arty-crafty fetish in its own right. Doubtless it can become so, but . . . [b]y having high ideals and applying them to a real situation there is a good chance of being efficient.

Some emotional appeals derive from persuasive aims secondary to that of moving the reader to do the task in a certain way. Brochures or owner's manuals, for instance, may aim to reassure the reader that he or she has made the right purchase or other choice. In "How to Use Your Kodak Instamatic X-35F Camera," such a persuasive aim seems to affect the organization of the discourse. There, initial description of materials may have been minimized to reassure the new owner of the Instamatic's simplicity. Because most "how to" writing, however, is writing to effect rather than to affect, such advertising aims are not central to it.

The most important arguments of "how to" persuasion are logical. As I suggested earlier, we can think of "how to" discourse as implicitly, by its pretensions to instruct, arguing an inductive hypothesis, "this is how to do" whatever. Indeed, the discourse sets up a series of steps or arrays a selection of entities with which the reader is to test (prove or disprove) that hypothesis. Within the main argument, at the level of sections, steps, paragraphs, sentences, clauses, and phrases, may be many subordinate arguments, implicit and explicit, inductive and deductive. Inductive arguments will be of the logical patterns, "If you do this, then that will happen." Deductive arguments will be of the logical pattern, "This is so; therefore you must do that." And all of these arguments, main and subordinate, depend at some level on statements about the world the signs of the discourse represent. If these statements are untrue, then the logical arguments will fail in their persuasive aim. By the pretensions of the discourse to instruct about the performance of a task in the world referred to, the reader is, as I have already suggested, cast in the role of tester of those statements about the world. Thus, the logical arguments of "how to" discourse, unlike those of other persuasion, must usually be derived from *true* deductive hypotheses and from sufficient and appropriately chosen inductive evidence, and must usually issue in *true* conclusions.

Suppose I write, in a set of instructions for conducting a kind of test in the oilfield, "Catch the sample from the valve in the lead line." Implicit in the last phrase of this instruction is the deductive enthymeme: "Sample valves are always located in the lead line; therefore the valve from which you will catch the sample is located in the lead line." The deductive premise here also happens to be an inductive generalization; presumably I have examined a large enough number of the valves in question to have inferred reliably that they are always located in lead lines. But suppose that the reader finds no valve in the lead line. My inductive generalization is wrong; my deductive conclusion is therefore wrong; and the reader can't find the sample valve. Since collecting the sample depends logically on finding the valve, and performing the test from my instructions depends logically on collecting the sample, my "how to" discourse may fail entirely because of a single logical error, a hasty generalization. Of course, this is an extreme example. The reader may notice or find out in some other way that the sample valve is, in fact, located in another position and proceed to follow the rest of my instructions. But my discourse has not ensured this result.

From this example, we can see clearly how the projection of the writer's knowledgeability and empathy, as arguments from character, actually depends on the logical argument. Imagine the response of the reader of my instructions when he cannot find the valve. He loses confidence in my knowledgeability and my empathy. Even if he finds the valve elsewhere and continues to follow my instructions, he will not trust them as he did before. He will know that I either did not know enough to generalize reliably for all cases where the valve is, or that, if I knew, I forgot that his experience might not be exactly the same as mine. At the very least, he will be wary for some new ignorance or lack of empathy in me which will cost him more time and frustration. Worse, he may begin to take all of my instructions approximately and make some irretrievable error. Or, if he has another source of instruction, he may prefer it over my discourse. In any of these cases, my discourse will have failed to some degree.

We may, then, think about "how to" discourse as a special kind of persuasion, used primarily to effect readers' performances of tasks. To this end, the discourse depends mainly on logical argument, which depends on accurate statement about the world of the task. The discourse does make some arguments from character and some emotional arguments, but these are not as important as they are in persuasion to affect. The most important arguments from character that the discourse makes are revealed through its logical arguments and statements about the world. Moreover, because of the discourse's use, the reader is continually in the position to verify empirically the validity of the logical arguments and the accuracy of the statements about the world. "How to" discourse is persuasion of peculiar honesty. The logical rigor of such discourse is comparable to that of scientific proof. In scientific proof, however, the demonstration of hypotheses about the world is an end in itself [2]. In "how to" discourse, the demonstration of hypotheses about the world is incidental, a means of enabling the reader's performance. This difference suggests one way, though not, I think, a comprehensive one, of distinguishing between scientific and technological writing generally.

CONCLUSION

The preceding view of the pragmatics of "how to" discourse completes one theoretical overview of this kind of writing. Whatever the merits of my particular theoretical view, the value of theory, in general, seems to me to be the value of any careful generalization — the value of systematizing knowledge about the objects of our interest, with the aim of knowing more about them. Knowing more about them, we may take more rational and critical approaches to reading and writing them and to constructing courses and curricula to teach them. Extending our knowledge of technical writing discourses seems to me particularly desirable insofar as the academic discipline of technical writing is concerned. It came into existence as a technology of language which has seemed to me in some respects to lack a science to draw on. (Though many scholars of rhetoric may be uncomfortable with the idea of a "science of language," I use the term *science* here merely in the old, general sense of *study* or *knowledge*.) Extending and systematizing our knowledge of technical writing would seem to require attention to its discourses from perspectives essential to their constitution as such. Semiotically-based discourse theory has seemed to me to provide such perspectives.

REFERENCES

1. C. Morris, Foundations of the Theory of Signs, in *Writings on the General Theory of Signs*, Mouton, The Hague, pp. 17-71, 1971.
2. J. L. Kinneavy, *A Theory of Discourse: The Aims of Discourse*, Prentice-Hall, Englewood Cliffs, New Jersey, 1971.
3. L. Rockas, *Modes of Rhetoric*, St. Martin's Press, New York, 1964.
4. J. Moffett, *Teaching the Universe of Discourse*, Houghton Mifflin, Boston, Massachusetts, 1968.
5. J. L. Kinneavy, J. Q. Cope, and J. W. Campbell, *Writing – Basic Modes of Organization*, Kendall-Hunt, Dubuque, Iowa, 1976.
6. R. Jakobson, Linguistics and Poetics, in *Essays on the Language of Literature*, S. Chatman and S. R. Levin (eds.), Houghton Mifflin, Boston, Massachusetts, 1967.
7. C. Morris, Signs, Language and Behavior, in *Writings on the General Theory of Signs*, Mouton, The Hague, pp. 75-397, 1971.
8. D. Stevenson, Mapping the Unexplored Area: Developing New Courses and Coherent Programs in Technical Communication, *Journal of Technical Writing and Communication, 8*, pp. 193-206, 1978.

CHAPTER 9

Scientific Writing as a Social Act: A Review of the Literature of the Sociology of Science

CHARLES BAZERMAN

It is generally recognized that writing is a social act — a communication between individuals and within groups; moreover, implicit in every writer's concern for audience is the realization that skilled writing relies on knowledge of the social context and intended social consequences of the writing. Yet sociological thought and knowledge have rarely been used to aid the study of writing, except for the politically important sociolinguistic studies of the difficulties particular dialect groups have in mastering the standard literate code [1–5].

Scientific and technical writing particularly lend themselves to sociological study because they serve limited functions within distinct communities. The discipline of sociology of science has, furthermore, done much to map out the structure of the scientific community and its activities. This essay will review the literature in the sociology of science to explore what light it may shed on scientific and technical writing and to see what questions it may raise for future study.

In its early years (1935 to 1960) the sociology of science was primarily concerned with the relations between society as a whole and the social institution of science: the effects of science on society, the social conditions under which science prospered, the attitudes with which society viewed science. Much of the seminal work was written by Robert Merton; his *Science, Technology, and Society in Seventeenth Century England* examines the interplay among Puritan values, economic expansion, military needs, and the growth of science [6]. "Science and the Social Order" [7] and "Science and Technology in a Democratic Order" [8] explore in more general terms the social attitudes that aid or impede the development of science. Bernard Barber's *Science and the Social Order* follows in this tradition by placing the social institution of science against other social institutions, such as the political order, business, and the university, in order to provide a macrocosmic view of the social role of science [9]. DeGré similarly examines science as an institution within the wider society [10]. In more recent years such interests have been channeled into policy studies — recommending, evaluating, and analyzing government initiatives in science and examining the extent and nature of sex discrimination within science.

Just prior to 1960, however, sociologists began to look into the social structure of the scientific community itself. Research focused on issues such as the values of science and their enforcement; the rise, structure, and interaction of specialties; rewards and competition; and the relationship between cognitive structure and social structure in scientific fields. These and similar issues bear directly, as the following pages will attest, on our understanding of scientific communication. This review will proceed in two parts. The first section will examine the major models of scientific activity and community in order to define the role that communication takes in each. Each model points to different features and functions of scientific writing. The second part of the review will apply specific concepts and findings of the sociology of science to well known issues in the study of writing: the writing process, textual form, the dissemination process, and audience definition and response.

THEORIES OF SCIENTIFIC ACTIVITY
WITH IMPLICATIONS FOR WRITING

Even the traditional view of scientific writing, stemming from Bacon [11] and fostered by the founding of the Royal Society [12], implies a social theory. According to Bacon, the social factors that inevitably impinge on the individual scientist and form the circumstances of his work are impediments to the search for objective truth and need to be eliminated through the procedures of scientific practice and communication. One must free one's mind and one's language from what Bacon calls the idols that inhabit them, so that reality may be impartially observed and accurately reported in a language that is transparent and unproblematic. Persuasion is extraneous, for any statement can be tested empirically. One should not write for a particular audience, but should rather attend to the objects under consideration, for all of humankind is capable of recognizing the truth clearly stated. The book of nature is open to all; by meticulously transcribing it the scientist is able to rise above the limitations of self and society.

The moment, however, that one thinks of language as something other than a transparent conveyor of accessible realities independent of the personality and consciousness of writer or reader, the sociology of the scientific paper becomes more complex. In "Is the Scientific Paper Fraudulent?" for instance, Medawar argues that the scientific paper distorts scientific thought because it does not at all represent the process of discovery [13]. Although the scientific paper gives the appearance that a scientist gathers objective observation until a conclusion rises inductively, Medawar argues that all observation is prejudiced and that discovery is distinctly different from proof, which is after-the-fact and deductive. Nor are the guesswork and groping that go into the formulation of a scientific idea represented in the crisp hypothesis, results, and conclusions of the formal paper. In comparing observations of laboratory work and published reports, Knorr and Knorr find that the formal report not only omits all the false leads and unsuccessful procedures but does not even discuss the factors that resulted in the choice of problem and the final set of procedures [14]; moreover, the report does not even provide enough information for another scientist to replicate the successful procedure. In addition, Toulmin has argued that, except in formal logic and mathematics, scientific writing does not follow the canons of formal deductive logic [15]. Finally, studies of diffusion, resistance, and evaluative judgment suggest that the claims of a scientific paper are accepted neither uniformly nor promptly [16—20], indicating that forces beyond the proof presented on the page act on the audience of the scientific community. If a scientific paper is not a complete account of a scientist's observations and doings, nor a tightly argued deductive proof of claims, nor an unproblematic conveyor of claims to be objectively evaluated fairly and promptly by a professional audience, what indeed is the scientific paper communicating, and to whom?

Contemporary accounts imply answers to these questions by examining the way scientific knowledge is created and modified through social processes. Ziman, for example, sees scientific knowledge as defined by the consensus of scientists [21]. Each new publication or statement is based on the existing consensus and strives to become accepted into that consensus. Ziman explains that dependence on prior consensus accounts for the heavy use of citation and a strong continuity of language from previous literature on the subject. On the other hand, impersonality of voice and technical language can be seen as attempts by the new contribution to appear as if it has already been accepted into the body of agreed-upon knowledge. The scientific paper makes the would-be contribution public, open to the evaluation and júdgment of the scientist's peers. After a period of evaluation — and being ignored is as much part of the process of judgment as explicit critiques or citation in the review literature — the work may become actively accepted consensual knowledge, cited and used in future work in the area.

The communal evaluation of scientific publications is considered from another perspective in Popper's concept of objective knowledge [22]. By *objective knowledge* Popper does not mean the knowledge produced by impartial scientists, for Popper recognizes that each scientist's subjectivity affects the claims he or she makes. Rather, Popper suggests that a scientific statement, once written, itself becomes an object upon which critical operations can be performed. Just as the spider web, once made by the spider, has an existence independent of the spider, so do scientific statements, once made, exist independent of the subjectivity of the maker. These statements, now objects in the world, can be examined according to the criterion of falsifiability, suggested by Popper in an earlier work [23]. That inspection by critical tests is crucial to the scientific endeavor. Because the body of all statements exists, for Popper, as something other than nature itself and other than the subjective consciousness of scientists, he calls the scientific literature the "third world," or knowledge that exists "without a knowing subject." The role Popper perceives for writing and publication in opening thought up for critical inspection beyond the circumstances of the statement's utterance is similar to the role literacy has in developing culture, as noted by the anthropologist Goody [24, 25] and the classicist Havelock [26, 27]. Similar also is Eisenstein's historical evaluation of the social and intellectual consequences of the invention of printing [28].

The continuous evaluation and reevaluation of statements by the scientific community, as Ziman suggests, lead to a changing consensus about what comprises accepted scientific knowledge. The state of that evolving consensus is important for what a scientist both says and sees, for in affecting the terms and manner of description, a change in the consensual understanding also affects the perception and conception of the phenomena being studied. As Hanson argues in *Patterns of Discovery* [29], all observations are theory laden, all perceptions are filtered through assumptions about the world. Thus each scientist's reports of observations must be understood as the product of explicit and implicit theory, the larger part of which is not the scientist's own invention, but which is received from the consensually shared knowledge of the time and the discipline. Lakatos, Toulmin, Kuhn, and Fleck each present models of how scientific statements are embedded within such received knowledge.

Lakatos suggests that a scientific community shares a research program consisting of methodological rules which define what is and is not valid and promising research [30]. A negative heuristic (the rules that point out what not to pursue) forms the "hard core" of the program, limiting the infinite possibilities for work into a coherent field with coordination of results and theory among members of the community. A positive heuristic gives the scientists guidance in wending their ways through the confusions and anomalies even within the limited field. The positive heuristic can evolve, resulting in a problem shift (or change of the scientific community's focus of attention) while still remaining within the research program defined by the negative heuristic. Indeed the vitality of a research program depends, according to Lakatos, on its ability to generate new problems for investigation. The research program will persist despite anomalies as long as the program keeps suggesting new research questions;

the anomaly itself may be considered as a new problem within the program. As inconsistencies add up, however, the program will either shift through attempts to rationalize anomalous findings or will wither as scientists chose to formulate their work according to more promising programs. Thus each scientific contribution is to be understood against the background of the existing research program, the problems the program proposes, and the evolution of the program in response to new findings. Consequently, in order to communicate the point and value of new work, the scientific writer would be well advised to understand how his or her new contribution fits within the continuity of the problems of the relevant research program. If Lakatos is right, adherence to accepted theory is not so necessary for an article's gaining acceptance as is adherence to the current research program. Even empirical data need to be sorted through the structure of the field's problems. Thus an article that expands a field's problems or redirects the research program is more consequential for the development of a science than the critical experiment that would presumably falsify one theory and verify a competing theory.

Toulmin proposes a Darwinian evolutionary model of knowledge [31]. Competing concepts proliferate; those best adapted to their time survive to be developed and modified in succeeding work, and those less well adapted fall into desuetude. At times one strong line of theory will come to dominate an area, but a change in conditions — whether intellectual, social, economic, or historical — may lead to a new proliferation of competing concepts. Science shares the foregoing with all branches of knowledge, but most scientific disciplines also fall into the more limited class of compact disciplines, characterized by five features.

1. The activities involved are organized around and directed towards a specific and realistic set of agreed collective ideals.
2. These collective ideals impose corresponding demands on all who commit themselves to the professional pursuit of the activities concerned.
3. The resulting discussions provide disciplinary loci for the production of "reasons," in the context of justificatory arguments whose function is to show how far procedural innovations measure up to these collective demands, and so improve the current repertory of concepts or techniques.
4. For this purpose, professional forums are developed, within which recognized "reason-producing" procedures are employed to justify the collective acceptance of novel procedures.
5. Finally, the same collective ideals determine the criteria of adequacy by appeal to which the arguments produced in support of those innovations are judged [31, p. 379].

Toulmin's view suggests that all knowledge-bearing documents, including scientific writing, should be understood within the conditions and goals of the period as well as against the competing contemporary claims. Further, a text should be seen as only one articulation of an evolving concept struggling to survive. The writer of knowledge-bearing texts needs to be aware of the current climate of conceptual competition and evolution as well as the history of the concept at issue. Furthermore, in writing for scientific as well as other compact disciplines, one should understand the continuity between the work at hand and other work in the discipline. More concretely from the writer's point of view, the writer must know the problems of the field, the ideals and ethos of the field, the accepted justificatory arguments, the institutional structure in which the knowledge is to be communicated, and the criteria of adequacy by which the innovative work will be judged.

According to Kuhn, under conditions of "normal science," a scientist's work and statements are dominated by contemporary assumptions about what science is and how one does it [32]. To describe the myriad shared features that define the accepted science of a period, Kuhn used the term *paradigm*, but changed its meaning from a model or exemplar used to conceive of phenomena to the entire complex of shared habits rarely raised to the level of explicit rules. Masterman has pointed out that Kuhn used the term *paradigm* in at least twenty-one different ways in *The Structure of Scientific Revolutions* [33]; Kuhn has since proposed the alternative terms *disciplinary matrix* (to indicate that what a discipline shares is more complex and something other than adherence to a particular theory [34]) and *exemplar* (to indicate concrete problem-solutions that determine tacit preferences). Scientific writing, then, in periods of normal science must be seen as the manifestation of the many particular habits of the time, such as typical modes of perception and problem definition, common formulations, earlier models of problem solutions, and styles of speculation. The scientist writing within a disciplinary matrix at a time of normal science seems to follow very closely in the footsteps of his colleagues. Moreover, because the shared features of a disciplinary matrix often lie below conscious articulation, writing within each discipline can only be fully understood by those who share the matrix. Communication between participants in separate disciplinary matrices is rife with misunderstanding and unresolvable conflict — unresolvable because there is no neutral terminology that will allow for determination of mutually acceptable criteria of adjudication. Thus, periods of revolutionary science, when no one view of what is proper science holds sway, are marked, according to Kuhn, by a breakdown in scientific communication, and scientists start to argue "like philosophers." [35] Such arguments are not resolved by evidence and one side's admission of defeat, but only by the emergence of a new generation of scientists with a marked preference for one of the matrices.

The consequences of Kuhn's theory for the nature of scientific writing in revolutionary periods are manifold. If Kuhn is correct, there should be clearly identifiable differences between the writing within two competing matrices. At the height of revolution, writing should take on a markedly argumentative, persuasive character. There should be clear evidence of miscommunication between members of the two matrices. The character of writing within a disciplinary matrix should also change as it loses or gains hold, either entering or leaving a period of revolution. Finally, if Kuhn is correct, a writer at a time of revolution would be wise to direct comments not so much at his opponents as at uncommitted third parties, such as young scientists entering the field; the argument should proselytize rather than attempt a definitive answer to the opposition.

Fleck's *Genesis and Development of a Scientific Fact*, first published in German in 1935 and obscured by the turmoil of the period until translated recently, anticipated many issues raised by current writers about the social influence on the context of scientific statements [36]. Fleck finds thought of any period dominated by a characteristic style emerging out of the contemporary "thought collective." The socially shared elements — or active elements, because they are the live carriers of the common culture — constrain what any scientist may find and determine the manner in which the scientist will express findings. However, in pursuing stylized intellectual work in accordance with the dictates of the thought collective, the scientist will run up against the resistances of empirical discoveries. Fleck calls these empirical resistances the passive elements of knowledge, because they are in a sense passively waiting for the scientist to chance into them. A passive element once discovered also becomes a constraint on scientific statement. A scientific fact is, indeed, the expression of such a passive resistance in the stylized terms actively determined by the contemporary thought collective. Fleck cites the example of the atomic weights of oxygen and hydrogen: no matter what one thinks hydrogen and oxygen to be and no matter what one perceives atomic weight to be (active elements in knowledge), once one assigns the atomic weight of sixteen to oxygen (also active), inevitably the atomic weight of hydrogen must be 1.008 (passively constrained). The passively determined ratio of the two weights is expressed as a fact in the stylized terms of modern chemistry. Until such empirical resistances are discovered, thought may be capricious, for the thought style may not be able to adjudicate among equally plausible claims, but a fact once discovered and expressed gives the scientist a solid point against which to fix an argument. The mark of modern science is its active pursuit of passive constraints, maximizing empirical experience to minimize thought caprice.

Fleck analyzes medical texts and diagrams from several different periods and cultures to illustrate how particular scientific statements may be viewed as the products of thought styles coming up against and contending with empirical resistances. Fleck's discussion suggests that a writer must rely on contemporary modes of statement while using new empirical experience as a heuristic for developing new forms of statement. Fleck also implicitly provides a method for reading scientific texts outside one's current thought collective, by distinguishing between the consequences of the thought style and those of the empirical resistances. Fleck's work, like Kuhn's, suggests the interesting program of identifying the particular features of discourse that characterize any particular thought collective. Finally, Fleck discusses the effect of popularization of science, noting how language, and consequently thought, becomes more concrete and definite as audiences outside the core scientific community are addressed.

These philosophers, Lakatos, Toulmin, Kuhn, and Fleck, suggest ways social processes shape the form and content of scientific statement. In contrast, a group of sociologists discuss the social structure and social mechanisms that allow and encourage the production of scientific statements. This group includes Merton [6, 37] and those who have followed his lead (including, among others, Cole and Cole [38], Cole [39], Gaston [40], Hagstrom [41], Storer [42], and Zuckerman [43]). Typical topics for Mertonian analysis include the value system (or ethos) of science, the extent and nature of deviance from that value system, the reward system and the importance of priority in the allocation of awards, the institutions of evaluation (e.g., organized skepticism and gate-keeping), social stratification and its function within the scientific community, and the accumulation of advantage (i.e., the process by which successful scientists gain the means to be even more successful). Many of these studies provide important insights into the context in which scientific writing takes place. Mertonians find that the chief reward of science is recognition for original and important work. In this claim we find a motive for persuasiveness in scientific papers, which must establish the priority and significance of the claims they present. However, other factors in the ethos and evaluative systems of science serve to restrain the desire for recognition and the tendency towards persuasion. Merton and his followers have turned to countable features of texts, particularly citations, in an attempt to gain quantitative indicators of social structure; their citation counts and other quantitative data provide substantial clues as to what actually is happening in the text, as will be discussed later.

Although Merton clearly recognizes that social issues inside and outside the scientific community affect the cognitive content of science, he is careful to keep a sharp distinction between social and cognitive aspects of science. On the other hand, some sociologists of science, particularly in Britain, are increasingly willing to see social issues dominating, if not explaining, the cognitive content of science. The differences between the British and American schools of sociology of science are discussed from the British perspective by Mulkay [44] and from the American perspective by Ben-David [45].

Taking the most radical epistemological position among the British sociologists of science is Barnes, who argues that a complete sociological account can and should be given of how scientific beliefs are developed and maintained, just like the complete sociological accounts of other belief systems [46]. The truth or falsity of a scientific claim should not affect the kind of sociological account needed to explain the claim. Barnes does not see the ethos of science as a mechanism encouraging the finding of truth [47]. He, indeed, accepts the full relativistic implications of a totally sociological explanation of scientific belief and claims that scientific knowledge has no more certain hold on truth than any other form of culturally determined knowledge [46]. Bloor takes the less radical position that although many scientific statements may be explained through logic and empirical testing, at crucial junctures logic and empiricism do not provide guidance, and crucial issues in dispute are settled by cultural preferences [48]. Drawing examples from mathematics and logic, Bloor demonstrates that major issues are answered by social negotiation rather than scientific reason. Least radical because they assume the truth of the findings of the field they investigate, Edge and Mulkay demonstrate in a detailed case study of the development of radioastronomy in Britain that the social context (both scientific and non-scientific) and the social structures that develop within a scientific field help shape the development, progress, direction, and knowledge of that field [49]. Elsewhere, Mulkay has criticized the view that scientific knowledge is privileged and has proposed a more thorough sociological approach to scientific knowledge [50].

What Bloor calls the "strong programme" in the sociology of science would lead to the view that social negotiation and the advancement of individual interests determine the nature of scientific communication. Working with this program and influenced by French phenomenology, some researchers have developed economic models of scientific activity in which the scientists shape the scientific paper to enhance its prospects in a market place that will assign it a value. Clearly the persuasion here is not tempered by ethos or critical evaluation. Among these researchers, Knorr considers the past literature as a set of scriptures, a source of cultural capital [51]; Latour and Woolgar [52], taking up the suggestion of Bachelard [53], consider even the equipment in the laboratory a reification of earlier literature, and consequently the result of social negotiation and a form of cultural capital.

SCIENTIFIC WRITING FROM A SOCIOLOGICAL PERSPECTIVE

The first half of this article has explored theoretical constructions of the social structure of science in order to suggest how a scientific paper might be conceived of in sociological terms. In all these theoretical constructions, no matter what their ultimate epistemological positions, the scientific statement is recognized as a social act within a social context. The remainder of this article will explore what the sociology of science tells us about the social context of scientific writing and the concrete influence of that context on the writing process and product. This exploration will focus on four main issues: the writing process, textual form, the dissemination process (including publication and audience structure), and audience response.

The Writing Process

In order to understand the process of scientific writing, we need to examine the relationship between writing and research activities. From one point of view, the two are coextensive.

The writing process may be said to begin long before the writer sets pen to paper; the moment one focuses attention to a topic with the hope that thinking and data-gathering will lead to a written statement, one starts to engage in activities that will shape what finally appears on the page. In the sciences this pre-writing stage is particularly long, while the actual writing-up stage is frequently very rapid. In *The Double Helix,* for example, Watson reports that almost two years were spent from the time he and Crick turned their attention to the structure of DNA until the time they were ready to write up their findings, while only little more than a week was needed for actual writing and revisions [54]. Pressures to establish priority lead to a great rush to print, cutting down the time available for writing up results, except in special circumstances (such as the case of Jodrell Bank, described by Edge and Mulkay [49]). Thus, to find the events, choices, and focusing of thought that shape the scientific paper, one must look to that long pre-writing stage of laboratory work.

Latour and Woolgar, working from observations of a biochemical laboratory, have suggested, in fact, that the entire laboratory activity is a process of inscription, gradually turning the materials under study into the words and symbols that appear in an article or other scientific communication [52]. They view the laboratory as a kind of factory; the raw materials of biological specimens, human power, electrical energy, the morning mail, and the like, are processed through experimental apparatus, equipment for extraction, labeling procedures, analytical machines, computers, and the word processing equipment of the front office in order to produce the marketable products called scientific communications which are shipped out in the afternoon mails. At each stage of this process of inscription, the product gets further and further from the raw object of study and more heavily encoded in symbolic languages. Latour and Woolgar are much concerned with the forgetting of the real object at each stage, but one could as well be concerned with what remains and how it is transformed to language at each stage.

Latour and Woolgar, following Garfinkel with modifications [55], also explore how in conversations scientists on a team construct tentative formulations of their subject in anticipation of what is likely to satisfy the colleagues who will be evaluating their work. Thus, laboratory conversation appears much like an early drafting or rehearsal procedure with the intent of creating a persuasive argument. Audience considerations appear to enter early and often into laboratory work.

Despite the close relationship between research activity and writing, Knorr emphasizes that the entire research process is not presented in the written product [51, 56]. Working from observations of research activities in a technological laboratory studying plant protein, she has found what she calls a process of constructive tinkering. With no fixed idea of what they are looking for to guide them in the design of experiments and observations, scientists are prone to tinker, that is, make a moment-by-moment "progressive selection of what works through what has worked in the past and what is going to work under present, idiosyncratic circumstances." [51, p. 673] Out of this tinkering, the scientist discovers an asset, something the scientist perceives as giving an advantage or handle in considering a problem; only then is the specific problem to be addressed selected and defined. Then the scientist moves backward in order to "make the stuff work." [51, p. 677] Such assets include what catches one's eye as a striking new idea when read in a paper. However, in another analysis Knorr and Knorr find that virtually nothing of the laboratory process of tinkering is carried over into the final report of findings [14]: the report of procedures is so incomplete as to be useless in replication, and all the unsuccessful probings and tinkerings are never mentioned. The asset or bright idea is taken as the given rather than the product; the only other item carried over from laboratory to article is the statistical chart of data. The article is constructed on different grounds, to be discussed below.

Bazerman, on the other hand, working from first-person accounts of sociological work, has found indications that formulations of research problems, hypotheses, data, and interpretation are made throughout the research process; some earlier formulations, in fact, linger to become part of the final statement [57]. From first recognition of a research problem to the final report there are many intermediary documents which, although not reaching closure on the solution, establish the terms of the problem under investigation, the procedures to be followed and later reported on, the selection of data, and the preliminary conclusions.

If the sociology of science has only recently gotten into the laboratory to notice the correlation between activities and final statement, the field has long been interested in problem selection and the focusing of attention. These are, in effect, the writer's first choice: what topic shall I write on? The sociology of science has considered how the choice of research topic is influenced by both the socio-economic factors apparently external to science and the cognitive and socio-economic factors internal to science.

Merton's early and continued interest in how research priorities are established forms a basis for understanding the intellectual background that shapes problem choice [58–61]. Only with an appropriate shared framework of knowledge substantially developed through prior discoveries will it become evident that a particular future discovery is conceivable, possible, and within reach, so that a priority race may begin with several aspirants aiming to be the first to reach the well-defined unknown. For example, the well known priority race for the structure of DNA, as recounted by Judson [62], depended on established theories of genetics, biochemistry, and molecular physics, as well as specific knowledge of proteins and X-ray diffraction techniques. Moreover, contemporary knowledge may so clearly point toward problems to be tackled and so fully provide ideas and information that may be pieces of the solution, that several scientists may come to the same or similar solutions at close to the same time, as in the case of Darwin and Wallace. According to Merton, multiple discoveries and near-simultaneous discoveries are frequent phenomena.

Zuckerman, in an extensive review of the literature on problem choice in science, explores in depth the types of cognitive assumptions that lead scientists to certain problems and away from others, including assumptions about theory, terminology, accepted scientific laws, and the riskiness of reputedly error-prone areas of investigation [63]. As a result, she says, scientific knowledge accumulates selectively. In an earlier study, for example, Zuckerman noted how greatly research had been constrained by the misnaming of bacteria as *schizomycetes* (i.e., reproducing only through asexual splitting) [64].

Other sociologists have given a variety of accounts of how problems are selected. Crane, in defining fashion in scientific problem selection, distinguishes between those cases where scientists flock to new problem areas for scientific reasons and those cases where social or economic factors influence the migration of attention; her analysis is tied to the formation of invisible colleges, to be discussed below [65]. Fell recounts the fashions, some of them recurring, in cell biology [66]. Stehr and Larson have found generational differences in areas of sociological specialization, indicating that the shared experience of each age cohort influences problem selection and distinguishes each cohort from all others [67]. Edge and Mulkay notice that the problem selection of radio-astronomers is influenced by, among other things, the equipment available and decisions about technological strategy, administrative styles of the research team, and the receptivity of different audiences [49]. Cozzens explores how reviews of the literature, in giving shape to the knowledge of a field, serve to identify problem areas for future investigation [68]. Gieryn discusses those considerations which would lead a scientist to continue with one line of research; he suggests that in general scientists shift attention to new problem areas only gradually [69]. Finally, Sullivan, White, and Barboni attribute the differences in problem selection they found among particle physicists of different nations to a kind of economic consideration based on potential recognition [70]: given current technology, knowledge and other resources, what significant findings is the team likely to achieve with priority? Similar economic calculations are discussed by Latour and Woolgar [52], Knorr and Knorr [14], and Knorr [51].

Because writing and research are part of the same overall process, which begins with attention and problem selection, the values (or ethos) governing the conduct of research have implications for writing. However, in applying the sociological concept of ethos to the production of scientific texts, we must remember that the sociological definition of ethos as a set of institutionally realized moral imperatives is not the same as the rhetorical definition of the term as the appearance of the author's character in the text as a persuasive element. There may well be a relationship between the two forms of ethos, but no simple correspondence can be assumed. In the seminal work on the topic, Merton finds a scientist's activity defined by four moral imperatives [8] : universalism (that knowledge claims and individual advancement be judged on impersonal cognitive criteria), communism (that knowledge be shared, even as recognition is given to the discoverer), disinterestedness (that conclusions be reached and advanced impartially, under threat of institutional sanction), and organized skepticism (that all claims be systematically judged according to current standards and knowledge of the field). Since this original formulation, other authors have suggested modifications [9, 41, 42, 71, 72], and some have challenged the basic conception by suggesting that deviance goes unpunished [73], that the norms exist only as after-the-fact justifications [45, 73], that the norms are irrelevant to the operation of science [45, 73], that each norm is balanced by a diametrically opposed counter-norm [74], that the norms do not differ from the norms of other fields [47, 75], and that the norms refer only to pure science and not applied [9, 42, 47]. Stehr reviews the history of the controversy and suggests a possible resolution [76]. Miller raises the issue of how the sociological concept of ethos might be applied to technological writing, but only after the scientific ethos is carefully distinguished from the technological [77].

Textual Form

The close relationship between writing activities and research activities suggests the value of a detailed analysis of scientific texts to determine how they function. However, serious study of the features of scientific texts has begun only recently. For a long time, texts were seen as the historical markers of discovery, as the method by which findings are made public for consensual evaluation, or as the measure of a scientist's career. The extent of textual inquiry was the common-sense questioning, like that by Weinberg [78], of the turgidity of scientific prose. Even though the theories of science as a social activity discussed earlier in this article had direct implications for the under-standing of scientific texts, only Fleck was led to the detailed analysis of texts, in order to give substance to the concept of thought styles. He finds striking examples of how different patterns and habits of expression result in different theories and conclusions [36]. Because Fleck's book was unnoticed until recently, no tradition of textual studies has developed from his work, and it has been left to the recent observers of laboratory activity to be drawn to the analysis of texts through their bafflement about how these texts relate to laboratory practice.

As part of their observation of activities in a biochemical laboratory, Latour and Woolgar closely examined the scientific texts produced therein [52]. They see these texts as moves in a game. In the process of establishing credibility and gaining credit, the tactical moves of a scientific paper help the scientist establish a position from which to continue the game. In particular, Latour and Woolgar consider two features of the texts. First, they characterize scientific statements as to how closely the statements appear tied to the circumstances of a particular laboratory, for such particularity makes the statement appear less fact-like and thus less credible. The statements which gain the most credit are those that seem to rise above the circumstances of their discovery in order to appear generally true. Latour and Woolgar analyze several texts to expose the strategies by which the scientists attempt to decrease the particularity of their own statements. Second, texts are examined to show how they change the rules of the game as they go. By introducing new criteria for credible work, an article is able simultaneously to discredit older work retrospectively, to promote the value of the work pursued by the article's authors, and raise the stakes for competitors, so that certain researchers may be forced out or prevented from playing the game. Each paper is part of the evolution of a scientific specialty, with each contributor trying to redefine the game to his liking and favor. Latour and Woolgar analyze the research literature on thyrotropin releasing factor (TRF) in detail in order to show the tactics by which each research team has pressed its own version of what constitutes credible work.

Woolgar elsewhere analyzes a different kind of scientific text, the auto-biographical account of discovery. In one study, he notes great variation in the discovery accounts of different participants in the same field [79]. After isolating some of the causes of the variation, Woolgar discusses insights into the discovery process revealed by the differences. In another study, he analyzes a single account closely to reveal the practical reasoning by which the scientist creates "a picture of the discovery process as a path-like sequence of logical steps toward the revelation of a hitherto unknown phenomenon." [80, p. 263] To do this the scientist must give the reader preliminary instructions on how the text is to be read and must employ externalizing, pathing, and sequencing devices.

Knorr and Knorr find that a text, rather than being an accurate summary of laboratory work, is a persuasive document intended to establish the value of the scientist's research within a particular market [14]. To do this the paper must first reconstruct the market, define the needs of the market, and identify the research being reported as the proper vehicle for the satisfaction of those needs. The paper must then fulfill the mandate it has constructed by demonstrating that its solution to the market needs was in fact achieved in the laboratory. There is no need for a complete and reproducible account of the work because detailed procedural instructions are communicated by personal contact, and methods will in any event be modified by later workers. The report need only present a plausible account of general events to establish that the solution has been realized.

Bazerman considers each text as mediating among four poles: the writer, the audience, the object under study, and the prior literature on the subject [81].

Features of the text can be explained in relation to one or more of these poles. In comparing texts from molecular biology, sociology, and literary studies, he finds various techniques by which the biological text subordinates its representation of writer, audience, and prior literature to its representation of the object under study. Although certain features of the scientific paper are directed toward persuasion of the audience, demonstration of the originality of the author's conclusions, and the reconstruction of prior literature, all these features are harnessed in the service of creating a symbolic representation of the object of study. The final criterion of all the features is the fit between object and language. In the sociological and literary texts other configurations of the four elements are achieved.

Qualitative citation studies shed light on the persuasive and argumentative uses scientists make of references and citations in advancing their own statements. Gilbert explores a variety of possibilities for strategic referencing, from displaying allegiances to borrowing capital from authoritative previous work [82]. Small investigates how in chemistry well known papers come to stand for specific concepts and procedures; reference to these works invokes a narrow meaning and stands in place of more complete explanation [83]. Moravcsik and Murugesan catalogue citations in theoretical high energy physics, finding, among other things, that about 40 per cent of references are perfunctory and that references tend to be affirming rather than negational by a 6:1 ratio [84]. Chubin and Moitra, using similar data from high energy physics, find varying citation patterns depending on the type of article or letter [85]. Spiegel-Rosing, in examining a sociological specialty, finds that the largest number of references are used to substantiate a statement or point to further information; only an almost miniscule number of references (0.4%) make negative evaluations [86]. Cole's taxonomy of citation types, also based on data from sociology, more fully explores the number of ways a reference can be used to substantiate a new argument — from use in the formulation of research problems to the interpretation of results [87].

The Dissemination Process

Once research activities have been completed and the written text has been given form, the social processes affecting scientific writing are far from over. The routes by which a scientific text reaches its readers are by no means straightforward; neither is the ultimate configuration of its audience, both inside and outside the author's specialty, nor are the mechanisms by which work will be evaluated. It isn't even evident whether the text will contribute to the overall evolution of science, and if so, how. Nonetheless, it is useful to consider how texts contribute to the continuing discourse of science, both for the interpreter of science and for the scientific writer trying to frame a statement that will wend its way through the intellectual labyrinth of the evaluation of his peers. Indeed every writing scientist must be an interpreter of the scientific literature, for the cumulative nature of science assumes that the new depends on the old. Even the old saw on the subject of intellectual debt, usually attributed to Newton, has a long and intricate history which Newton capitalized on, as Merton discusses in the amusing study *On the Shoulders of Giants* [88].

There are two major routes by which scientific knowledge is disseminated. The first is formal publication in print, which will be discussed later. The second, informal exchanges among scientists, is less publicly visible, but nonetheless important. As Menzel noted as early as 1959, scientists frequently gain important information through personal contacts, often in an unplanned, accidental manner [89]. Price then suggested that these informal communications among scientists actually form organized networks of researchers active in closely related areas; to describe this network phenomenon, Price revived a term from the time of the founding of the Royal Society — "invisible colleges." A study by Price and Beaver suggests that invisible colleges consist of the most productive workers closest to the research front surrounded by a floating membership of less productive workers [90]. Large groups of collaborators play a crucial role in communicating information, although non-collaborating scientists still have access to most of the information. Gaston documents the crucial role of informal communication in high energy physics because of the rapid change in the research front [40]; Gaston notes that older scientists seem to rely more heavily on informal communication than younger ones, and experimentalists more heavily than theorists. Other structural features of the invisible college in high energy physics are also described. Crane has provided an extensive study of the characteristics of information networks in science, noting among other things different styles and extents of participation in invisible colleges [17]. Griffith and Mullins note that invisible colleges tend to be more highly organized if the group is formulating a radical conceptual break with the rest of its field [91]. In addition to being associated with theoretical breaks, such highly organized networks tend to have acknowledged intellectual and organizational leaders, geographical centers, and a brief period of intense activity.

The most permanent and public method of disseminating scientific information is through formal publication in print. The following discussion of this method considers two issues: the referee system, which determines which texts will enjoy publication, and the configuration of the audience, which actually uses published texts. Generically, the referee system is a form of gatekeeping (whether the metaphor is drawn from St. Peter or Kafka depends on the studies you read). Zuckerman and Merton describe the history, rational function, and variations of the referee process throughout the sciences and humanities [92]; they note that even from the beginning of journal publication with the *Transactions of the Royal Society* there has been some attempt to control quality through the use of referees. Ben-David examines the role of national academies and other intellectual institutions in helping to establish standards of scientific work and in developing consensus on promising problems and methods [93]. Where national academies have developed strong methods of quality control, such as in Germany in the early nineteenth century, science flourished. Only when monopoly conditions later developed did German science lose ground to French. Zuckerman and Merton also find, as of 1967, a differential pattern in rejection rates depending on discipline [92]: in those fields with strong consensus as to what constitutes significant work competently produced (such as physics, geology, and linguistics), up to 80 per cent of the manuscripts are accepted for publication; in fields with low consensus, such as history, language and literature, and philosophy, up to 90 per cent of manuscripts are rejected. Also, in different fields there seem to be different editorial policies: in high rejection fields editors state they would rather run the risk of overlooking some good work than of publishing inferior work; in high acceptance fields, where shared standards are likely to prevail, editors are more willing to publish borderline work.

There is some disagreement about whether the review process is biased. Zuckerman and Merton's examination of the archives of *Physical Review* revealed that no identifiable bias appeared in the review process [92]. Crane, on the other hand, does notice a correlation between prestige of referees and prestige of authors in journals in sociology and economics [94]. Crane interprets this correlation as a result of similarities in training rather than the influence of personal ties. Abramowitz, Gomes, and Abramowitz evaluated the effect of cognitive bias on psychologists acting as referees [95]. The psychologists were asked to evaluate an empirical study contrasting the psychological well-being of student political activitists and non-activitists; all versions of the paper were identical, except that in half the copies references to activists and non-activists were switched in the findings and discussion sections. When asked to evaluate specific features of manuscript quality such as methodology and writing, the referees exhibited no significant bias; but when asked to consider the statistical analyses, conclusions, overall manuscript quality, and publishability, the referees exhibited strong bias in favor of the article that supported their own political leanings.

The referee process used in the evaluation of grant proposals submitted to the National Science Foundation has also been the subject of conflicting studies. Mitroff and Chubin review the debate [96], focusing on the conflicting studies of Hensler [97], who finds significant biases in the peer review process, and Cole, Rubin, and Cole [98], who find the process on the whole fair.

A number of studies of stratification in science suggest some of the possible influences in the review process. One cause may be the accumulation of advantage. The seminal work on this subject is Merton's discussion of the Matthew Effect [99], named after the passage in the Gospel of Matthew which describes how "unto every one that hath shall be given, and he shall have abundance." In a more recent essay, Merton gives an anecdotal account of how accumulation of advantage has worked in the career of Thomas Kuhn [100]. Allison and Stewart have also found statistical evidence of accumulation of advantage in several fields [101]. The most comprehensive study by Cole and Cole finds that the most rewarded and recognized scientists are indeed those who have contributed the most, that those physicists who have gained most prestige are in a position to receive more communication and thus are able to proceed in their own work in a more informed and efficient manner, that important papers are recognized quickly no matter what the status of the author, and that almost all significant work gains recognition over a period of several years, although the middle-range work of more prestigious authors is likely to gain more rapid initial recognition than equal work of less well known colleagues [38]. Finally, Cole and Cole find no obvious signs of significant ethnic or sex discrimination. In a more recent study, Cole does locate a number of points where sex discrimination enters science [39]. Other major studies on stratification include Zuckerman's study of Nobel Prize winners [43], Zuckerman's consideration of the function of stratification [102], Zuckerman and Merton's study of the role of age in the structure of the scientific community [103], Mulkay's analysis of the role of the scientific elite [104], and a recent article by Hargens, Mullins, and Hecht which suggests that the differing structures of research areas affect the role and extent of stratification [105].

Although the gatekeeping system prevents many texts from getting published, the number of those that are published seems to grow exponentially. Several authors, including Price [106], Crane [17], Storer [42], Weinberg [78], Ziman [21], and the Committee on Scientific and Technical Communication of the National Academy of Science [107], have discussed the effects and proposed solutions to the so-called knowledge explosion. One obvious effect is that scientists must select the texts they read; they cannot read them all. Their collective decisions determine the configuration of the audience for a published scientific text.

Citation studies, some of which are discussed below, suggest that most scientists attend to a limited set of articles that tend to correspond to the structure of their specialty and their network of professional and personal contacts. The implications of who reads and cites whose research are large. Consider the case of radioastronomy, as documented by Edge and Mulkay [47]. Radioastronomy developed out of military radar groups during World War II. After the war two major research groups were established in Britain at Jodrell Bank and Cambridge to investigate celestial phenomena the military groups had incidentally noted. Early publications were in journals of technical radio engineering. The work of radioastronomers was virtually ignored by optical astronomers, nor did the radioastronomers attend much to the more long-standing literature of optical astronomy. It was as if there were two heavens — the radio and the visual — which had nothing to do with each other. The single exception of some early interchange over meteors occurred only because at the time optical astronomers generally left observations of meteors to amateurs. Because of the lack of interchange, the application of radio techniques to astronomical questions was for a time stunted and radioastronomers spent substantial time rediscovering things long known to optical astronomers. Moreover, even within the radioastronomy community, each group seemed to proceed on different tracks, paying greater attention to its own findings, with self-citation rates being particularly high. Storer has discussed the difficulties that lead to the low degree of transfer of information among different scientific disciplines [108].

Studies of citations (which papers refer to which other papers) and co-citations (which two papers are repeatedly cited together in third documents) can aid in describing the configuration of the audiences that uses scientific texts. The earlier statistical work by Price observes that in tightly structured fields a large number of references are to a limited number of very recent articles, which seem to represent a research front [106, 109]. In different fields there are different amounts of scatter of citations and different citation half-lives for articles. A more recent study by White, Sullivan, and Barboni explores the interdependence of theory and experiment at a time of revolutionary change (the discovery of parity violation) in the physics of weak interactions [110]. Co-citation studies, such as those by Small [111]; Small and Griffith [112]; Griffith, Small, Stonehill, and Dey [113]; and Garfield, Malin, and Small [114] have begun to map out how the social structure of specialties changes in the wake of publications reporting discoveries that reshape the field. They have measured communications within and between a wide number of specialties, both those that are rapidly changing and those that are more slow moving. Through co-citation mapping they have been able to create graphic representations of the structure of specialties over time. Moreover, a study by Mullins, Hargens, Hecht, and Kick [115] shows that the networks of communication revealed by co-citation closely resemble networks revealed by other measures of interaction, such as personal contact and awareness of each other's work. A recent article by Lenoir has suggested using co-citation clustering in conjunction with blockmodeling techniques to explore further the relationship between specialty structure as revealed in print and as revealed in personal contact and awareness [116]. Most of the citation and co-citation studies have been made possible by the data of the Institute for Scientific Information, publishers of the *Science Citation Index, Social Science Citation Index,* and *Humanities Citation Index.* The prefaces to these indexes by editor Garfield frequently point out features of the social structure revealed by the citation data; these prefaces have been collected [117].

The communication patterns within technological fields differ from patterns in the sciences. An early article by Marquis and Allen finds that for many reasons, including obligation to an employer, technologists are less likely to rely on and disseminate findings through public print sources [118]. Price further explores the "papyrophobic" character of technology to discover ways in which diffusion of technology and the interaction between science and technology can be increased [119]; he recommends rapid turnover and transfer of personnel so that young technologists will bring the newest scientific findings and the older technologists will carry their expertise with them to the new work site. Ben-David, on the other hand, believes that the way to increase technological use of scientific findings is to encourage entrepreneurial opportunities for technologists, who are likely to know best which scientific knowledge is most applicable [120]. The Price essay discussed above is part of a volume called *Factors in the Transfer of Technology,* edited by Gruber and Marquis [119]; it also includes an article by Toulmin, extending his ideas on scientific evolution [31] to show how scientific findings and innovative techniques are diffused to technology; and one by Allen, generally showing that technological information is transferred poorly, that literature is not used as a primary channel of communication, that translation problems are common in transferring information across informational boundaries, and that the better performing groups rely on the resources of their own laboratories. Allen's comprehensive study on the subject, *Managing the Flow of Technology*, focuses largely on communications within a single organization, considering such factors as organizational structure and architecture; although the limited and troublesome roles of literature and communication among organizations are fully documented, all his recommendations concern internal organization [121].

Audience Response

When a scientific text has reached an audience, through direct or circuitous channels of dissemination, the audience has the opportunity to respond in several ways. Until recently, studies of reception have been limited to cases where there has been initial resistance to or rejection of ideas later accepted [16–20], the implicit assumption being that other instances of acceptance and rejection were based on rational judgments and further experimental evidence. Latour and Woolgar's investigations into the microprocesses through which judgments are developed and expressed, however, suggest that there is much to be learned about how readers, particularly scientific readers, form judgments about their reading, both upon immediate reading and upon long-term development of beliefs about their specialty [52]. In more general terms, Gilbert speculates about the process by which judgments regarding research findings are rendered [122]: when claims are accepted, they serve as models on which to base new research, thereby becoming temporarily adopted as scientific knowledge. At this moment it remains unclear how much social negotiation and reconstruction of the literature — in the manner described in Berger and Luckmann's *The Social Construction of Reality* [123] — actually takes place in science.

A number of historical studies have examined how the formulation or claim of one scientific text can emerge to dominate a field for some time. In his book on the Copernican Revolution, Kuhn emphasizes the collapse of prior beliefs through the accretion of anomalies and the emergence of the new theory out of a period of confusion [124]. Elkana notes the confusion in terminology that prevented the discovery of conservation of energy until appropriate terminology lent precision to the concept of energy [125]. Cole observes the role of the theory in producing puzzles to be solved [87], in legitimating and interpreting empirical work, and in generating further theoretical innovations; a theory that proves useful in all these ways may outlast anomalous empirical findings. Crane finds that the main factors affecting how a theory was received in theoretical high energy physics were its breadth and testability — how many kinds of observations and with what level of testable predictiveness the theory covered [126].

One feature of acceptance first noticed by Merton is that although accepted claims are at first explicitly recognized through citation, as the claim grows older it is no longer explicitly referred to, but rather is implicitly incorporated into the argument of other scientific texts, becoming an assumption rather than a specific source [127]. Messeri has examined this process of obliteration by incorporation by using case material from the acceptance into standard geological knowledge of plate tectonics and sea-floor spreading [128].

One final case study should remind us that however we conceive scientific writing, scientific texts, and the processes of dissemination and reception, our conception must always be grounded in an understanding of the contemporary social and intellectual conditions that surround any act of statement making. Mendel has long been cited as a legendary example of a scientist whose work was ignored because it did not fit the scientific orthodoxies of his time. Brannigan, however, now finds that Mendel was far from originally ignored or rejected in the 1860's [129]. His work was recognized and well cited by his contemporaries as a substantial, although far from revolutionary, contribution to the field of hybridization. Moreover, from Mendel's comments, his limited publishing ambitions for the work, and his satisfaction with the reception, it appears that the scientific reception matched his own estimation of his work. Only later, in a turn-of-the-century debate on evolution, was Mendel reinterpreted as making a major contribution to the theory of genetics. Only in retrospect, in light of this new interpretation, did Mendel's contribution appear to be ignored.

CONCLUSION

The consequences of any scientific paper for our understanding and control of nature, for future work in science, and even for our retrospective reconstruction of the knowledge and history of a discipline are the result of complex social processes we have barely begun to explore. In the same way, how a scientific text emerges from a social web of human motivations, intentions, and actions holds many mysteries. We can see that intentions and consequences meet through the printed text, but until we sort out the web of social action that surrounds the text, we cannot know fully what the piece of scientific writing is or does.

Postscript

After this review was written, but before it went to press, several essays relevant to scientific discourse appeared. Knorr-Cetina has brought together in a book length essay her theories on the constructed nature of scientific statements and knowledge [130]. Garfinkel, Lynch, and Livingston have closely analyzed the talk identifying an astronomical discovery [131]; Morrison has examined "telling-order designs" in texts of didactic inquiry [132]; and Yearley has analyzed the persuasive elements in an early nineteenth century geological text [133]. Bazerman has discussed the problems arising from political science's attempt to institute an idealized version of the scientific paper [134] and has examined the forces and choices shaping some articles by the physicist A. H. Compton [135]. Gilbert and Mulkay have released the first results of their research program examining discourse practices in a biochemical research area [136–141]; and Mulkay has argued for the importance of discourse studies for an understanding of science [142].

REFERENCES

1. B. Bernstein, *Class, Codes, and Control,* Routledge and Kegan Paul, London, 1970.
2. W. Labov, *Language in the Inner City,* University of Pennsylvania Press, Philadelphia, Pennsylvania, 1972.
3. R. Hoggart, *The Uses of Literacy,* Chatto and Windus, London, 1957.
4. D. Olson, From Utterance to Text: The Bias of Language in Speech and Writing, *Harvard Educational Review, 47,* pp. 257-281, 1977.
5. D. Olson, Oral and Written Language and the Cognitive Processes of Children, *Journal of Communication, 27,* pp. 10-26, 1977.
6. R. Merton, *Science, Technology, and Society in Seventeenth Century England,* Howard Fertig, New York, rpt. 1970.
7. R. Merton, Science and the Social Order, *Philosophy of Science, 5,* pp. 321-337, 1938; reprinted in [37], pp. 254-266.
8. R. Merton, Science and Technology in a Democratic Order, *Journal of Legal and Political Science, 1,* pp. 115-126, 1942; reprinted in [37], pp. 267-278.
9. B. Barber, *Science and the Social Order,* The Free Press, Glencoe, Illinois, 1952.
10. G. DeGré, *Science as a Social Institution,* Random House, New York, 1955.

11. F. Bacon, *The Advancement of Learning*, W. Wright (ed.), Clarendon, Oxford, 1900.
12. D. Stimson, *Scientists and Amateurs: A History of the Royal Society*, Schuman, New York, 1948.
13. P. B. Medawar, Is the Scientific Paper Fraudulent?, *Saturday Review*, pp. 42-43, August 1, 1964.
14. K. D. Knorr and D. W. Knorr, *From Scenes to Scripts: On the Relationship between Laboratory Research and Published Paper in Science*, Research Memorandum No. 132, Institute for Advanced Studies, Vienna, 1978.
15. S. Toulmin, *The Uses of Argument*, Cambridge University Press, London, 1958.
16. B. Barber, Resistance by Scientists to Scientific Discovery, *Science, 134*, pp. 596-602, 1961; reprinted in *The Sociology of Science*, B. Barber and W. Hirsch (eds.), Free Press, New York, pp. 539-556, 1962.
17. D. Crane, *Invisible Colleges: Diffusion of Knowledge in Scientific Communities*, University of Chicago Press, Chicago, Illinois, 1972.
18. S. S. Duncan, The Isolation of Scientific Discovery: Indifference and Resistance to a New Idea, *Science Studies, 4*, pp. 109-134, 1974.
19. R. Merton, *Sociological Ambivalence*, Free Press, New York, 1976.
20. G. Stent, Prematurity and Uniqueness in Scientific Discovery, *Scientific American, 227*, pp. 84-93, 1972.
21. J. Ziman, *Public Knowledge*, Cambridge University Press, London, 1968.
22. K. Popper, *Objective Knowledge: An Evolutionary Approach*, Oxford University Press, Oxford, rev. ed., 1979.
23. K. Popper, *The Logic of Scientific Discovery*, Hutchinson, London, 1959.
24. J. Goody, *The Domestication of the Savage Mind*, Cambridge University Press, London, 1977.
25. J. Goody and I. Watt (eds.), *Literacy in Traditional Societies*, Cambridge University Press, London, 1968.
26. E. Havelock, *The Greek Concept of Justice*, Harvard University Press, Cambridge, Massachusetts, 1978.
27. E. Havelock, *Origins of Western Literacy*, Ontario Institute for Studies in Education Monograph Series, *14*, Toronto, 1976.
28. E. Eisenstein, *The Printing Press as an Agent of Change*, Oxford University Press, Oxford, 1978.
29. N. R. Hanson, *Patterns of Discovery*, Cambridge University Press, London, 1958.
30. I. Lakatos, *The Methodology of Scientific Research Programs*, Cambridge University Press, London, 1978.
31. S. Toulmin, *Human Understanding: The Collective Use and Evolution of Concepts*, Princeton University Press, Princeton, New Jersey, 1972.
32. T. Kuhn, *The Structure of Scientific Revolutions*, University of Chicago Press, Chicago, Illinois, 1962, 1970.
33. M. Masterman, The Nature of a Paradigm, in *Criticism and the Growth of Knowledge*, I. Lakatos and A. Musgrave (eds.), Cambridge University Press, London, pp. 59-89, 1970.

34. T. Kuhn, Second Thoughts on Paradigms, *The Essential Tension*, University of Chicago Press, Chicago, Illinois, pp. 293-319, 1977.
35. T. Kuhn, Logic of Discovery or Psychology of Research?, in *Criticism and the Growth of Knowledge*, I. Lakatos and A. Musgrave (eds.), Cambridge University Press, London, pp. 1-23, 1970; reprinted in [34], pp. 262-292, 1977.
36. L. Fleck, *Genesis and Development of a Scientific Fact*, F. Bradley and J. Trenn (trans.), University of Chicago Press, Chicago, Illinois, 1979; reprinted from the German original published by Benno Schwabe, Basel, Switzerland, 1935.
37. R. Merton, *The Sociology of Science: Theoretical and Empirical Investigations*, N. W. Storer (ed.), University of Chicago Press, Chicago, Illinois, 1973.
38. J. Cole and S. Cole, *Social Stratification in Science*, University of Chicago Press, Chicago, Illinois, 1973.
39. J. Cole, *Fair Science*, Free Press, New York, 1979.
40. J. Gaston, *Originality and Competition in Science: A Study of the British High Energy Physics Community*, University of Chicago Press, Chicago, Illinois, 1973.
41. W. Hagstrom, *The Scientific Community*, Southern Illinois University Press, Carbondale, Illinois, 1965.
42. N. Storer, *The Social System of Science*, Holt, Rinehart, and Winston, New York, 1966.
43. H. Zuckerman, *Scientific Elite: Nobel Laureates in the United States*, Free Press, New York, 1977.
44. M. Mulkay, The Sociology of Science in Britain, in *The Sociology of Science in Europe*, R. Merton and J. Gaston (eds.), Southern Illinois University Press, Carbondale, Illinois, pp. 224-257, 1977.
45. J. Ben-David, The Emergence of National Traditions in the Sociology of Science: The United States and Great Britain, *Sociological Inquiry, 48*, pp. 197-218, 1978.
46. B. Barnes, *Scientific Knowledge and Sociological Theory*, Routledge and Kegan Paul, London, 1974.
47. S. B. Barnes and R. G. A. Dolby, The Scientific Ethos: A Deviant Viewpoint, *European Journal of Sociology, 2*, pp. 3-25, 1970.
48. D. Bloor, *Knowledge and Social Imagery*, Routledge and Kegan Paul, London, 1976.
49. D. Edge and M. Mulkay, *Astronomy Transformed: The Emergence of Radio Astronomy in Britain*, John Wiley and Sons, New York, 1976.
50. M. Mulkay, *Science and the Sociology of Knowledge*, George Allen and Unwin, London, 1979.
51. K. D. Knorr, Producing and Reproducing Knowledge: Descriptive or Constructive?, *Social Science Information, 16*, pp. 669-696, 1977.
52. B. Latour and S. Woolgar, *Laboratory Life: The Social Construction of Scientific Facts*, Sage, Beverly Hills, California, 1979.
53. G. Bachelard, *Le materialisme rationnel*, P. U. F., Paris, 1953.
54. J. D. Watson, *The Double Helix*, Atheneum, New York, 1968.

55. H. Garfinkel, The Rational Properties of Scientific and Common Sense Activities, *Studies in Ethnomethodology*, Prentice-Hall, Englewood Cliffs, New Jersey, pp. 262-283, 1967.

56. K. D. Knorr, Tinkering Toward Success: Prelude to a Theory of Scientific Practice, *Theory and Society*, 8, pp. 347-376, 1979.

57. C. Bazerman, Constructing Written Knowledge, Seminar on Sociology-of Science, Columbia University, New York, 1979.

58. R. Merton, Priorities in Scientific Discovery, *American Sociological Review*, 22, pp. 635-659, 1957; reprinted in [37], pp. 286-324.

59. R. Merton, The Behavior Patterns of Scientists, *American Scientist*, 58, pp. 1-23, 1969; reprinted in [37], pp. 325-342.

60. R. Merton, Singletons and Multiples in Science, *Proceedings of the American Philosophical Society*, 105, pp. 470-486, 1961; reprinted in [37], pp. 343-370.

61. R. Merton, Multiple Discoveries as Strategic Research Site, *European Journal of Sociology*, 4, pp. 237-249, 1963; reprinted in [37], pp. 371-382.

62. H. Judson, *The Eighth Day of Creation*, Simon and Schuster, New York, 1979.

63. H. Zuckerman, Theory Choice and Problem Selection in Science, *Sociological Inquiry*, 48, pp. 65-95, 1978.

64. H. Zuckerman, Cognitive and Social Processes in Scientific Discovery: Recombination in Bacteria as a Prototypical Case, unpublished manuscript, 1975.

65. D. Crane, Fashion in Science: Does it Exist?, *Social Problems, 16*, pp. 433-440, 1969.

66. H. B. Fell, Fashion in Cell Biology, *Science, 132*, pp. 1625-1627, 1960.

67. N. Stehr and L. Larson, The Rise and Decline of Areas of Specialization, *The American Sociologist*, 7, pp. 3-6, 1972.

68. S. Cozzens, Operationalizing Problems and Problem Areas, paper presented at the meeting of the Society for the Social Studies of Science, Toronto, 1980.

69. T. Gieryn, Problem Retention and Problem Change in Science, *Sociological Inquiry*, 48, pp. 96-115, 1978.

70. D. Sullivan, D. White, and E. Barboni, The State of a Science: Indicators in the Specialty of Weak Interactions, *Social Studies of Science*, 7, pp. 167-200, 1977.

71. A. F. Cournand, The Code of the Scientist and Its Relationship to Ethics, *Science, 198*, pp. 699-705, 1977.

72. H. Zuckerman, Deviant Behavior and Social Control in Science, in *Deviance and Social Change*, E. Sagarin (ed.), Sage, Beverly Hills, California, 1977.

73. M. Mulkay, Norms and Ideology in Science, *Social Science Information*, 15, pp. 627-656, 1976.

74. I. Mitroff, Norms and Counter-Norms in a Select Group of the Apollo Moon Scientists: A Case Study of the Ambivalence of Scientists, *American Sociological Review*, 39, pp. 579-595, 1974.

75. M. Mulkay, Some Aspects of Cultural Growth in the Natural Sciences, *Social Research*, 36, pp. 22-52, 1969.

76. N. Stehr, The Ethos of Science Revisited: Social and Cognitive Norms, *Sociological Inquiry*, 48, pp. 172-196, 1978.

77. C. R. Miller, The Ethos of Science and the Ethos of Technology, paper presented at the Conference on College Composition and Communication, Washington, D.C., 1980.
78. A. Weinberg, *Reflections on Big Science*, M. I. T. Press, Cambridge, Massachusetts, 1967.
79. S. Woolgar, Writing an Intellectual History of Scientific Development: The Use of Discovery Accounts, *Social Studies of Science, 6*, pp. 395-422, 1976.
80. S. Woolgar, Discovery: Logic and Sequence in a Scientific Text, in *The Social Process of Scientific Investigation*, K. Knorr, R. Krohn, and R. Whitley (eds.), D. Reidel Publishing Company, Dordrecht, Holland, pp. 239-268, 1981.
81. C. Bazerman, What Written Knowledge Does: Three Example of Academic Discourse, *Philosophy of the Social Sciences, 11*, pp. 361-388, 1981
82. G. Gilbert, Referencing as Persuasion, *Social Studies of Science, 7*, pp. 113-122, 1977.
83. H. Small, Cited Documents as Concept Symbols, *Social Studies of Science, 8*, pp. 327-340, 1978.
84. M. Moravcsik and P. Murugesan, Some Results on the Function and Quality of Citations, *Social Studies of Science, 5*, pp. 86-92, 1975.
85. D. Chubin and S. Moitra, Content Analysis of References: Adjunct or Alternative to Citation Counting?, *Social Studies of Science, 5*, pp. 423-441, 1975.
86. I. Spiegel-Rosing, Science Studies: Bibliometric and Content Analysis, *Social Studies of Science, 7*, pp. 97-113, 1977.
87. S. Cole, The Growth of Scientific Knowledge: Theories of Deviance as a Case Study, in *The Idea of Social Structure*, L. Coser (ed.), Harcourt Brace Jovanovich, New York, pp. 175-220, 1975.
88. R. Merton, *On the Shoulders of Giants: A Shandean Postscript*, Free Press, New York, 1965.
89. H. Menzel, Planned and Unplanned Scientific Communication, in *The Sociology of Science*, B. Barber and W. Hirsch (eds.), Free Press, New York, pp. 417-441, 1962.
90. D. Price and D. Beaver, Collaboration in an Invisible College, *American Psychologist, 21*, pp. 1011-1018, 1966.
91. B. Griffith and N. Mullins, Coherent Social Groups in Scientific Change, *Science, 177*, pp. 959-964, 1972.
92. H. Zuckerman and R. Merton, Institutionalized Patterns of Evaluation in Science, *Minerva, 9*, pp. 66-100, 1971; reprinted in [37], pp. 460-496.
93. J. Ben-David, Organization, Social Control, and Cognitive Change in Science, in *Culture and Its Creators*, J. Ben-David and T. N. Clark (eds.), University of Chicago Press, Chicago, Illinois, pp. 244-265, 1971.
94. D. Crane, The Gatekeepers of Science: Some Factors Affecting the Selection of Articles for Scientific Journals, *The American Sociologist, 2*, pp. 195-201, 1967.
95. S. Abramowitz, B. Gomes, and C. Abramowitz, Publish or Politic: Referee Bias in Manuscript Review, *Journal of Applied Social Psychology, 5*, pp. 187-200, 1975.

96. I. Mitroff and D. Chubin, Peer Review at the NSF: A Dialectical Policy Analysis, *Social Studies of Science, 9,* pp. 199-232, 1979.
97. D. Hensler, *Perceptions of the National Science Foundation Peer Review Process: A Report on a Survey of NSF Reviewers and Applicants,* NSF 77-33, National Science Foundation, Washington, D.C., December 1976.
98. S. Cole, L. Rubin, and J. R. Cole, Peer Review and the Support of Science, *Scientific American, 237,* pp. 34-41, October 1977.
99. R. Merton, The Matthew Effect in Science, *Science, 159,* pp. 56-63, 1968; reprinted in [37], pp. 439-459.
100. R. Merton, The Sociology of Science: An Episodic Memoir, in *The Sociology of Science in Europe,* R. Merton and J. Gaston (eds.), Southern Illinois University Press, Carbondale, Illinois, pp. 3-141, 1977.
101. P. Allison and J. Stewart, Productivity Differences Among Scientists: Evidence for Accumulative Advantage, *American Sociological Review, 39,* pp. 596-606, 1974.
102. H. Zuckerman, Stratification in American Science, *Sociological Inquiry, 40,* pp. 235-257, 1970.
103. H. Zuckerman and R. Merton, Age, Aging, and Age Structure in Science, in *A Sociology of Age Stratification* (Vol. 3 of *Aging and Society*), M. Riley, M. Johnson, and A. Foner (eds.), Russell Sage Foundation, New York, pp. 292-356, 1972; reprinted in [37], pp. 497-559.
104. M. Mulkay, The Mediating Role of the Scientific Elite, *Social Studies of Science, 6,* pp. 445-470, 1976.
105. L. Hargens, N. Mullins, and P. Hecht, Research Areas and Stratification Processes in Science, *Social Studies of Science, 10,* pp. 55-74, 1980.
106. D. Price, *Little Science, Big Science,* Columbia University Press, New York, 1963.
107. Committee on Scientific and Technical Communication of the National Academy of Sciences, *Scientific and Technical Communication: A Pressing National Problem and Recommendations for Its Solution,* National Academy of Sciences, Washington, D.C., 1969.
108. N. Storer, Relations Among Scientific Disciplines, in *The Social Contexts of Research,* S. Nagi and R. Corwin (eds.), John Wiley and Sons, New York, pp. 229-268, 1972.
109. D. Price, Networks of Scientific Papers, *Science, 149,* pp. 510-515, 1965.
110. D. White, D. Sullivan, and E. Barboni, The Interdependence of Theory and Experiment in Revolutionary Science: The Case of Parity Violation, *Social Studies of Science, 9,* pp. 303-328, 1979.
111. H. Small, A Co-Citation Model of a Scientific Specialty: A Longitudinal Study of Collagen Research, *Social Studies of Science, 7,* pp. 139-166, 1977.
112. H. Small and B. Griffith, The Structure of Scientific Literatures I: Identifying and Graphing Specialties, *Science Studies, 4,* pp. 17-40, 1974.
113. B. Griffith, H. Small, J. Stonehill, and S. Dey, The Structure of Scientific Literatures II: Toward a Macro- and Microstructure for Science, *Science Studies, 4,* pp. 339-365, 1974.

114. E. Garfield, M. Malin, and H. Small, Citation Data as Science Indicators, in *Toward a Metric of Science: The Advent of Science Indicators,* John Wiley and Sons, New York, 1978.
115. N. Mullins, L. Hargens, P. Hecht, and E. Kick, The Group Structure of Cocitation Clusters: A Comparative Study, *American Sociological Review, 42,* pp. 552-562, 1977.
116. T. Lenoir, Quantitative Foundations for the Sociology of Science: On Linking Blockmodeling with Co-Citation Analysis, *Social Studies of Science, 9,* pp. 455-480, 1979.
117. E. Garfield, *Essays of an Information Scientist,* ISI Press, Philadelphia, Pennsylvania, 1977.
118. D. Marquis and T. Allen, Communication Patterns in Applied Technology, *American Psychologist, 21,* pp. 1052-1060, 1966.
119. D. J. Price, The Structures of Publication in Science and Technology, in *Factors in the Transfer of Technology,* W. H. Gruber and D. G. Marquis (eds.), M.I.T. Press, Cambridge, Massachusetts, pp. 91-104, 1969.
120. J. Ben-David, Scientific Entrepreneurship and the Utilization of Research, in *The Sociology of Science,* B. Barnes (ed.), Penguin, London, pp. 181-187, 1972.
121. T. Allen, *Managing the Flow of Technology,* M.I.T. Press, Cambridge, Massachusetts, 1977.
122. G. Gilbert, The Transformation of Research Findings into Scientific Knowledge, *Social Studies of Science, 6,* pp. 281-306, 1976.
123. P. Berger and T. Luckmann, *The Social Construction of Reality,* Doubleday, New York, 1966.
124. T. Kuhn, *The Copernican Revolution,* Harvard University Press, Cambridge, Massachusetts, 1957.
125. Y. Elkana, *The Discovery of the Conservation of Energy,* Harvard University Press, Cambridge, Massachusetts, 1974.
126. D. Crane, An Exploratory Study of Kuhnian Paradigms in Theoretical High Energy Physics, *Social Studies of Science, 10,* pp. 23-54, 1980.
127. R. Merton, *Social Theory and Social Structure,* Free Press, New York, pp. 27-30, 1968.
128. P. Messeri, Obliteration by Incorporation: Toward a Problematics, Theory, and Metric of the Use of Scientific Literature, paper presented at the Convention of the American Sociological Association, San Fransciso, 1978.
129. A. Brannigan, The Reification of Mendel, *Social Studies of Science, 9,* pp. 423-454, 1979.
130. K. D. Knorr-Cetina, *The Manufacture of Knowledge: An Essay on the Constructivist and Contextual Nature of Science,* Pergamon Press, Oxford, 1981.
131. H. Garfinkel, M. Lynch, and E. Livingston, The Work of a Discovering Science Construed with Materials from the Optically Discovered Pulsar, *Philosophy of the Social Sciences, 11,* pp. 131-158, 1981.
132. K. L. Morrison, Some Properties of "Telling-Order Designs" in Didactic Inquiry, *Philosophy of the Social Sciences, 11,* pp. 245-262, 1981.

133. S. Yearley, Textual Persuasion: The Role of Social Accounting in the Construction of Scientific Arguments, *Philosophy of the Social Sciences, 11*, pp. 409-435, 1981.

134. C. Bazerman, Getting the Damn Parts to Fit Together: Strategies in Writing a Science of Politics, paper presented at the Convention of the American Political Science Association, New York, 1981.

135. C. Bazerman, Forces and Choices Shaping a Scientific Paper: Arthur H. Compton, Physicist as Writer of Non-Fiction, paper presented at the meeting of the Society for the Social Studies of Science, Atlanta, Georgia, 1981.

136. N. Gilbert and M. Mulkay, Contexts of Scientific Discourse: Social Accounting in Experimental Papers, in *The Social Process of Scientific Investigation*, K. D. Knorr, R. Krohn, and R. Whitley (eds.), D. Reidel Publishing Company, Dordrecht, Holland, pp. 269-296, 1981.

137. M. Mulkay and N. Gilbert, Putting Philosophy to Work: Karl Popper's Influence on Scientific Practice, *Philosophy of the Social Sciences, 11,* pp. 389-408, 1981.

138. N. Gilbert and M. Mulkay, Experiments are the Key: Participants' Histories and Historians's Histories of Science, paper presented at the meeting of the Society for the Social Studies of Science, Atlanta, Georgia, 1981.

139. M. Mulkay and G. Gilbert, Joking Apart: Some Recommendations Concerning the Analysis of Scientific Culture, paper presented at the meeting of the Society for the Social Studies of Science, Atlanta, Georgia, 1981.

140. N. Gilbert and M. Mulkay, Warranting Scientific Belief, *Social Studies of Science, 12*, pp. 383-408, 1982.

141. M. Mulkay and N. Gilbert, Scientists' Theory Talk, unpublished paper, 1981.

142. M. Mulkay, Action and Belief or Scientific Discourse? A Possible Way of Ending Intellectual Vassalage in Social Studies of Science, *Philosophy of the Social Sciences, 11*, pp. 163-172, 1981.

PART FOUR
Historical Perspectives

CHAPTER 10

Style as Therapy in Renaissance Science

JAMES STEPHENS

In Europe, the period between 1500 and 1700 was a fertile one for science, or "natural philosophy." The explosion of knowledge was so dramatic that few could keep up with it or absorb fully its implications for the way men would live and think in the future. Nor surprisingly, scientists of the period found it more difficult to communicate their findings persuasively than to conduct their experiments. Men like Paracelsus (1493-1541), Copernicus (1473-1543), Francis Bacon (1561-1626), and Galileo (1564-1642) were frightened of publication. They feared the human mind because of its allegiance to superstition and untenable values and knew that the nature of their material compelled them to develop a style of address which would gently coax intelligent readers into the circle of knowledge. A soothing manner of communication, as Kepler (1571-1630) said, has always been an "excellent remedy" for intellectual disease [1, p. 75]. It works as a form of therapy for the mind by mediating between reader and writer, by both exposing and clothing shocking ideas adroitly, so that the receiver is slowly led to understand them as the writer intends. Renaissance scientists discovered, in fact, that their modes of discourse were crucial to their larger success. Style, they came to see, must be curative as well as communicative; it must remedy the ills of the human mind while simultaneously sweetening the pill with a feast of words and figures, and with pleasing arrangements of material, designed to alleviate the pain of confronting new truths. Kepler hardly exaggerates when he complains that, in this momentous time, everything depends on "the exigencies of . . . speech." [2, p. 6]

Thus, while forcing every thinking man to reconstruct his world view, the Renaissance scientist took great pains to provide emotional and psychological relief by means of style. Since the new philosophers, as Bacon acknowledged, lacked "any art or precepts to guide them in putting their knowledge before the public" [3, p. 61], their task was formidable, and their achievements as authors varied enormously in both literary power and public acceptance. Some of them overcame the barriers erected naturally by the human mind itself (both their own and their readers'), largely because they appreciated Bacon's point that the mind is a false mirror, "receiving rays irregularly" and distorting "the nature of things by mingling its own nature with it." [4, v. 4, p. 54] And, because the mind, as Galileo said, cannot apprehend or assimilate ideas unless "stimulated by images of things acting on it from without" [5, p. 23], the strategies of style adopted by most Renaissance scientists became ever more figurative. As the complexity of their ideas increased, their styles gained in concreteness and pictorialism. Ironically, most of them employed familiar images of what they thought was false, usually from biblical or mythological sources, as a means of ingratiating themselves with readers who might, in time, come to accept what the scientists knew was true. Copernicus used the language of Hermetic alchemy, a "familiar language that can be retained by all" [6, p. 37], while Kepler conceded that anyone with a radical thesis must seem to adopt "as his own not only true and traditional views but also absurdities and falsities." [2, p. 6] Even Francis Bacon, sharp critic of most scientific writing and father of the plain English prose style, came to see that the new learning had its best chance to prevail if delivered to an unsuspecting world by a rhetorical method which "muffles her head and tells tales." [4, v. 3, p. 225]

Though most of these scientists remained evasive about where their beliefs left off and their rhetoric began, three daring and frankly rhetorical forms of intellectual therapy gained acceptance with them: each of these strategies of style exploits a popular and revered system of knowledge, and each seeks subtly to convert the central images of that system into rhetorical patterns which might work on behalf of the new learning. In addition to the use of these three systems — medieval alchemical lore, classical myth, and Christian doctrine — we find increasing clarity and integrity of style, as we move from scientific writings of the early Renaissance to those of the seventeenth century. The best scientists managed to strengthen their readers' faith in older systems of knowledge while broadening their capacity to accept another, apparently congenial, philosophy of nature. John Donne was not alone among intellectuals of the time in praising the styles of the new experimental scientists, as a "physick of the understanding," a medicine which goes down smoothly and yet has wondrous therapeutic results [7, pp. 10-11].

Without examining in detail the style of any Renaissance scientist, the following pages offer a preliminary survey of the strategies which, like generals, they formulated to ensure a successful conclusion to their march upon the human mind. The rationales offered by individual scientists for their own manners of address are of particular interest, and we note that all of them seemed to learn from the failures and successes of their predecessors. The focus here, as in most scientific works of the period, is on the common and, of course, related image systems of medieval alchemy, classical mythology, and Christian doctrine.

ALCHEMY AND SCIENTIFIC STYLE

The medieval pseudo-sciences, particularly astrology, provided clusters of imagery which proved useful to many new scientists who wished to gain a hearing for views inimical to mystical Hermeticism. Medicine and chemistry, for example, had traditionally been regarded as godless disciplines, largely because the pagans, Aristotle and Galen, remained the chief authorities. Paracelsus and his followers thus found it helpful to invent a myth of medicine which incorporated virtually all the popular and "pious" sciences and linked them with religion in a systematic way. Just as astrology, numerology, physiognomy, and chiromancy were justified by men as the revelation of God's hand in nature, Paracelsus argued, so should the new experimental chemistry and medicine. He and such disciples as Giordano Bruno (1548?-1600), John Dee (1527-1608), and Thomasso Campanella (1568-1639), suggested that writers on the new chemistry should resurrect the tradition of natural symbolism so central to ancient Egyptian magic. Ancient Egypt, they asserted, was the last culture to have preserved science and religion in harmony with one another, and to have done so by a natural supernaturalism founded on hieroglyphic images drawn entirely from commonly observed objects in nature and the heavens.

The medieval and Renaissance chemists might have succeeded in bridging the gap between religion and science; had they done so, it would have been a feat accomplished by figures of speech. As it was, those very forms defeated the Paracelsans and obscured for centuries their real contributions to knowledge. Paracelsus's first principle, in both scientific discovery and communication, is that imagination is all. Science has its source in man's imaginative powers, he says, because it is through them that God inspires His chosen priests, the chemists, and reveals to them His creation in all its mathematical and chemical splendor. The true scientist is God's earthly surrogate, and like God, can (if he is a chemist) produce useful things from an impure mass, being somehow gifted with the power of discerning images latent in the elements of material reality. Paracelsus thus employs the old arts of star-reading, numerology, even animal symbolism and dream lore, in a deliberately oracular style which imitates the scriptures but is frankly calculated to further his own career as a serious and highly productive experimental chemist. He goes so far, moreover, as to claim that his very style of argument is God's gift to mankind, mysteriously sent to Paracelsus, a man whose middle name was "Bombastus."

In other words, Paracelsus claimed that he had been divinely inspired to express his laboratory findings in a suitable figurative language. Though most of the beliefs subsequently attributed to him, including the doctrines of the Egyptian God, Thoth, or Hermes, were almost certainly never held by him, his style is so undiscriminating in its use of allusions that no reader can ever be sure. He seems to employ such alchemical notions as the Philosopher's Stone, the transmutation of base metal into gold, and the mystical language of stars almost exclusively as figures of speech, to enchant the reader with what is, after all, mundane information on minerals and gasses [8, v. 2, p. 250]. He emphasizes as a matter of course that these figurative words are used both to clarify and to serve as a code for his fellow travellers [8, v. 2, p. 5], and he asserts more than once that nature itself constitutes "the only true life of man." [8, v. 2, pp. 6-9] Though his language, rich and strange, has made all his readers wonder about his meaning and beliefs, Paracelsus knew it as a divine gift which enabled him to reveal to all discerning thinkers "how the concordances are discovered by us in the Valley of the Shadows." [8, v. 2, p. 90]

Of more significance is Paracelsus's insistence that all general conclusions be grounded firmly in natural experimental evidence, another doctrine which affected his style. Metaphors and symbols, though welcome, may not be made in his system of communication except from confirmed natural data. He does not offer "a pompous parade of words," he promises, "but marvelous speculations and new operations . . . confirmed by full proof and experimentation." [8, v. 1, p. 4] He will replace "mere similitudes," the staple of Ciceronian rhetoric, with stars, plants, metals, and gasses, and allow the reader to draw from those concrete realities and their properties any abstract truths they care to find. Having demonstrated in the laboratory, for example, that most things in nature have a core or essence that may be extracted and employed for higher purposes, he seeks to present this news by comparing essences to human souls and himself to Christ; or, as often is the case, he uses Hermetic terminology to show that the elements we can feel and touch have the same magical (that is, medicinal) properties that are attributed to the "signatures," the Philosopher's Stone, or the zodiac. His form of medicine was highly suspect, and he attempted to justify it by linking it to religion and all the popular sciences.

As Michel Foucault sees the phenomenon of Paracelsus, it is a rhetorical, rather than an intellectual, oddity. Men in the Renaissance knew very well that analogy is a rhetorical figure, never a material reality. The new scientists simply chose, for very practical reasons, to continue using traditional figurative strategies, expecting audiences of the proper accomplishment to see at once how they were applied and for what purposes. Though it seems to us that early Renaissance learning is "made up of an unstable mixture of rational knowledge, notions derived from magical practices, and a whole cultural heritage whose power and authority had been vastly increased by Greek and Roman authors," we fail, Foucault says, to observe that men in those days quite genuinely regarded the world as an assemblage of "signs that must be deciphered," signs which are themselves "no more than forms of similitude." [9, p. 32] The candid use of schemes and tropes, then, seems less peculiar when we know that the user sees *everything* as a rhetorical figure, a word uttered by God. If we are astonished to find a serious chemist equating medicine with the purgation of sin, transmutation of base metals with the Resurrection, the Hermetic Emerald Tablet with the Ten Commandments, and even salt, sulphur, and mercury (key elements) with the Christian Trinity, we have failed to comprehend the author or his world. Finally, we must agree that, though Paracelsus obscured with his style more than he brought to light, Carl Jung's judgment of him is essentially correct: he was "on the track of a process of psychic transformation that is incomparably more important for the happiness of the individual than the possession of the red tincture." [10, p. 160]

Many scientists and mathematicians in the next two centuries imitated the Paracelsan manner in their efforts to bridge the gaps between old and new modes of thought. Even Copernicus, Kepler, and Bacon, voices for modernism, spoke frequently in Hermetic terms. John Dee, a brilliant mathematician, sought to hide his numbers under the cover of an alchemical monad; his *Monas Hieroglyphica* (1564) claims to teach readers how to draw mystical truths from material objects, and its true subject, Dee implies, is the alchemical quest for God in nature [11]. Similarly, Giordano Bruno felt forced to adopt a flamboyant and mysterious style in his defense of Copernicanism. His works of highly modern scientific philosophy include dialogues between Egyptian gods, allusions to secret number symbolism, small jokes that depend on a reader's familiarity with magical traditions, and a consistent use of Hermetical terminology as a point of reference. Bruno was very well received by intelligent men of his age, however, and, as Frances A. Yates has shown so convincingly, was a powerful influence for years thereafter. His *Spaccio della bestia trionfonte* (1584), for example, brought Egyptian magical symbols into a context of new Western thought, and, through what Yates has called its "dramatic style," became "an operative work on the formation of the Elizabethan Renaissance." [12, p. 234] Combining a style loaded with ancient configurations with a fresh and exciting message of science, Bruno thrilled his readers, even while sealing his own doom. Accused of heresy, he was burned at the stake in 1600.

SCIENTIFIC USES FOR CLASSICAL MYTHOLOGY

Clearly, some different mode of scientific communication was needed, and the theorists of the early seventeenth century began to exploit the formal, more perspicuous, and frankly figurative style of the Greeks, perceiving there something superior to Paracelsan bombast. The most important aspect of this reform is a new conception of how figurative language should work in natural philosophy. The ongoing and incisive critique of Paracelsan style conducted by Francis Bacon at the turn of the century signalled an important shift. Bacon, who is always credited with ringing the bell that brought the new world to order, greatly admired the Paracelsans' theories and their experimental results, and he acknowledged that "there is no proceeding in invention of knowledge but by similitude." [4, v. 3, p. 218] By the same token, of course, failure to analogize properly or coherently is certain to lead to untenable conclusions. The difference between the style of a philosopher and that of an ordinary writer must be that the former never fails to display his figures for what they are: devices of style. On this essential requirement, Paracelsus fails to earn Bacon's respect; all Bacon's complaints about his alchemical predecessor are on the grounds of faulty style and its role in obscuring truth. One of the reasons Bacon worked so hard on behalf of a new style for science was the example of Paracelsus, a scientist whose style was his undoing.

Bacon notes, for example, that there are two classes of scientists, workers and theorists. In his effort to belong to both, Paracelsus allowed his rich theoretical imagination to overwhelm the reasonable conclusions he reached in the laboratory. The results were predictable; he compromised his value to modern science by writing a lot of colorful but fantastic nonsense. His terminology, over the course of two thousand written pages, becomes so cloudy and furtive that it prevents readers from determining when they are meant to take key words and doctrines literally. Though he may like the notion of dividing the natural elements into two classes, sulphurous and mercurial, Bacon indicts Paracelsus for "monstrous follies" of imagination in his treatment of those mundane materials [4, v. 5, p. 369].

On another occasion, Bacon objects to Paracelsus because he fails completely to understand the way figurative language could work in scientific communication. The alchemist, Bacon thought, was right to attempt the reform of rhetorical demonstration by grounding the figures in observable reality, but he went badly astray in reducing the Bible, and most other written history, to alchemical handbooks. He thus overlooked the obvious truth that real communication in words must be based on either analogy or accepted convention, and that the distinction between the two must be clear in any work which succeeds as rhetoric. In other words, a man of science is obligated to signify in one way or another the mode in which key terms are meant to operate; this Paracelsus fails to do. Rather than employ fables to clarify or persuade, Paracelsus indulges his imagination and uses those rhetorical devices to drag his reader down to "vast and bottomless follies." [4, v. 2, p. 641] Bacon devoted his later years to demonstrating how ancient fables, enigmas, parables, and analogies might be exploited in the interests of science, and all along the way he employs Paracelsus as a symbol for Western man of divine imagination perverted.

The most common flaw in Paracelsus's writing, in fact, is his habit of allowing emblems or pictures to come between his laboratory evidence and his audience's perception of it, a rhetorical error that Bacon deplores. Since both scientists emphasized inductive logic as the key to knowledge, both were concerned with the invention of new memory systems which might allow men to store their specific findings until axioms might be drawn from them. Moreover, both concluded that the best appeals to memory were word pictures and figures of speech, vivid sensory experiences which could be easily recalled. Although Paracelsus had a chance to achieve useful reform, Bacon charges, he severely abused the scientific and rhetorical arts of memory. Not only does the alchemist fail to give the essential definitions which would render his arguments coherent, but, what is worse, he mangles his experimental evidence by making it stand as texts for emblems, rather than employing the emblems to contain and communicate the evidence. That is, the experimental results simply become grist for the rhetorical mill in the works of Paracelsus; they remain entirely unclarified by the figurative language in which they are encased and have no impact on the reader. An excellent illustration, Bacon says, is the Paracelsan conception of man as a microcosm. Man, he says, "is now a microcosm, or little world, because he is an extract of all the stars and planets of the whole firmament, from the earth and the elements; and so he is their quintessence." [8, v. 2, p. 285] This "ancient emblem" was never meant to be taken seriously as empirical truth, Bacon claims. Though it is most useful in medicine, especially to calm the minds of ignorant men, no true scientist should employ it for any reason other than to gain entrance into the thoughts of his readers; that accomplished, the emblem should be quietly abandoned [4, v. 4, p. 380]. Bacon thought nature was "a kind of second Scripture" [4, v. 4, p. 261], and should be written of reverently; but there comes a time in all scientific writing when all "ornaments of speech," elegant disposition of parts, and things "philological" are omitted in favor of a style of "chastity and brevity." [4, v. 4, pp. 254-255] It is hardly surprising then that, to Bacon, Paracelsus's lengthy and frequent discussions of the microcosm, and microcosms within microcosms, seem inappropriate to a treatise on chemical extraction. Bacon's last word on the matter is simply that a philosopher's imagination must work "to second reason, and not to oppress it." [4, v. 4, p. 456]

In fact, his final word was the *New Atlantis*, a work published posthumously in 1627. There Bacon parodies the alchemists mercilessly, joking about everything from the symbolic props to the philosopher-priest's blue mantle and peach-colored shoes. As a candid fiction on behalf of the new science, the *New Atlantis* is a good example of the second stage at which scientific language employed the figurative forms of traditional poetry and rhetoric. The entire first book has an alchemical aura of Utopian fable-making, but the second book treats the reader to nothing more than a straightforward list of numbered aphorisms on the experiments and instruments that must be assembled for the scientific revolution that is imminent. Bacon had learned to exploit the formal myths of the classical tradition, such as the Platonic notion of a lost Atlantis, for his own new ends.

Thus, in his fragment *On Principles and Origins,* he explores in great detail the myth of Cupid, or Eros, as a means to explaining a complex theory of natural creation. In the *Advancement of Learning* and the *De Augmentis Scientiarum,* the God Pan is evoked at elaborate length to explain "the nature of things," and the image of Atalanta chasing golden balls informs both the *Advancement* and the *New Organon.* Many of the *Essays* update the messages of classical mythology, including those in the fables of Hercules, Prometheus, Metis, Pandora, Proserpine, and Paris. The new scientist, Bacon knew, cannot "drop all arts and subterfuges." "Frenzied" man must be "beguiled," and a wise philosopher will force himself to develop a "mild" style which has "in it an inherent power of winning support." [3, p. 62] As Bacon says in *The Refutation of Philosophies,* readers must never be pushed into a "direct, abrupt encounter with things themselves." [3, p. 103] In the same work, however, he rejects the Paracelsan mode of "shameless fancy" and "endless deceits." [3, p. 123]

Obviously, Bacon preferred instead to adapt the images of ancient myth to his purposes, seeing, no doubt, that they had a better chance than alchemical figures to be perceived for what they are. *The Wisdom of the Ancients* (1609) is a genuine work of mythography which re-tells ancient stories in order to illustrate and dramatize the new doctrines of moral, civil, and natural science. Bacon admits frankly to exploring the "region of cloud and darkness, the secret recesses of remote antiquity," but not "for the value of the thing." He knew well "what solemnity it would add to new discoveries to connect them with remote antiquity." [3, pp. 86-87] Such a method is safe, because the "vulgar apprehension" will perceive no more in it than amusing tales, while those of "deeper intellect" may use the myths as vehicles to greater things [4, v. 6, p. 690]. Thus, according to James Spedding, Bacon decided, as part of his continuing effort to "treat popular prejudices of all kinds with the greatest courtesy and tenderness," to employ many favorite stories on behalf of the new science [4, v. 3, p. 174]. As it is, no scientist could avoid using the myths, or something like them, Bacon claims, because the effort to throw new light on any matter requires a writer to go the way of the ancients "and call in the aid of similitudes." [4, v. 6, p. 698]

The similitudes in the *Wisdom of the Ancients,* his most popular work, are ingenious indeed. The tale of Orpheus is "best understood as referring to natural philosophy," for the scientist uses his powers for "adjustment of parts in nature, as by the harmony and perfect modulation of a lyre." [4, v. 6, p. 721] Coelum, oldest of the Gods, represents "an enigma concerning the origin of things, not much differing from the philosophy afterwards embraced by Democritus"; he stands for "the concave or circumference which encloses all matter," while Saturn is "matter itself." [4, p. 723] The fable of Proteus tells us all about "the secrets of nature and the conditions of matter" [4, p. 725], whereas, in the fate of Daedalus we may read of "mechanical skill and industry, together with its unlawful artifices and depraved applications." [4, p. 734]

Cupid "I understand to be the appetite or instinct of primal matter," Bacon says, or "to speak more plainly, *the natural motion of the atom*; which is indeed the original and unique force that constitutes and fashions all things out of matter." [4, p. 729] The myth of the Sphinx is "an elegant and a wise" description of science itself; the sphinx seems monstrous only because it is baffling, posing "a variety of hard questions and riddles." Yet, we may, like Oedipus, gain "a kingdom" if we can answer the riddle [4, pp. 755-757]. Two luckless women, Cassandra and Proserpine, were particularly appealing to Bacon; the former was undoubtedly an image of people who speak too plainly, as if they lived *"in the republic of Plato and not in the dregs of Romulus"* [4, p. 702], and the latter's fate surely is that of us all, confined in darkness and ignorance [4, p. 759].

Galileo, to name but one of Bacon's major contemporaries, understood perfectly what Bacon was doing; he saw that no scientist can succeed with the public unless he merges rhetoric with scientific method to create an enchanting, memorable style. Like Bacon, Galileo grounded his imagery in concrete and observable reality so that the invisible world became to his readers as palpable as a statue of the goddess Minerva. Also like Bacon, who chided himself for staying too long in the "theatre," Galileo was embarrassed by his literary style. At one point, he compares his *Dialogue on the Great World Systems* to a giddy and digressive poem, a typical man-made invention in its incoherence (in contrast with the geometric perfection of the heavens); we move along, he says, with almost "as much liberty as if we were telling stories." [13, p. 176] The *Dialogue*, as Giorgio de Santillana says, plants a "charge of dynamite" precisely because its rhetoric is "on the level of educated public opinion." [14, p. 187] And, even in a work of the purest scientific purpose, *On Motion*, Galileo will pause to exclaim: "Heavens! At this point I am weary and ashamed of having to use so many words to refute such childish arguments." [15, p. 58] Like Paracelsus and Bacon before him, Galileo sought to transcend "mere similitudes" by engraving on his readers' minds both the objects of the observed world and the symbolic significance those objects might hold for men of philosophic or spiritual inclination. He will strive "by every artifice," he promises, to make Copernican astronomy seem the truth [13, p. 6].

Galileo also seems to agree with Bacon, who argues that, if men's passions and imaginations "were brought to order," there might be no further use "of persuasions and insinuations to give access to the mind, but naked propositions and proofs would be enough." [4, v. 4, p. 456] Since there is no alternative, however, Galileo replaces the ancient gods and goddesses with real objects in the heavens, teaching the new astronomy as if it were a fairy tale. Each of the deities who contributes his name to a heavenly body is allowed to retain his name and its symbolic implications. Thus, Saturn is a "decrepit little old man" with two servants (rings); Jupiter becomes a king with "a guard of satellites"; Venus remains "the mother of loves." His style, Galileo admits, is calculated to make him accessible and to prove, in roundabout fashion indeed, that astronomers ought not to be regarded as cranks, "men of no wit, and little better than absolute fools." [16, p. 102] It is little wonder then that Galileo chose, in his popular works, to write as a poet, explaining his findings as Dante or Petrarch would explain their own unseen discoveries, and leaving open "fields . . . for Epsody's," or digressions [13, p. 176]. The point is, he says, to imitate Copernicus, "as if I were his Zany," or mask [13, p. 146]. It is a direct challenge to mystical philosophy, and "such-like trifles." [13, p. 469] With heavy irony, Galileo suggests that such a style will soothe the minds of those to whom the new astronomy is incomprehensible or threatening.

SCIENTIFIC STYLE AND CHRISTIAN DOCTRINE

Much more soothing, of course, were Galileo's very serious efforts to square science with Christianity, a task that required great rhetorical gifts. He believed that his discoveries clarified God's intentions, rendering them manifest to all who look. Asserting that "It is much more a matter of faith to believe that Abraham had sons than that the earth moves," he believed sincerely that science opens "the road to the discovery of the true sense of the Bible." [5, pp. 168-169] In those works which make the case, Galileo creates a new style for science that was to remain a model at least through Darwin's time, a style which asks men to use their imaginations in the way that belief in the Christian God requires. In one popular work, he presents himself as a writer who imitates the scriptures, even while re-interpreting them. The scientist is a "starry messenger," a decoder of God's and nature's complex ciphers, a reader of the "vast book" of Creation. That book, nature, he argues in *The Assayer,* cannot be read until "one first learns to comprehend the language and read the letters in which it is composed." The language must be mathematical, moreover, because its characters "are triangles, circles, and other geometric figures." [5, p. 238] Later in *The Assayer*, he asserts that whatever is not open to mathematical demonstration exists only in the subjective mind. Taste, odor, and color, for example, are "nothing more than names" and exist only in the sensitive being [5, p. 276]. In preparing his notes on this matter, due to be delivered to Cardinal Bellarmine, Galileo said in perfect sincerity: "We believe that Solomon and Moses and all the other holy writers knew the constitution of the universe perfectly well, as they also knew that God did not have hands or feet or wrath or prevarication or regret." [5, p. 169]

Thus, in the *Letter to the Grand Duchess Christina,* his most dignified rhetorical plea for the rights of scientists, Galileo can speak of his experiments as "aids in the true exposition of the Bible." We must move out of the world of superstition and ignorance by allowing ourselves to see that "the holy Bible and the phenomena of nature proceed alike from the Divine Word, the former as the dictate of the Holy Ghost and the latter as observant executrix of God's commands." The difference between the Bible and the scientist's work, however, is that the former is a work of language which accommodates itself to every man, while nature "is inexorable and immutable" and does not care a whit "whether her abstruse reasons are understandable to men." Truly religious men, then, will begin their search for God "not from scriptural passages, but from sense experiences and necessary demonstrations." [5, pp. 182-183] In his letter to Castelli, Galileo says: "I add that the words *The sun also riseth, and the sun goeth down, and hasteth to the place where he ariseth* were written by Solomon, who not only spoke by divine inspiration, but was a man wise above all others, and learned in the human sciences and in the knowledge of all created things, which wisdom he had from God." [5, p. 164] The strategy of style is apparent in the works of Galileo. He will link his physics, a science of unseen phenomena and movement, with Christian doctrine, a body of beliefs that requires even more imagination of its adherents. The two are clearly "appropriate aids" to man's search for truth [5, p. 183].

Passages of this sort led Galileo's friend, Johannes Kepler, to proclaim him a Hercules who dragged Saturn "down to earth and exposed it to the gaze of all." The telescope has become for all men "a sort of ladder" for scaling "the furthest and loftiest walls of the visible world" and caused us all to fall in love again with Venus, to be enchanted by "Mercury's magic wand" (the telescope itself) [16, pp. 81-111]. Equally significant to Kepler was Galileo's splendid, oracular writing. His "very style attests to the soundness of his judgment" and proves that he loves God because he cherishes nature, "the abode of Christ." Comparing Galileo to God, Kepler says, "you caused the sun of truth to rise, you routed all the ghosts of perplexity together with their mother, the night." Kepler implies that his friend taught him of the "undisclosed treasures of Jehovah" in a manner unmatched by his own extensive theological training. He states flatly that Galileo's work filled him with a "surging love of God" that gave him courage to proceed with his politically dangerous experiments [2, pp. 11-18]. When we consider that astronomers relied more on their rhetorical abilities than on their scientific instruments for the immediate success of their work, Kepler's is a remarkable testament to Galileo's genius.

These illustrations from Kepler's writing reveal that his style, which Galileo found repellent, is far more rambling and otiose than his mentor's. Yet he learned from Galileo, as one critic has said, "to muffle the metaphysicists in their own jargon," and, at the same time, to prepare "less prejudiced minds for a wild leap into the unknown." [17, p. 49] Though Kepler apologizes often for his "diffuse and independent way of discussing nature," and admits to lightening "the hard work and difficulty of a subject by mental relaxation, conveyed by the style," he also proclaims that "the revered mysteries of sacred history are not a laughing matter to me." [2, pp. 5, 40, 48] He thus can describe the three laws of planetary motion as images of the Christian Trinity, or assert that the sun is God, or even, at one point, suggest that the soul or formative principle of every snowflake is a symbol of God for all to behold: "without doubt the authentic type of these figures exists in the mind of God the Creator and shares His eternity." [18, p. 37] A final passage from Kepler sums up both his thought and his style: "Geometry is unique and eternal, and it shines in the mind of God. The share of it which has been granted to man is one of the reasons why he is the image of God." [2, p. 43] We can understand easily enough why Albert Einstein wrote of Kepler's "marvellous achievement" in demonstrating that real knowledge is a combination of external evidence and internal response to that evidence; it cannot "spring from experience alone but only from the comparison of the inventions of the intellect with observed fact." [19, p. 27] Kepler's triumph as a stylist is that he never confuses verbal wit (inventions of his intellect) with the "wit" in nature (observed fact).

A soothing style, as Kepler said, is an "excellent remedy" for intellectual and imaginative distress [1, p. 75]. All the scientists of the Renaissance attempted to provide this relief for their disturbed readers, and they were increasingly successful. Though Paracelsus and his followers blurred the distinction between physical and spiritual worlds, and between literary and experimental materials, men like Bacon took up the cause and fought for it in a manner of greater purity and candor. The true achievers of the Renaissance, Galileo and Kepler among them, found that Paracelsus was right about at least one thing: an appropriate style does seem to develop, as if by divine dispensation, just when one has something that must be said. Their styles are genuinely a "physick of the understanding."

REFERENCES

1. J. Kepler, *Kepler's Somnium,* E. Rosen (ed. and trans.), University of Wisconsin Press, Madison, Wisconsin, 1967.
2. J. Kepler, *Kepler's Conversation with Galileo's Sidereal Messenger,* E. Rosen (ed. and trans.), Johnson Reprint Corporation, New York, 1965.
3. F. Bacon, *The Philosophy of Francis Bacon,* B. Farrington (ed. and trans.), University of Chicago Press, Chicago, Illinois, 1966.
4. F. Bacon, *The Works of Francis Bacon,* 14 volumes, J. Spedding, R. L. Ellis, and D. D. Heath (eds.), Friedrich Fromann Verlag, Stuttgart-Bad Canstatt, 1963.
5. G. Galileo, *Discoveries and Opinions of Galileo,* S. Drake (ed. and trans.), Doubleday and Company, Garden City, New York, 1957.
6. N. Copernicus, *De Revolutionibus Orbium Coelestium,* Librairie Felix Alcan, Paris, 1934.
7. J. Donne, *Essays in Divinity,* E. Simpson (ed.), The Clarendon Press, Oxford, 1952.
8. Paracelsus (Theophrastus Bombastus von Hohenheim), *The Hermetical and Alchemical Writings of Paracelsus the Great,* A. E. Waite (ed. and trans.), University Books, New Hyde Park, New York, 1967.

9. M. Foucault, *The Order of Things: An Archeology of the Human Sciences*, Pantheon Books, New York, 1970.
10. C. G. Jung, Paracelsus as a Spiritual Phenomenon, *The Collected Works of C. G. Jung*, Princeton University Press, Princeton, New Jersey, Vol. 13, pp. 109-189, 1968.
11. J. Dee, A Translation of John Dée's "Monas Hieroglyphica" (Antwerp, 1564) with an Introduction and Annotations by C. H. Josten, *Ambix, 12*, pp. 84-221, 1964.
12. F. A. Yates, *Giordano Bruno and the Hermetic Tradition*, Routledge and Kegan Paul, London, 1964.
13. G. Galileo, *Dialogue on the Great World Systems*, G. de Santillana (ed.) and T. Salusbury (trans.), University of Chicago Press, Chicago, Illinois, 1953.
14. G. de Santillana, *The Crime of Galileo*, Time, Inc., New York, 1962.
15. G. Galileo, *On Motion and On Mechanics*, I. E. Drabkin (ed. and trans.), University of Wisconsin Press, Madison, Wisconsin, 1960.
16. G. Galileo, Letters and Anagrams, reprinted in *The Sidereal Messenger*, E. Carlos (ed. and trans.), Dawson's of Pall Mall, London, 1880.
17. J. Lear, Introduction and Interpretation, *Kepler's Dream*, University of California Press, Berkeley, California, pp. 1-78, 1965.
18. J. Kepler, *The Six-Cornered Snowflake*, C. Hardie (trans.), The Clarendon Press, Oxford, 1966.
19. A. Einstein, Johannes Kepler, *Essays in Science*, A. Harris (trans.), The Philosophical Library, New York, 1934.

CHAPTER 11

Bacon, Linnaeus, and Lavoisier: Early Language Reform in the Sciences

JAMES PARADIS

— In correcting their language, they reason better.

Antoine Lavoisier
*Elements of Chemistry in a
New Systematic Order* (1793)

As early as the seventeenth century, Robert Boyle had called into question the scholastic tradition of natural science by suggesting that experimentalists consider shaping language anew:

> For my part, that which I am solicitous about is, that what nature hath made things to be in themselves, not what logicians or metaphysicians will call them in terms of his art; it being much fitter in my judgement to alter words, that they may better fit the nature of things, than to affix a wrong nature to things that they may be accommodated to forms of words . . . [1, p. 41].

This willingness to view language as a flexible, changing construct of the senses rather than as a perfected artifact of the reason amounted to a reversal of the traditional concept of language. To Boyle, the experimenter was no longer the interpreter of a received tradition of speculation, but was now the innovator, who was obliged to verify the terms of his or her inquiry. Rather than seeking new applications for old terms, the investigator invented new language, attempting always to make a better fit between his own terms and the "nature of things."

This view of language was not unique to Boyle. Francis Bacon, William Harvey, Isaac Newton, Carolus Linnaeus, and Antoine Lavoisier all reflected a new self-consciousness about language and emphasized the need for semantical innovations. Technical vocabularies, they assumed, could be constructed through careful definition to provide systems of broadly accepted distinctions. It was the obligation of the investigator to command assent: the new language must reflect the particulars of human experience and sensation in a manner that was clear, precise, and self-evident. To Bacon, Linnaeus, and Lavoisier, this requirement was so fundamental a part of the concept of science that inventing language became an essential methodology — the necessary accompaniment to inventing evidence through observation and experiment.

I should like in this paper to consider how certain special word groups, namely, the technical name, term, and classification system, were adopted as the practical instruments of this program to renovate and to manufacture scientific language. These three word groups, which I take to be the main elements of any specialized scientific lexicon, can be traced to many origins in Aristotelian logic and natural science, the Greek mathematical tradition, and the innumerable speculative disciplines of metaphysics, magic, and alchemy. But it was not until the Renaissance that the fit between language and things was critically reviewed. It was at this juncture that the technical word took on new status as the literary unit of sense experience and began seriously to condition the directions taken in scientific discourse.

Because *nomenclatures, classification systems,* and *terminologies* are now sometimes used synonymously to refer to technical words in general, we must recall that they nearly always have separate origins and semantical functions in disciplines. Indeed, when we examine groups of technical words carefully, we find that their original functions have largely been retained.

- Technical *nomenclatures* are catalogues that name and briefly characterize the main physical units or subjects — for example, specific organisms or substances — of a field of specialized interest.
- *Classification systems,* on the other hand, are made up of words that group entities by reference to one or more of their common characteristics. Because these classes are often specified by several criteria, they typically take the form of descriptive matrices or models, against which individuals can be compared.
- *Technical terminologies,* the third group, may be viewed as word systems that support the names and classes of a given discipline by supplying its working generalizations. Terms take the form of characteristics such as the *stamen* or *calyx* of a flower, and they identify and define such phenomena as *acceleration, compound,* and *electrolyte.* Typically, the technical term

is matched with a definition that isolates one or more variables on which distinctions of degree or relationship may be based. These variables can, of course, be derived in different ways. Terms based on physical variables such as weight, materials, morphology, and functions can be resolved into units of measurement — degrees, percentages, grams, centimeters.

I would like to begin by examining Francis Bacon's critique of language and his call in the *Novum Organum* for semantic reform of the received lexicon of natural science. I will then review some of the lexical innovations leading to the work of Càrolus Linnaeus, whose integrated name, term, and classification system furnished one important prototype of a modern scientific lexicon. I will conclude by considering some of the terminological reforms of Antoine Lavoisier and by suggesting how Lavoisier's ideas about scientific language drew on the thinking of his predecessors and inspired the first modern scientific textbook, which set down the terms of a new discipline.

BACON'S THIRD IDOL

Francis Bacon was one of the first to argue that exact science needed a new basis for collaboration. The student of natural science, he held, required a language of observation and experiment, with standard terms that would transform the minute detail of human experience into a conceptual structure that could be shared by many individuals. Much of the confusion in natural science, Bacon argued in his *Advancement of Learning* (1605) and *Novum Organum* (1620), could be traced to the florid style of academic disputation and to the vague words of the received tradition. The renovation of scientific letters, he held, should therefore be twofold. First it should be stylistic. Natural scientists should cultivate a plain style of prose, in self-conscious reaction against the pseudo-Ciceronian ideal that had overwhelmed the universities. In addition, it should be semantic. The key words of the sciences, whether Aristotelian, hermetic, or vernacular in origin, should be carefully reviewed by investigators, who should determine in what sense such words had analogues in observable things.

Although much has been written about Bacon's stylistic reform [2–4], which was most forcefully advocated in the early *Advancement of Learning*, little attention has been given to the terminological reforms proposed in the *Novum Organum*. Yet, the renovation of scientific terminology was in many respects the most important measure of Bacon's program for the reform of scientific letters. For no methodology or stylistic reform could perfect an arbitrary and ill-defined stock of terms.

Bacon's call for terminological reform shared the skeptical spirit of Montaigne, who had held that "nothing comes to us except falsified and altered by our senses." [5, p. 454] Bacon similarly distrusted the senses: man was not the scale by which to measure nature. "The testimony and information of the sense has reference always to man," Bacon warned, "and it is a great error to assert that the sense is the measure of things." [6, p. 21] Bacon thus began his proposal for a new organon or system of knowledge with the assertion that "the primary notions of things which the mind readily and passively imbibes, stores up, and accumulates . . . are false, confused, and overhastily abstracted from the facts." [6, p. 3]

Language, the embodiment of human experience, became the natural focus of Bacon's efforts to reform human knowledge. The terms of scientific discourse, Bacon observed, were often barriers to scientific learning. Of the four idols that Bacon believed stood in the path to knowledge, the third idol, the faulty language of the marketplace, was the most deceptive, because people wrongly believed that "their reason governs words." Yet, Bacon noted, "words [also] react on the understanding." [6, p. 56]

The faulty terms of the marketplace, which included those of the received tradition, made natural knowledge "sophistical and inactive," Bacon held [6, p. 56]. Such words were of two kinds:

1. fanciful words for things that did not exist; and
2. "unskillful abstractions." [6, p. 57]

Of these, fanciful terms such as "fortune," "Prime Mover," and "Element of Fire" had no discernible counterparts in the world of physical experience and were therefore easiest to eliminate.

Faulty abstractions posed a more formidable barrier, because they were based on observable phenomena. "Like a false mirror," Bacon noted, the human understanding "discolors the nature of things by mingling its own nature with it." [6, p. 48] Men gave body and permanence to such distortions through the affirmations of language. The term "humid" was an instance, Bacon argued, of the diffuseness of human abstractions. It encompassed processes and qualities as different as those of dispersion, attachment, and liquidity, and was used to characterize substances as diverse as glass, dust, and flame. Hence, it was "nothing else than a mark loosely and confusedly applied to denote a variety of actions which will not bear to be reduced to any consistent meaning." [6, p. 57] Although "humid" could be said to derive from sense experience, it had no standard definition and was linked to no measurable variables.

The language of science, Bacon held, should begin with physical experience. The words closest to unique, discernible objects were the least faulty; words based on abstract qualities were, by the same reasoning, the most faulty. The least flawed terms of the received sciences were the nouns that named concrete things, particularly those species of objects and materials that were grossly and immediately apparent to the senses. Somewhat less accurate were the verbs, which identified states and processes, where time was an inherent part of the concept. Least valid were the qualities, the words that could not be reduced to any constant meaning or definition:

There are . . . in words certain degrees of distortion and error. One of the least faulty kinds is that of names and substances, especially of lowest species and well-deduced (for the notion of *chalk* and that of *mud* is good, of *earth* bad); a more faulty kind is that of actions, as *to generate, to corrupt, to alter*; the most faulty is of qualities (except such as are the immediate objects of the sense) as *heavy, light, rare, dense,* and the like. Yet in all these cases some notions are of necessity a little better than others, in proportion to the greater variety of subjects that fall within the range of human sense [6, p. 58].

The terms in Bacon's rough scale of semantic precision vary in visual concreteness. Such simple generic substances as chalk and mud represented tangibles that for Bacon were self-evident. The abstraction *earth*, on the other hand, was theory-laden: the four *elements*, of which it was one, could not be reduced systematically — that is, through definition — to the simple genera of the material world. Actions and qualities such as "to corrupt" and "dense" could not be defined in terms of gross, measurable physical sensations. Such actions and qualities, not being isolable, depended for their significance on the substances in which they inhered and from which they could not easily be distinguished. They were entirely the artifices of language, having no object status in the external world; in Bacon's view, they could neither be counted nor measured.

The terms of natural science could be improved, Bacon held, if they were progressively linked to observable objects. Language, in this respect, should be under the stress of continual refinement. In the received tradition of natural history, he observed, "nothing [is] duly investigated, nothing verified, nothing counted, weighed, or measured . . . and what in observation is loose and vague, is in information deceptive and treacherous." [6, p. 95] Terms, he held, should be narrowed through definition and fixed to clear, measurable sense impressions, after which they could be used to define new terms. Beginning with precise and well-defined terms, the natural scientist could inductively build new generalizations. Elementary words for objects and substances could logically be generalized into more abstract classes that characterized them. The generic units of human experience could then be manipulated in discourse. These genera, unlike many in the received tradition of natural science, could consistently and logically be reduced to their experiential origins.

The most basic activity of Bacon's proposal for terminological reform was, thus, to name and to describe simple physical entities. "To resolve nature into abstractions is less to our purpose than to dissect her into parts," he noted [6, p. 53]. He recommended the techniques of close observation and cataloguing. The natural scientist was to expand his field of consideration to commonplace, elementary phenomena, as well as to "things that are mean or even filthy — things which (as Pliny says) must be introduced with an apology." [6, p. 109] Bacon compared this broad program of inventory-taking to collecting and arranging materials in a warehouse. Moreover, since so "great a number and army of particulars" would emerge from such cataloguing activities and possibly "confound" the understanding, he recommended that "all the particulars which pertain to the subject of inquiry [should], by means of Tables of Discovery, apt, well-arranged, and, as it were, animate, be drawn up and marshalled." [6, p. 97] Such generic grouping and tabular arrangement of terms, Bacon believed, would reveal the materials of nature in a fundamental order upon which higher abstractions could be based.

Bacon's recommendations of the use of instruments and experiments in scientific inquiry also had considerable implications for the expansion and refinement of scientific language. Because instruments magnified the senses, they also enabled the investigator to extend the physical terms of the sciences beyond the boundaries of the senses. Many instruments, in addition, standardized the terms of description, for the investigator would tend to describe diverse phenomena in terms of the instrument itself, making use of scales and units that converted processes to numbers. Motion in its many manifestations could, for example, be measured with a clock, and the terms of motion defined in standard units of time. Experiments would have additional effects on language, for they gave a reproducible structure to experience. "All truer kind of interpretation of nature," Bacon held, "is effected by instances and experiments fit and apposite; wherein the sense decides touching the experiment only and the experiment touching the point in nature and the thing in itself." [6, p. 53] The investigator was thus discouraged from elaborating a system of metaphors for the unseen. An experiment required standard terms of description if its apparatus and results were to be reproduced by others.

In effect, Bacon externalized language by making it an object, whose fit with the physical world could be studied and refined. The scientific lexicon became in Bacon's view a center of intellectual growth and consolidation, a great conceptual matrix that held scientific discourse to the concrete particulars of observable nature. Lexicon building was to Bacon an indispensible methodology, alternately extending the focus of scientific discourse outward to the physical objects and processes of nature, and then consolidating bodies of observed fact into summary generalizations and definitions. The two activities of specification and generalization were fundamentally opposed to one another, establishing a useful tension in which the scientific lexicon was continually being reviewed and adjusted. Observation and analysis generated ever more detail; definition and synthesis continually consolidated the same. Such a fluctuating lexicon was in Bacon's view "animate," constantly in motion.

OTHER SEVENTEENTH-CENTURY TERMINOLOGICAL TRENDS

Bacon's critique of the state of scientific letters strongly influenced the standards of language adopted by the later experimentalists and by members of the Royal Society. After Bacon, we find in scientific letters an almost universal concern about accuracy in language. The language of chemistry, Boyle argued in his *Sceptical Chymist* (1661), must be rendered in the concrete and measurable terms of physical experience. Similarly, natural philosophers like Harvey and Newton paid considerable attention to the processes by which they derived the terms of their respective discourses.

Harvey's treatise on circulation, *De Motu Cordis* (1628), which appeared two years after Bacon's death, was clearly in the Baconian rhetorical spirit of physical demonstration and experiment. Harvey drew attention to his own stringent empiricism, his "using greater care every day, with very frequent experimentation, observing a variety of animals and comparing many observations." [7, p. 26] Terminologically, the work was conservative. Harvey confined himself to the received anatomical language of Galen, Vesalius, and Fabricius. Within that tradition, however, Harvey systematically analyzed and reduced the hypothetical content of terms. Anatomical structures previously defined in terms of spiritual fluxes were now defined in terms of physical functions, many of which could even be crudely quantified.

Much of Harvey's terminological reduction was transacted through analogical reasoning, Harvey arguing that similar anatomical structures demonstrated similar functions. If the valves of the right and left ventricles were nearly identical in structure, he asked, "why say they are for the purpose of impeding the escape and reflux of spirits in the left but of blood in the right? The same structure cannot be suited to hinder in a similar way blood as well as spirits." [7, p. 17] Harvey thus methodically reversed the direction of term derivation, redefining the older anatomical terms on the basis of objects and processes that were within the range of his own physical observations.

Like Harvey, Newton was fastidious about terms. He took immense care in the composition of the *Principia Mathematica* (1686) to set down the context and methodology of its terminological structure. Although a committed experimentalist in the mode of Boyle, Newton drew much of his language from the older mathematical tradition of physical speculation. Newton followed a method of terminological idealization or modelling that had passed from Euclid's *Elements*, through the works of Archimedes, to the statics and dynamics of Galileo's new sciences. Newton idealized through definition. He identified the essential quantities and relationships of such concepts as *force* without entering into a discussion of their physical characteristics. "The accelerative quantity of a centripedal force," he wrote, "is the measure of the same, proportional to the velocity which it generates in a given time." [8, p. 4] Such a Newtonian force was not a real phenomenon but a mathematical quantity. It described dynamic changes in bodies (themselves points) that moved along perfect mathematical lines. "The reader is not to imagine," Newton warned, "that by [*forces*] I anywhere take upon me to define the kind or manner of the action, the causes or the physical reason thereof, or that I attribute forces, in a true and physical

sense, to certain centres (which are mathematical points)." [8, pp. 5-6]
Newton's *force* was a convenience of mathematical expression, a term without a
real analogue in experience. It enabled him to establish a relationship between
time, motion, and direction, without having to define their formal and material
properties, their causes, or their ends.

To connect this ideal world to the real world of the experimentalist, Newton
argued that his system could be considered dualistically. One could imagine two
sets of terms, one set absolute and mathematical and another set relative and
physical. For example, *time, space, place,* and *motion,* could be considered
either "absolute" or "relative." Newton's distinction resembled that between a
Euclidean line and its corporeal approximation. The former was purely the
linguistic product of definition (the shortest distance between two points); the
latter was the physical species, as drawn, for example, on a piece of paper.
"Absolute time," Newton argued, was perfect, "flow[ing] equably without
relation to anything external," while "relative time" was "some sensible and
external (whether accurate or unequable) measure of duration by means of
motion . . . such as an hour, a month, a year." [8, p. 6]

Newton's terminological dualism connected the language of the *Principia* with
the world of the senses. The Newtonian system was open to, indeed, depended
upon, experimental verification. Newton owed his theory partly, if not largely,
to his own extensive program of observation and experiment, in which he applied
such instruments as the telescope and pendulum to the study of celestial and
terrestrial motion. If his abstract terms enabled him to transcend the limitations
of human sense by rarefying the objects and processes of the physical universe
and manipulating the resulting abstractions in mathematical discourse, the same
terms could ultimately be traced back to their empirical and experimental origins.

It was not only the model of successful scientific speculation provided by
investigators like Harvey and Newton that recommended the new scrutiny of
language; the development of professional societies was perhaps as potent a force
for lexical reform. Thomas Sprat reported that members of the Royal Society,
many of whom viewed Bacon's *Novum Organum* as their essential text, had
agreed to strive after "the primitive purity, and shortness [of language], when
men deliver'd so many things, almost in an equal number of *words.*" [9, p. 113]
The reduction of words to object equivalents was a return to the Baconian
injunction to "dissect [nature] into parts." Such a program emphasized the
analytical and cataloguing activities of investigating and encouraged conservatism
in the coinage of abstract terms. Jonathan Swift was to turn this principle to
satirical account in *Gulliver's Travels* by describing an experimentalist discourse
at the Academy of Lagado — his Lampoon of the Royal Society — that
proceeded solely as a silent exchange between two men, showing one another
physical objects drawn from immense bags they carried on their backs.

Under Henry Oldenburg's editorship, the Royal Society's *Philosophical
Transactions,* which began publication in 1665, weighed and gradually

standardized an immense body of terminology in the sciences, trades, and medicine. The motto of the Society, *Nullius in Verba* ("On the Word of No Man"), demanded physical proof as the condition of assent, a principle that moved Oldenburg to include enough detail in the papers of his new periodical to establish a basis for verifying the results. These first scientific articles set many of the rhetorical standards for modern scientific discourse [10, pp. 72-73]. The periodical journal, which rapidly established itself in the late seventeenth century as one of the primary methods of technical publication, became the literary mechanism *par excellence* of Baconian collaborative science, because it created an entirely new kind of international audience whose members could speak to one another through the medium of print. The public exchange of observations and ideas, made possible through the serial publication of what Robert Boyle called "experimental essays," exerted an irresistible pressure to standardize the terms of scientific discourse [1, p. 303].

THE DEVELOPMENT OF DESCRIPTIVE BOTANY

Descriptive botany, although not destined to become the most glamorous of the modern scientific interests, was the field in which many of the descriptive problems peculiar to the sciences were initially worked out. Few traditions so galvanized the semantical issues Bacon raised as did the tradition of botanical field observation. The plant kingdom, long the focus of practical medicine, agriculture, and the crafts, had been the object of much experimentation with naming and classifying technique. Such linguistic experimentation was motivated by the communication problems faced by scholars and naturalists who wished to connect bodies of fact, drawn from many accounts, with thousands of specific organisms, many of which closely resembled one another. The matching of specific names and great numbers of factual observations posed one of the most formidable challenges of all to the representation of science in language.

Classification schemes were the oldest of the scientific linguistic systems, their origins going back to Aristotelian methodology. In his *Historia Animalium*, Aristotle had investigated the problems of large-scale verbal enumerations by attempting to find some systematic way of arranging physical data on the differentiating characteristics of animals [11]. Elsewhere, notably in the *Metaphysics*, he had discussed the philosophy of classification and followed the Platonic method of dividing higher categories by means of *differentiae* (distinguishing characteristics) into subaltern genera and further dividing these into more simple genera, until some particular species was attained. Although the *Historia Animalium* was not an effort at systematic classification, Aristotle did arrange organisms in part by reference to *differentiae* drawn from such variables as *habitat, locomotion, heat, reproduction, diet,* and *morphology.* The Aristotelian method of dividing general categories into more specific categories on the basis of *differentiae* became standard practice for field naturalists all the way down through Linnaeus.

Field botanists drew in particular, however, on the Greek descriptive traditions of Theophrastus and Dioscorides, who had each known and described several hundred kinds of plants. To the early record of Greek botany, medieval botanists contributed the study of plant morphology and thus extended the basis for plant description by differentiating a variety of root, leaf, and floral characteristics. By the beginning of the seventeenth century, field naturalists such as Andrea Cesalpino (1524-1603) and Casper Bauhin (1560-1634), had undertaken ambitious programs to codify botanical nature in language. Cesalpino established a method of classifying plants on the basis of a small number of common root and fruit characteristics; Bauhin experimented with the convention of binomial nomenclature and identified some 6,000 new species of plants.

As knowledge of plant structure and functions expanded, two approaches to classification eventually developed. Restricting the criteria for classification to a small number of easily identified features, as Cesalpino and others had done, became known as *artificial classification*, because its primary purpose was not to show relationships among organisms so much as to establish a convenient convention for naming them. More comprehensive classification schemes that took into account a broad range of functional and structural *differentiae* were known as *natural classification*, because they attempted not only to identify organisms, but also to reveal natural relationships among them.

Whatever their many practical and philosophical motives, the various plant naming schemes of the Renaissance all attempted to establish a verifiable relationship between language and things, between a given name and its living counterpart in the field. In principle, objects did not merit names until they could be routinely isolated in the field on the basis of a set of suitably precise terms. However, since few seventeenth-century botanists were familiar with the names and terms of hundreds of other observers, much less the precise criteria upon which such distinctions were based, botanists were under considerable pressure to invent linguistic mechanisms and hierarchies that could bring the giant plant lexicon under some systematic control.

Of the many lexical experiments of the seventeenth century, few were more intriguing or instructive than John Wilkins's baroque *Essay Towards a Real Character and a Philosophical Language* (1668). Commissioned by the Royal Society in 1662 to prosecute a design for a "universal language," Wilkins, a follower of Bacon and friend of Boyle, attempted to solve once and for all the problem of semantical imprecision that Bacon had determined to be one of the most formidable barriers to exact knowledge. By grouping names into some twenty Baconian "Tables" that corresponded to what he imagined were the primary categories of the phenomenological world, Wilkins believed he could create a lexical system whose physical arrangement would reflect the essential relationships among natural phenomena. The place of an entity in the lexicon was the key to the entity's logical relationship with all other elements of the system; it was also the key to the status of its natural counterpart in the great chain of existence.

> The principle of design aimed at in these Tables is to give a sufficient enumeration of all such things and notions, as are to have names assigned to them, and withall so to contrive these as to their order, that the place of everything may contribute to a description of the nature of it, denoting both the General and the Particular difference whereby it is distinguished from other things of the same kind [12, p. 289].

Although Wilkens's work confused Platonic abstractions with empirical categories of physical objects, his program nevertheless reflected the linguistic objectives of the seventeenth-century systematic botanist.

These objectives included:

1. determining what kinds of subjects merited names;
2. establishing a formal and practical naming convention;
3. finding one or more *differentiae*, common to the subjects of the system, on which to base descriptive terms;
4. systematically basing the names of things on the available descriptive terminology; and
5. discovering principles of grouping that would arrange thousands of names and, by proxy, their attendant characterizations, into hierarchies.

These objectives rarely were met in any set sequence in a given discipline. The selection of variables upon which to base term definitions, the slow building of new terms upon established terms, the development of a broadly accepted naming convention: all these developments required that the work of many precise observers be scrupulously coordinated.

Descriptive methodology became the main interest of both John Ray (1627-1705) and Carolus Linnaeus (1707-1778), whose respective contributions to natural and artificial classification established many of the semantic standards upon which modern technical lexicons are based. Ray's natural system of classification followed Aristotle's practice of grouping animals on the basis of a matrix of morphological and functional variables. Ray based his categories of plants on developmental distinctions between monocotyledons (one seed leaf) and dicotyledons (two seed leaves), as well as on morphological variations in root, flower, and leaf characteristics. The need for extensive physical profiles of plant species made the execution of a comprehensive classification system problematic in Ray's time.

Natural classification of the kind attempted by Ray required an immense body of descriptive information that, even when obtained, was by no means easy to reduce into principles of grouping and hierarchical arrangement. For example, if three plant specimens, P_1, P_2, and P_3, shared characteristic A, yet P_1 and P_2 alone shared characteristic B, and P_1 and P_3 alone shared characteristic C, then, in principle, the classifier had reason to arrange them in one, two, or even three separate categories. As the number of considered characteristics expanded, and the number of candidate species mounted into the thousands, the difficulties of arriving at a clear and consistent classification system increased dramatically. Natural classification also required an extensive and well-defined terminology of plant parts in order to enable others to follow and to apply the distinctions that were being made. Such a terminology could be constructed only after thorough structural and functional examination of a great number of plants, which, at Ray's time, remained to be carried out. Moreover, a natural system of classification was inevitably difficult to apply in the field, based as it was on so many different features, some of which only an expert could easily distinguish. The greatest problem facing the descriptive methodologist was that of devising a lexicon sufficiently useful to thousands of individuals to establish the system as the standard. Many sophisticated naming and classification schemes had failed and would fail merely because, whatever their merits, they did not simplify the task of communication.

THE LINNAEAN METHODOLOGY

Carolus Linnaeus, born in 1707, some two years after Ray's death, solved problems in nearly every major aspect of systematics. Building upon the work of Cesalpino, Bauhin, Ray, and hundreds of early cataloguers, Linnaeus devised the first lexical system to standardize the names of plants and to integrate the three components of a specialized technical lexicon — the nomenclature, terminology, and the classification system. The Linnaean lexical system not only demonstrated for the first time how an invented nomenclature-terminology code could provide a key to the diverse literature of a given scientific tradition, but it also revealed how a specialized lexicon could be used to restrict the terms of scientific discourse and, thus, to define, focus, and consolidate a particular field of inquiry. Such restricted lexical domains were eventually to be widely recognized as essential to all specialized fields of science and applied science.

What distinguished Linnaeus from his predecessors was his unique linguistic imagination and his intuitive understanding of the relationships between words and objects. He viewed knowledge almost exclusively from the perspective of semantics and descriptive method. "All real knowledge which we possess," he asserted, "depends upon METHOD; by which we distinguish the similar from the dissimilar. The greater the number of natural distinctions this method comprehends, the clearer our idea of the things. The more numerous the objects which employ our attention, the more difficult it becomes to form such a method; and the more necessary." [13, p. 188]

The Linnaean method was guided by one primary object: "to link together a single distinct *concept* and a distinct *name*." [14, p. 273] If a well-developed system of concept-name relationships was not made a priority in the sciences, Linnaeus held, as Bacon had more than a century before him, "the abundance of objects would overwhelm us and all exchange of information would cease through lack of common language." But naming, the essential act of knowledge, was also profoundly difficult. It required the consolidation and correlation of many different sources and levels of information:

> To determine the essential characteristic of the SPECIFIC NAME is no light task; indeed, it demands an accurate knowledge of many *species*, a most scrupulous investigation of their *parts*, the choice of *differential characters*, and then the proper use of *Terminology*, that they may be expressed most concisely and surely [14, pp. 154-155].

Naming was a comprehensive activity that required an initial act of analysis or dismantling, a subsequent selection of *differentiae* or variables, and then the careful synthesis and application of terms. Such complex linguistic activity, Linnaeus held, was essential to establishing clear domains of plant, animal, and chemical knowledge.

Although he shared John Ray's preference for natural classification, Linnaeus concluded early in his career that the factual basis for such a system did not yet exist in botany. The alternative, he calculated, was to discover some single characteristic common to all plants from which a series of "differential characters" could be developed. He found such a characteristic in the sex organs of plants.

Cesalpino had been the first to use flower and fruit organs as the basis of plant classification. This approach gained further justification as a means to classify after the French botanist, Sebastien Vaillant, whose work Linnaeus had studied carefully, described the sexual function of floral parts. Because reproduction was essential to all life forms, Linnaeus reasoned that the sex organs constituted a universal botanical characteristic, and that the relatively complex structure and configuration of flower parts must of necessity be highly consistent for each given plant species. The floral complex, including the male stamens and female pistils, varied sufficiently among plants to provide a principle of differentiation, and it provided a highly visible focal point to which all field observers could readily refer.

Linnaeus's strategy for designing a controlled lexical system occupied some thirty-five years of his life. He began by describing plants in the field and determining their broad categories of *differentiae*. Much of this initial work was carried out in the *Systema Naturae* (1735) and the *Critica Botanica* (1737). Linnaeus expanded and refined his descriptive terminology in order to establish a clear and unequivocal physical basis for characterizing both the names and the classes of plants. He arranged and characterized plant genera in the *Genera Plantarum* (1737); he did the same for plant species in the *Species Plantarum* (1753). In the latter work, he first applied his binomial method of naming. Linnaeus's published works were designed to be used together; for example, the species listed in the *Species Plantarum* could be located in the *Genera Plantarum* for their full generic descriptions.

The Linnaean descriptive terminology consisted of words, each defined by reference to the variable morphological feature of a plant part. These terms furnished the basis for other semantical distinctions.

In the *Genera Plantarum*, for example, Linnaeus provided a set of terms that distinguished seven major morphological areas of the flower, including the *calyx, corolla, stamen, pistil, pericarp, seed,* and *receptacle*. These morphological distinctions were further broken down into some twenty-six morphological distinctions, each assigned a term:

> We have described of the CALYX: 1. the *Involucre*; 2. the *Spathe*; 3. the *Perianth*; 4. the *Ament*; 5. the *Glume*; 6. the *Calyptre*; of the COROL: 7. the *Tube* or Claws; 8. the *Border*; 9. the *Nectary*; of the STAMENS: 10. the *Filaments*; 11. the *Anthers*; of the PISTIL: 12. the *Germ*; 13. the *Style*; 14. the *Stigma*; of the PERICARP: 15. the *Capsule*; 16. the *Silique*; 17. the *Legume*; 18. the *Nut*; 19. the *Drupe*; 20. the *Berry*; 21. the *Pome*; of the SEED: 22, 23, and its *Crown*; of the RECEPTACLE: 24. the *Flower*; 26. the *Fruit*. Thus, there are more parts, more letters here, than in the alphabets of language. These marks are to us as so many vegetable letters; which, if we can read, will teach us the characters of plants . . . [13, p. 192].

Floral parts were said by Linnaeus to be his *alphabet*, with which he could characterize any plant species, genus, or class. Collectively, this group of terms placed high on the Baconian scale of semantical precision. As a group, the terms also constituted an idealized flower, to which all other specific flowers could be compared. Idealization meant focusing on only a selected set of features and ignoring hundreds of other features. One gained in return economy, precision, and consistency of description.

The Linnaean flower and fruit parts, some of which have since altered in meaning, were carefully defined relative to one another. For example, the *perianth*, Number 3, referred to "that green cup which incloses and supports the bottom of the *corolla*." [14, p. 94] Basing the definitions of new terms on those of existing terms, gave the terminology a high internal consistency and helped to build up a semantic texture. The definition of *perianth* extended the meaning of *corolla*, which was now partly characterized by its physical position relative to the *perianth*. This principle of interlocking definitions helped to restrict the lexical domain to terms already sanctioned in the discipline, and, thus, to build upon established descriptive information.

What most distinguished Linnaeus's terminology from earlier systems, however, was its limitations, with some minor exceptions, to distinctions of quantity, shape, placement, and proportion. This radical restriction of terminological distinctions to a set of defined adjective-variables referred all descriptions to gross and highly visible features and thereby eliminated more subtle distinctions of quality and function that, as Bacon had warned, might be open to conflicting interpretations. Hence, Linnaeus insisted that the twenty-six morphological distinctions should be described exclusively in terms of four "immutable mechanic principles: *Number, Figure* [shape], *Situation* [placement], *Proportion* [size relative to other parts]." [13, p. 193] To assist this descriptive process, Linnaeus developed an extensive Latin terminology of descriptive adjectives to which the taxonomist was to refer. *"Lanceolatus,"* for example, was an adjective for *"Figure"* that referred to a shape "oblong, but gradually tapering towards each extremity and terminating in a point." [14, p. 94] Many of these descriptive adjectives were further elucidated by illustrations in works such as the *Systema Naturae.* By restricting his adjectives to "mechanic principles," Linnaeus avoided the qualitative distinctions of color, odor, and taste, as well as the unsatisfactory characteristic of size, which was difficult to determine for an organism subject to varying conditions of growth. Given his twenty-six morphological distinctions, his four mechanical principles, and well over 100 descriptive adjectives, Linnaeus had many thousands of possible descriptive combinations, enough, he noted, to "distinguish the genera so certainly from each other, that nothing more is wanted." [13, p. 193]

In addition, the Latin medium of Linnaean description placed even greater distance between the characterizations of plants and what Bacon had called the language of the "marketplace." Latin terms were not likely to change casually in meaning, according to patterns of popular usage. Furthermore, Latin was accessible to an international community of plant taxonomists and field naturalists, whose familiarity with a quite limited number of adjectives and nouns would suffice to gain them access to the Linnaean catalogues. The highly restricted Linnaean term thus gained additional stability, even though it was typically manipulated among many other words of the vernacular.

In the *Systema Naturae,* Linnaeus applied his terminology to the problem of grouping plants. He first sorted plants into twenty-four Classes, on the basis of the number and configuration of the *stamens* (male organs). For example, the Class *Triandria* consisted of hermaphroditic plants, such as *Crocus sativus,* whose flowers exhibited three stamens; Class *Pentandria* consisted of hermaphroditic plants, such as *Nicotina tabacum,* whose flowers exhibited five stamens; and Class *Dioecia* consisted of plants, such as *Cannabis sativa,* whose male and female organs were found in separate flowers confined to separate plants. Linnaean Orders, the next lower level of generalization, were determined by the number of pistils (female organs) characteristic of the flower. Orders *Monogynia, Digynia,* and *Trigynia,* for example, corresponded to plants that exhibited flowers with one, two, and three pistils. Thus, the crocus, a flower with three stamens and one pistil, belonged to the Class *Triandria,* Order *Monogynia.* Such distinctions of Class and Order, each based as it was on one selected morphological characteristic, were entirely distinctions of convenience, with little theoretical justification. Hence, as Linnaeus readily admitted, they constituted "artificial" categories.

The Linnaean Genus was described in terms of the full twenty-six morphological distinctions for flower parts, outlined in the *Genera Plantarum.* To derive or typify each genus of plant, Linnaeus began with several individual candidate species, selected through inspection, and carefully listed the morphological characteristics of their floral parts. After comparing the full descriptions of the individual species, he then eliminated those characteristics that varied from species to species, thus arriving at the diagnosis of the generic character of the group.

The generic description, in effect, "selected" the physical detail that distinguished one Genus from another. Hence, it was a model. In the *Genera Plantarum,* the Genus *Crocus* was listed as follows (in translation):

> *Triandria Monogynia* [3 stamens on hermaphroditic plant; 1 pistil]
> 55. CROCUS
> Cal[yx]. *Spathe* one-leaved.
> Cor[ol]. *Tube* simple, long. *Border* six-parted, erect; the divisions
>   egg-oblong, equal.
> Stam[ens]. *Filaments* three, awl'd, shorter than corol. *Anthers* arrow'd.
> Pist[il]. *Germ* beneath, roundish. *Style* thread-form, the length of the
>   stamens. *Stigmas* three, convolute, saw'd.
> Per[icarp]. *Capsule* roundish, three-lobed, three-celled, three-valved.
> Seeds numerous, round [13, p. 194].

Because the generic diagnosis was confined to the terminology Linnaeus had developed, the terms and class names were effectively integrated to form a closed lexical system. Like the parts terminology Linnaeus had constructed for a generalized flower, the generic description constituted an idealization. But it was physically more detailed and less abstract than the ideal flower, because its parts were now described in terms of specific *numbers, figures, situations,* and *proportions* that could be traced to specimens in the field.

The Linnaean Species was the most particular classificatory distinction that Linnaeus universally applied to plants. As a concept, *species* was, at best, a clouded distinction in the mid-eighteenth century. To Linnaeus, the various species were the natural forms of a divinely created nature. More pragmatically, however, each species had certain distinctive morphological and functional characteristics that enabled one to describe the hierarchy of botanical nature.

The most comprehensive and systematic Linnaean catalogue of plant species was the *Species Plantarum*, considered by many the first modern classification system. Its most renowned feature was its binomial nomenclature, which Linnaeus now universally applied to the identification of species. The binomial "*Crocus sativus*," for example, established a permanent name that was unique and unequivocal. It could be manipulated easily in a sentence because it was limited to two words; yet, the two-word name was a proxy for the full characterization. The effect of this unique naming system was to condense considerable information into fixed, representative names. Binomial names were also, in most instances, connected to a physical specimen preserved in a herbarium, a specimen that furnished the phenomenological standard of the species characterization.

In addition to the binomial name, Linnaeus included a short "phrase name," which for *Crocus sativus* was "crocus spatha univalvi radicalli, corollae tubo longissimo." This provided a quick field diagnostic; for example, "corollae tubo longissimo" referred to the elongated tubular petals characteristic of *Crocus sativus.* Linnaeus listed as well the other works of botanical literature to which the naturalist could refer for more extensive characterizations. This measure provided a key to the history of the species name and enabled scholars who used the Linnaean species catalogue to find the previous descriptive work and illustration of many earlier scholars.

Each catalogue entry for a species included the following:

1. a binomial name to identify the generic group and the specific name of a plant;
2. a diagnostic phrase name of some ten to fifteen terms and adjectives for quick field identification;
3. a synonymy to coordinate the Linnaean species with other noteworthy species descriptions in the literature; and
4. a brief reference to the known habitats of the species.

The entire entry for a species rarely exceeded fifty words. The entry for *Crocus sativus,* the first of two species of the genus *Crocus,* was as follows (in the original botanical Latin):

> Triandria Monogynia
> CROCUS
> *sativus* 1. CROCUS spatha univalvi radicali, corollae tubo longissimo.
> Crocus floribus fructui impositis: tubo longissimo.
>   *Roy. lugb.* 41. *Hort. ups.* 15. *Mat. med.* 27.
> Crocus flore fructui imposito. *Hort. cliff.* 18. . . .
> *Habitat in* Alpibus Helveticis, Pyrenaeis, Lisitanicis
> Tracicis.
> *Bulbocodium* 2. CROCUS . . . [14, p. 36].

This format was repeated throughout the *Species Plantarum,* thus standardizing even the physical layout of a species characterization.

With the description of close to 6,000 species of plants in the *Species Plantarum,* Linnaeus's design for a descriptive system was essentially complete. This immense network of linguistic distinctions was tightly organized around a relatively small number of strictly defined terms, names, and classes; the specific name of each plant was individually characterized by the species epithet, yet linked to the system through the generic name. Each plant was positioned in such a way that it could be viewed logically in the grid of terminological distinctions and hierarchical relationships.

When we survey the elaborate apparatus supporting a distinction as simply and intuitively arrived at as that of the common crocus, it is difficult to suppress a feeling of astonishment at the lengths to which Linnaeus had gone to formalize the distinction in language. Indeed, the crocus of common experience and the Crocus of the Linnaean system are radically different. The vernacular version is a phenomenonological unity, with a full range of colors, scents, and accidental characteristics — such as missing petals, broken stamens, and other irregularities — all viewed within the context of an environment. Its shape or distinguishing characteristics are impressed upon the senses in innumerable ways, as various as each individual experience. Its contextual possibilities are infinite. The common crocus is not, then, formally restricted by definition or, indeed, by language.

The Crocus of the Linnaean system is, in essence, a legal entity, circumscribed by definition in terms that, as we have seen, are restricted to the prescribed distinctions of *number, figure, situation,* and *proportion.* This version of the Crocus is an idealization, identical in many respects to the "absolute" terms of the Newtonian world. The Linnaean world, like that of the *Principia*, is one of great symmetry and order, an ideal world that is entirely the artifice of language. We can view the Linnaean lexicon as a warehouse (to return to Bacon's idea of naming and arranging natural objects), from which we may extract the standard semantical distinctions with which to build a frame around the crocus. But if the Linnaean Crocus is uniquely and specifically placed within the taxonomical system, that place itself is no different in kind from the thousands of similar places that formally locate the species. Indeed, these places are framed according to descriptive formulae in order to achieve a familiar and predictable result; we understand, by analogy, the nature of thousands of similar species distinctions, the subjects of which we may never have seen. We believe these species exist because we can see them in the familiar terms of other, known species. We thus have a powerful analytical tool that enables us to extend language to unfamiliar phenomena, and thereby to convert the phenomena to elements in our system. Linnaeanism was a vigorous linguistic effort to convert "unknown" plants into the formal components of the accepted lexicon.

The achievement of Linnaeus was, thus, a linguistic one. He demonstrated how terminology, nomenclature, and classification systems could be used in concert to define a lexical domain and a specialized professional perspective. By the end of the eighteenth century, researchers in a great variety of fields had become aware of the successes of Linnaeus in standardizing the language of botany. Many sought to emulate him by applying his descriptive principles to other domains of nature; others, such as Cuvier, found his methods inadequate to the organization of the zoological world. But specialists who reviewed the example of Linnaeus, increasingly understood that language was a *tool* of the understanding no less powerful than experimental method itself.

LAVOISIER'S TEXTBOOK

The role of language in giving order to the sciences was nowhere so dramatically illustrated as in the innovations in chemical nomenclature that culminated, late in the eighteenth century, in the work of Antoine Lavoisier.

Lavoisier invented a modern discipline not with a succession of published experiments, but, rather, with a textbook — the *Elements of Chemistry* (1793). This work scrupulously set down the language of chemical discourse: Lavoisier carefully defined elementary terms in reference to quantifiable variables; he presented a new nomenclature system for naming chemical substances; and he classified substances, according to types of reactions and their characteristic products.

Lavoisier's science was a linguistic phenomenon that reflected three important developments in chemical science of the eighteenth century. The first was the reform of the old nomenclature for chemical substances and the publication by Lavoisier and several members of the French Academy of a new chemical synonyma. The second was the experimental tradition of chemistry, which Lavoisier reviewed partly in order to establish a clear physical basis for chemical language. The third was Lavoisier's invention of his textbook, which synthesized experimental and linguistic elements into a teaching manual. The purpose of this manual was to provide the novice means of systematic entry into the discipline.

Throughout his years of study in chemistry, Lavoisier clearly considered himself a student of the methodology of technical language. In collaboration with his colleagues, Guyton de Morveau, Antoine Fourcroy, and Claude Berthollet, he carefully studied, with a view to reform, the traditional nomenclature of chemistry. Partly inspired by the successes of Linnaeus, Lavoisier and his colleagues endeavored to unify the many naming schemes of the chemical tradition by constructing a "new language agreeable to all the different systems and capable of satisfying the opinions of all parties without adopting any in particular." [16, pp. 13-14] This effort culminated in the seminal *Method of Chymical Nomenclature* (1787), a synonyma, arranged in tables, in which the older names of substances were listed beside matching columns of new names (see Table 1). This philosophical and reformist effort was meant to provide a new basis for all chemical discourse and, indeed, thought. "It was not until we had reviewed every part of chymistry," Lavoisier noted in his introductory "Memoir" to the *Nomenclature*, "and maturely studied the metaphysic of languages, and the conformity of ideas with words, that we ventured to present this general Nomenclature." [16, pp. 4-5]

In his introductory "Memoir," Lavoisier applied certain philosophical ideas of Abbé Condillac to the problems of scientific language [17, pp. 168-172]. The sciences, Lavoisier suggested, were the products of the logic of language as much as they were the results of the logic of experiment. Languages, he argued, were really "analytical methods."

> Languages are intended, not only to express by signs, as is commonly supposed, the ideas and images of the mind; but are also analytical methods, by means of which, we advance from the known to the unknown, and to a certain degree in the manner of mathematicians . . . [16, pp. 4-5].

Table 1. Lavoisier's Synonyma (Selections)

Chemical Terms	
Ancient Names	New Names
Acid marine, dephlogisticated	Oxygenated muriatic acid
Acid of chalk	Carbonic acid
Acid of charcoal	Carbonic acid
Acid of nitre, dephlogisticated	Nitric acid
Acid of nitre, phlogisticated	Nitrous acid
Acid of phosphorous, dephlogisticated	Phosphoric acid
Acid of phosphorous, phlogisticated	Phosphorous acid
Affinities	Chymical affinities or attractions
Air, atmospheric, or common air	Atmospherical or common air
Air, dephlogisticated of Dr. Priestley	Oxygen gas
Air, factitious	Carbonic acid gas
Air fire, Scheele's	Oxygen gas
Air fixed, of Dr. Black	Carbonic acid gas
Air, pure	Oxygen gas
Air, solid of Hale's	Carbonic acid gas
Air, vital	Oxygen gas
Calces, metallic	Metallic oxyds

Languages were held by Lavoisier to be "instruments invented by men to facilitate the operations of the mind." Lavoisier thus took a heuristical view of scientific language; the structures erected by the descriptive methodologist pointed the way to new discoveries.

Lavoisier's main argument in the "Memoir" was that the sciences followed a natural logic that distinguished the general from the particular. "According to the natural order of ideas, the title of *class* and *genus*," he noted, "is that which reminds one of the properties common to a great number of individuals; the title of *species* is that which indicates the particular properties of certain individuals. This natural logic belongs to all the sciences, and we have attempted to apply it to chymistry." [16, pp. 13-14] Genus and species distinctions, when applied to the materials of chemistry, suggested the formal grouping of material substances. Hence, in the *Nomenclature*, the generic concept of *Metallic Oxyds* encompassed such species as *Oxyd of Mercury*. This two-part, binomial nomenclature was reinforced by the new concept-term, the chemical *compound,* as well as by the experimental finding that the *Oxyd of Mercury* decomposed, under the stress of intense heat, into a gas (called *Oxygen* by Lavoisier) and mercury. Language thus knit together the theoretical and experimental dimensions of chemistry.

In addition to studying the principles of language, Lavoisier also carefully reviewed the experimental tradition of chemistry. Perhaps the most famous innovation of the *Nomenclature* was its substitution of the name "oxygen gas" for the gas Priestley had discovered and named "dephlogisticated air." *Phlogiston,* the very element of fire that Bacon had argued in his *Novum Organum* was an invalid abstraction, had traditionally been associated with the phenomenon of burning. Never successfully isolated, phlogiston was assigned a negative weight to account for the increased weight of burned substances. Having familiarized himself with Priestley's experiment for isolating the gas that supported burning, Lavoisier was able to synthesize mercuric oxide by roasting mercury in air. He was then able to demonstrate that it was a compound formed partly from a component of air, and that the process of formation left behind Black's "fixed air" (carbon dioxide), which did not support burning. Lavoisier then decomposed his mercury compound, following Priestley's experiment, and he thus isolated the elementary substance it had taken from the air. Hence, the substance in question was identical to Priestley's *dephlogisticated air.* Lavoisier named the substance *oxygen gas.* He further deduced that other metallic compounds belonged to the same class of reactions, whereby specific substances were formed from metals and oxygen gas. This class of compounds became the *Oxyds.*

The *Chymical Nomenclature* was thus based on the extensive experimentation of Lavoisier, its terms and names deriving from empirical distinctions Lavoisier had made in his own laboratory. The new language, consequently, was well-grounded in experimental knowledge. Although, as Humphrey Davey noted, the language of the synomyna could not be said to be free of theoretical distinctions, it was in principle far less speculative and hypothetical than previous chemical nomenclature. Lavoisier and his colleagues eliminated a great number of names that originated in the metaphorical descriptive systems of alchemy. "The terms of *oil of tartar by the bell, oil of vitriol, butter of alimony, butter of arsenic, flowers of zinc,* &c.," Lavoisier noted, "are . . . ridiculous, because they give birth to false ideas, because, properly speaking there does not exist in the mineral kingdom, and especially in the metallic, either butter, or oil, or flowers." [16, p. 17] Systematically and without ceremony, Lavoisier and his colleagues, eliminated the old, colorful language of alchemy and replaced it with the generic language of compounds — acids, bases, and salts.

Increasingly in the late 1780's, Lavoisier found his work on the *Chymical Nomenclature* leading to a full elaboration of chemical terminology and a broad classification of compounds, all within the new theoretical context of chemical combination. The study of semantics led irresistibly to the linguistic codification of chemistry and the founding of a descriptive system or discipline. "Thus, while I thought myself employed only in forming a Nomenclature," Lavoisier recalled, "and while I proposed to myself nothing more than to improve the chemical language, my work transformed itself by degrees, without my being able to prevent it, into a treatise on the elements of chemistry." [18, p. xi] The result became Lavoisier's new textbook introduction to chemistry: the *Elements of Chemistry in a New Systematic Order* (1793).

Lavoisier's *Elements*, which cited Bacon's injunction to trace concepts back to their physical sources, rigorously unified the lexical and experimental traditions of chemistry. Names of substances were carefully listed in conformity with the *Nomenclature*, terms were clearly defined, and classes of phenomena were organized according to their end products. "The term *oxidation* or *calcination*," Lavoisier noted, "is chiefly used to signify the processes by which metals exposed to a certain degree of heat are converted into oxides by absorbing oxygen from the air." Other terms for chemical operations and methods were carefully explained, including those for *sublimation, crystallization, evaporation, solution, filtration,* and *distillation.* This careful description of technique, together with the systematic arrangements of classes of compounds, including acids, bases, and salts, not only unified the lexical and experimental dimensions of chemistry, but it also provided the student of chemistry the means to duplicate the results of classical chemical experiments.

Lavoisier viewed his treatise as a teaching tool. The novice could learn the essential distinctions and processes of chemical science only after he or she carefully studied a special language, designed to hold one to the main terms, logic, and focus of the discipline. Lavoisier's treatise taught technique, as well. Such preliminary measures focused specialist interests on the matrix of language and thus restrained the enthusiast from arbitrary departures from the established system:

> A language perfectly well-composed, a language agreeable to the successive and natural order of ideas, must occasion a necessary and immediate revolution in the method of teaching: it will not permit the professors of chymistry to deviate from the line of nature; and they must either reject the nomenclature or irresistibly pursue the delineated course. It is thus that the logic of the sciences is necessarily connected with their language [18, p. 6].

Lavoisier's textbook gave an intellectual order to chemistry by integrating terminology, nomenclature, and classes of chemical compounds and by merging the experimentalist and linguistic traditions of the sciences. These accomplishments were essential steps in the synthesis of a modern technical discipline.

CONCLUSION

By the beginning of the nineteenth century, constructing new scientific lexicons had become one of the preoccupations of scientific specialists. New names and terms, the astronomer John Herschel noted in 1831, were the foundations of disciplines. They provided the "nuclei or centres about which information may collect into masses." [19, p. 135] His contemporary, the Victorian mathematician and philosopher of science William Whewell, concluded that "almost every step in the progress of science is marked by the formation of a technical term." [20, p. xlviii] These views held scientific language to be in flux — or "animate," as Bacon had called it — the investigator continually extending language in an effort to codify the natural world.

Two basic, yet conflicting, goals in the natural sciences seem to have driven word invention to new levels in the seventeenth and eighteenth centuries. On the one hand, the desire to describe and thus to preserve new distinctions arrived at through close observation and experiment led to a sustained collective effort by investigators to expand the means of physical description. On the other hand, the requirement of independent verification demanded by the scientific community led to the formal definition and lexical systematization of new distinctions, so as to correlate them with existing knowledge. The tensions between these two activities created conditions under which language was continually being recreated in formal definitions that changed as new evidence became available. This activity of defining occupied no small portion of the discussions mounted in the professional literature, and it ultimately gave rise to the phenomenon of textbooks, which became increasingly central to the transmission of science in the nineteenth century.

Formal definition provided the consistency and semantical precision that to a descriptive methodologist like Linnaeus was a vital feature of all science. Such word systems reduced ambiguity and inconsistency by standardizing the verbal referents to natural phenomena. By limiting the characterizations and definitions of words to gross physical distinctions, the scientific lexicographer made his or her words useful to large numbers of specialists. This process of limiting the semantic possibilities of words, called *stripping* by the linguist Leonard Bloomfield [21, pp. 46-47], reduced terms to measurable variables. The lexicon-builder could manipulate terms in mathematical operations. Stripping provided a bridge between the domains of the physical and mathematical worlds and could be viewed as a method of idealizing objects and processes.

Stripping the meaning of a term thus had the effect of modelling, the word-inventor in effect selecting only detail believed relevant to his or her distinction. This process of semantical reduction was one of the roots of all specialization in knowledge, for it created a closed system of verbal reference that admitted the relevance of only selected kinds of information. This was the essence of the model or the matrix, which set the descriptive standard for all comparisons. A matrix of characteristics such as Linnaeus's idealized flower set the standard against which all other phenomenological flowers could be compared. Such a model sustained the topical focus of a discipline and guaranteed that casual, possibly irrelevant distinctions would not easily enter into its working vocabulary.

Terms, names, and classes also concentrated meaning. When the botanist cited a name such as *Crocus sativus,* he or she cited by proxy its entire characterization, as well as the degrees of relationship it had with other organisms by virtue of its generic position in the vast nomenclature of botany. A term such as Lavoisier's *oxidation* was a proxy for its definition. Such words condensed substantial detail into units that could be manipulated logically, descriptively, and often mathematically. Hence, a paragraph of a technical discussion would, in effect, concentrate a remarkable volume of formally defined distinctions and relationships. Such concentration of meaning has been identified by Bloomfield as one of the distinguishing characteristics of scientific prose [21, p. 39].

Although the formal words of the scientific lexicon were to a considerable degree fixed in their significance, this rarely was permanent, as the histories of such words as *species, heat,* and *acid* tell us. Indeed, the value of the specialist lexicon seems to reside partly in its susceptibility to change, given new physical evidence. In his 1865 study of scientific methodology, the experimentalist Claude Bernard observed:

> When we create a word to characterize a phenomenon, we then agree in general on the idea that we wish it to express and the precise meaning we are giving it: but with later progress of science, the meaning of the word changes for some people, while for others, the word remains in the language with its original meaning. . . . Our language, in fact, is only approximate, and even in science, it is so indefinite that if we lose sight of phenomena and cling to words, we are speedily outside reality [22, p. 188].

To Bernard, as to most modern scientists, language itself was neither absolute nor without ambiguity. It was always to the phenomena that the investigator must return for essential meaning. Yet, without the conceptual order afforded by a specialized lexicon, a modern scientific discipline, incorporating the specific work of many minds, would have been impossible to imagine.

REFERENCES

1. R. Boyle, *Works,* T. Birch (ed.), 2nd ed., Vol. 1, London, 1772.
2. R. Adolph, *The Rise of Modern Prose Style,* M.I.T. Press, Cambridge, Massachusetts, 1968.
3. B. Vickers, *Francis Bacon and Renaissance Prose,* Cambridge University Press, London, 1968.
4. M. Cross, *Style, Rhetoric, and Rhythm,* J. M. Patrick, R. O. Evans, J. M. Wallace, and R. J. Schoeck (eds.), Princeton University Press, Princeton, New Jersey, 1966.

5. M. Montaigne, *The Complete Essays*, D. Frame (trans.), Stanford University Press, Stanford, California, 1957.
6. F. Bacon, *The New Organon and Related Writings*, F. H. Anderson (ed.), Bobbs-Merrill, Indianapolis, Indiana, 1975.
7. W. Harvey, *Exercitatio Anatomica De Motu Cordis*, C. Leake (trans.), C. Thomas Publishing Co., Springfield, Illinois, 1970.
8. I. Newton, *Mathematical Principles*, A. Motte and F. Cajori (trans.), Vol. 1, University of California Press, Berkeley, California, 1934.
9. T. Sprat, *History of the Royal Society*, J. Cope and H. Jones (eds.), Washington University, St. Louis, Missouri, 1958.
10. M. Purver, *The Royal Society: Concept and Creation*, M.I.T. Press, Cambridge, Massachusetts, 1967.
11. Aristotle, *Historia Animalium*, A. L. Peck (trans.), Vol. 1, Harvard University Press, Cambridge, Massachusetts, 1965.
12. J. Wilkins, *An Essay Towards a Real Character and a Philosophical Language*, 1668, rpt. Scholar Press, 1968.
13. C. Linnaeus, from *Genera Plantarum*, in *Cambridge Readings in the Literature of Science*, W. Dampier and M. Whetman (eds.), Cambridge University Press, London, pp. 188-195, 1928.
14. C. Linnaeus, *Species Plantarum: A Facsimile of the First Edition* (1735), Vol. 1, W. Stearn (ed.), The Ray Society, London, 1957.
15. C. Linnaeus, *Species Plantarum*, in *A Facsimile of the First Edition* (1735), Vol. 2, W. Stearn (ed.), The Ray Society, London, 1957.
16. G. Morveau, A. Lavoisier, C. Berthol[l]et, and A. Fourcroy, *Method of Chymical Nomenclature*, J. St. John (trans.), G. Kearsley, London, 1788.
17. M. Crosland, *Historical Studies in the Language of Chemistry*, Dover, New York, 1962.
18. A. Lavoisier, *Elements of Chemistry in a New Systematic Order*, R. Kerr (trans.), 2nd ed., William Creech, London, 1793.
19. J. F. W. Herschel, *A Preliminary Discourse on the Study of Natural Philosophy*, Longman's, London, 1831.
20. W. Whewell, *The Philosophy of the Inductive Sciences*, Vol. 1, J. W. Parker, London, 1840.
21. L. Bloomfield, *Linguistic Aspects of Science, International Encyclopedia of Unified Science*, Vol. 1, No. 4, University of Chicago Press, Chicago, Illinois, 1939.
22. C. Bernard, *An Introduction to the Study of Experimental Medicine*, H. C. Greene (trans.), Dover, New York, 1957.

PART FIVE
Redefinition

CHAPTER 12

What's Technical About Technical Writing?

DAVID N. DOBRIN

It is a peculiar question. Similar questions with this form (what's medical, what's legal) have a trivial answer (nothing) because the words "medical" or "legal" designate a clearly defined discipline. To the extent that the question is meaningful for these words, the adjective has the force of a noun: medical writing is writing about medicine. There is, however, no discipline of technics. "Technical," rather, has the force of an adjective; there is something about the writing itself which is technical. The conjunction of adjective and noun actually brings out the ambiguity in "writing": it can be a thing (a piece of writing) or an activity (an act of writing). In the first case, "technical writing," the technicality is in the piece; in the second, the adjective shades off into an adverb: one doesn't write technics but "writes technically."

An adequate answer to the question, "What's technical about technical writing?" is a definition of technical writing, and, quite naturally, there have been many of them. Interestingly enough, the problems of previous definitions turn on the linguistic ambiguity of the term. Some definers choose to define "technical writing," some to define "writing technically." The choice, whether conscious or unconscious, determines the definer's project.

TECHNICAL WRITING

Common sense gives an obvious way to define "technical writing": collect many pieces of technical writing and find the characteristics they share. This is Fred MacIntosh's method in "Teaching Writing for the World's Work." [1] Originally speaking to English teachers interested in technical writing, he wishes to impress upon them the importance and variety of technical writing, so he lists some forty different purposes and forms of technical writing. He could list more. The bulk would be warranted if the list were exhaustive, but it is not. Writing only from his (admittedly large) experience, he does not include what he does not know. The result is unwieldy, yet incomplete; after reading this article, if we wish to resolve whether a piece of writing is technical, we're still best off asking MacIntosh.

If one does not list all the characteristics of these pieces, one must describe the determining characteristics by dividing them into large categories. A natural grouping is format, style, and content. (Some choose only one of these as the defining characteristics [2–4].) After examining hundreds of pieces of technical writing, John Walter uses precisely this division. According to Walter, each piece of technical writing he saw:

1. Had specific rhetorical modes and formats which were pitched to specific readers. (FORMAT)
2. Had a specialized vocabulary and an objective style. (STYLE)
3. Had primarily technical content. (CONTENT) [5]

Patrick Kelley and Roger Masse use the same categories, but conflate them, primarily because they overlap:

> Technical writing is writing about a subject in the pure sciences or the applied sciences in which the writer informs the reader through an objective presentation of facts [6].

Their definition may seem to cover only content, but Kelley and Masse make clear elsewhere that "objective presentation" and "inform" refer to style and format. Both definitions speak to people who know less about technical writing than the authors, Walter's to those less experienced than he, and Kelley and Masse's to technical writing students. Both have enormous intuitive appeal. They are simple. The categories are familiar. They are the sort of definitions we give to friends who want to know what it is we do.

The trouble is that they are simple because they define a difficult concept in terms which are equally difficult and then leave those terms undefined. Any gritty tackling of technical writing must surely decide what "objective" is, what "facts" are, what "technical" is, and what "presentation" (as opposed to "argumentation") is. In what way are the formats and readers "specialized"? But neither Kelley and Masse nor Walter grapples with these terms; they simply refer us for examples to the technical writing they have encountered. Without distortion, neither definition would count environmental impact statements as technical writing (because their subject is nonscientific and they are by law directed toward any reader), but both would count fraudulent scientific works such as Velikovsky's *Worlds in Collision* (highly technical, informative, and directed toward astronomers). The authors would surely resolve the case of Velikovsky not by redefining "objective" but by returning to their experience and then adding "truth" as a characteristic to the definition of technical writing. Again, this elaboration seems obvious. Yet a piece of technical writing, like natural speech, contains much that is neither true nor false: indicators of structure, hypothetical statements, recommendations, and even statements made in good faith but untrue. This criterion of truth requires yet further elaboration, or reference once again to authority, before it can be understood.

The definitions all break down, apparently because their authors have not explained themselves sufficiently. Yet I do not think further elaboration would prove fruitful. The method is faulty. The definers of technical writing don't collect systematically. Instead, they rely on a vast experience to govern the formulations they give us: they use a retrospective, intuitive, conservative procedure. They assume that something called technical writing exists, that it will change slowly, and that the bounds of their experience approximate the bounds of the corpus. They assume, in other words, that their experience is sufficient to comprehend (in both senses of the term) the texts they assemble and that those texts are in fact what technical writing is. But there is no reason to believe that their experience is complete, nor to believe that we can get at their experience in its totality with a few well-chosen words. So why should we depend on that experience for a definition?

WRITING TECHNICALLY

The definers of "technical writing" look at texts; the definers of "writing technically" look at the encounter which produces the texts. The aim of this method is straightforward: to find whatever is unique about the way the mind grapples with a technical subject and then converts that grappling into writing.

There are many such definitions [7–11]. I will discuss three, the most sweeping of which is John Harris's:

Technical writing is the rhetoric of the scientific method [12, p. 135].

Thus, whether writing is technical is determined by its own way of handling a subject, "quantitatively rather than qualitatively, and objectively rather than subjectively." [12, p. 135] A closely related definition, indeed a metaphorical restatement without the gestures toward rhetoric and science, is Charles Stratton's. A technical writer in

a particular art, science, discipline, or trade . . . helps audiences approach subjects [13, p. 10].

Thus, a technical writer should render his own act of writing invisible because technical writing is communication, not self-expression, and the information itself is far more important than the writer's attitude toward it.

In both definitions, what is unique about the act is its objectivity. Bringing a reader close to a subject is the result of objectivity, and handling information quantitatively is a way of gaining objectivity. The objectivity desired is of two kinds: the formal (the collection of such linguistic devices as impersonality with which a speaker performs an objective role) and the epistemological (the mental processes which formal objectivity conventionally designates). Neither Harris nor Stratton distinguishes the two.

Sharing these assumptions is a third definition of writing technically. Earl Britton, however, adds one very interesting criterion. Not only must writing technically be objective, it must be univocal.

> The primary, though certainly not the sole, characteristic of technical and scientific writing lies in the effort of the author to convey one meaning and only one meaning in what he says [14, p. 11].

Furthermore, while both Stratton and Harris would admit as technical writing something which is linguistically dense, Britton would not. He explains why in an analogy which appears frequently in his writing. For Britton, writing is like music. If one wants complexity in a piece of music, one writes a symphony; if one wants to wake up soldiers, one plays reveille on a bugle. Literature is a symphony; technical writing is a bugle call.

The three definitions say technical writing is a noble vocation. The technical writer speaks with the care of the scientist, the humility of a saint, the clarity of a bugle call. Frankly, I suspect more flattery than truth. Partly, it is because the definitions, like much flattery, are difficult to pin down. Their language is imprecise. I have difficulty understanding what Harris means by "rhetoric" and "science," what either Harris or Stratton means by "objective," and how technical writing is like music.

RHETORIC, SCIENCE, AND TECHNICAL WRITING

For Harris, technical writing is the rhetoric of the scientific method. Yet recent work in the history of science (by commentators ranging from Popper to Kuhn) provides a fairly accurate distinction between scientific and technical writing. Scientific writing makes a truth claim; technical writing does not. Moreover, the truth claim of any individual scientific statement is only provisional, and the statement is presented as such. In technical writing, on the other hand, the individual statement can be certain, because the whole is unconcerned with truth. Let me explain. A scientific statement presents itself to a self-regulating discourse, which as a whole makes a truth claim. The statement is provisional because it asks to be evaluated in terms of the rest of the discourse (which includes not merely other statements, but the methods of experimentation, the modes in which data are constituted, the means of confirming theses, the epistemological models underlying the theory, and the conventions of nomenclature). If the statement is satisfactory, it is accepted, and once it is accepted it ramifies the claim of the whole. So situated, the claim of the statement is always universal, never contingent. To invalidate the statement, "Table salt is more stable than free sodium and chlorine," requires a refutation of the whole system in which "salt," "stable," "sodium," and "chlorine" mean something. With the refutation, all the words and statements, procedures and theories, must be reformulated. On the other hand, a technical statement, like "Nut A fits on bolt B," does not refer to all the rest of the discourse. If the statement were found to be invalid (but how would one invalidate it?), the rest of the discourse would still stand. The statement is ineffective rather than invalid; the failure is in the quality control department, not in the discourse. If the statement about salt were found in technical writing (I doubt it would), it would still not make a universal truth claim; it would be contingent, referring only to this salt at this time in these circumstances.

I do not mean by this distinction to imply that science is either logical or true. If it were, Harris's Comtian leap — claiming that something based on science is scientific — might be justified. But most philosophers of science are unwilling to make either claim for it. Science can only be logical or true if it provides some purely logical way of resolving the question of whether a scientific observation should be admitted to its discourse, that is, if there were a scientific method. Apparently there is not. Instead, a claim for admission is rhetorical, and scientists are *persuaded* to admit a particular observation. (See Charles Bazerman's essay, p. 156 of this volume.) Now Harris seems to have this understanding of science, or so his use of the word "rhetoric" indicates. But if he does have this understanding, there's no warrant for his belief that technical writing is scientific. Worse, his definition hides an important distinction between scientific and technical writing: that each has its own modes of demonstration. The modes of technical writing are concerned with the instrumental and contingent, those of science with the discursive and universal. Since they have different modes and make different claims, the yoking is very weak; the claim that the scientific method defines writing *technically* is simply cooptation.

FORMAL VERSUS EPISTEMOLOGICAL OBJECTIVITY

Perhaps the most obvious link between the scientific and the technical is that they both appear to be objective, a fact that all three definers of writing technically seize upon as crucial. For all three, both kinds of objectivity — the formal and the epistemological — are necessary to technical writing; no definer distinguishes the two. Yet the relationship is merely conventional. Being

objective does not require me to use the linguistic devices which often designate
that objectivity — such as not using "I" or using the passive voice. I find it
troubling that all three seem to think it does. In writing, a subjectivity mediates
audience and content. It seems to me that to disguise the mediation by using
formal objectivity requires a warrant from the reader. He or she must know and
accept both the fact and the nature of the mediation. To imply that formal
objectivity confers epistemological objectivity on the subjectivity mediating is
naive — and dispiriting. Worse, it encourages unwarranted uses of formal
objectivity. Naive audiences might believe a statement so couched. But even if
the reader is ready to warrant formal objectivity, I'm not sure how ready the
technical writer should be to take the reader up. Why should a subjectivity
disappear from technical writing? If the visible presence of a subject
automatically moves the audience "farther away" from the object of the
discussion, why do human teachers like myself still present themselves to
students as they present the subject? The stipulation of objectivity as a form in
technical writing is merely another way of coopting the authority of science.

UNIVOCALITY

The last "scientific" stipulation is Britton's requirement that technical
writing be precise: ideally each speech act has "one meaning and only one
meaning." Britton's notion requires some stringent limitations of what is to
count as meaning, which his analogy does not provide. Britton assumes that
complexity inheres in speech itself — symphonies or poetry are complex,
technical writing or bugle calls are simple. But surely complexity is an agreement
on interpretive procedure; one agrees with the author that one will seek certain
sorts of meaning in certain sorts of situations. Reveille performed in a concert
hall is to be complex; Beethoven's Fifth played over loudspeakers at Fort Bragg
is simple. So if Britton's writer wishes to mean one and only one thing, he must
specify the procedure; moreover, that specification must itself be unambiguous.

We can identify some elements of that interpretive procedure. For one, it
must be able to enumerate meanings, fitting apprehension into discrete
categories. Words have primary and secondary meanings, implies Britton, or, to
continue his metaphor, primary tones and harmonics. The procedure separates
the two. The meaning of the word "rock" can be only that thing on the ground,
once the procedure has been applied. The procedure enables us to identify and
eliminate other meanings such as those established by the speaker's experience
("rock" from a geologist doesn't mean quite the same as "rock" from a child),
the cultural context ("rock" before 1953 has a different flavor from that of
"rock" now), the philology of the word, and the sound of the word. The
soldier hearing the loudspeakers at Fort Bragg is told to listen only to the
message, "Wake Up," and does so, according to Britton. He does not hear the
other messages in the bugle call: the insistence that each listener is uniform with

respect to the speaker; the affirmation of a continuing authority; the promise and provision of a visceral reward when the listener cedes his individuality.

Obviously the soldier — or the technical reader — at least picks up the secondary along with the primary tones. To separate the two requires special equipment — assent in the first case or a heightened attention in the second — as well as instructions from the author to use this equipment. Yet even if we are instructed to move into an information processing mode and we are capable of doing so (and how technical writing tells us to treat it as information is worthy of much study), I wonder if we actually can do so. Language is not information. The image of language as discrete units comes from our picture of the dictionary, in which each word has "n" meanings. But dictionaries exist to describe language; their descriptions cannot be substituted for a particular word as if a sentence were a mathematical equation. Those who have attempted to treat language as lexically determinate, to treat the sentence as a concatenation of dictionary definitions, mostly developers of artificial languages and computer translation equipment, have failed [15—17].

Exactly how we do understand language is not at all clear. But it is clear that the procedure which can find the "one and only one" meaning works by placing the word into various contexts to see if it fits. The ways we discover context are, however, extraordinarily complex. When I come up to a STOP sign, it seems that I am being confronted with a univocal message. It's not that simple. To decide what the word means in this situation, I must look at its physical location to see if it applies to me: "You stop here." I must consult the current usage of the sign. STOP in Massachusetts is a suggestion, not an order: "You should consider stopping here." I must decide whether STOP has been superseded by other rules: "You should consider stopping here unless there's an ambulance in back of you." The message grows as I apply contexts. For the message to be univocal and unequivocal, therefore, the procedure should specify the contexts I bring to the interpretation. It can't. There are too many contexts; they can be applied in too many ways. We do understand messages — we generally stop at stop signs — but not because the communication has specified how or because the author of the stop sign has intended only one meaning. We understand because we apply an experienced intuition to make pretty good guesses. And when we do so, we are frequently guided by those secondary meanings which Britton wishes to eliminate.

Apparently Britton is actually recommending a high level of specificity in technical writing. By "one and only one meaning" he means that we should distinguish which of several plausible meanings we actually do mean. If I say that a pen is easier to use than a pencil, I should specify whether I mean physically easier to grasp, psychologically more restful to me, or generally more responsive as I attempt to make smooth, graceful lines. If I mean all three, I should say so. It's hard, however, to tell how to apply Britton's recommendation. If he is enjoining us to write so that we're unlikely to be misunderstood by a good reader, his injunction scarcely applies only to writing technically. If the special characteristic of technical writing is that it always specifies, the injunction is a recipe for ponderousness. Surely preferable to a labored specificity is a grace which risks ambiguity. But even if ponderousness is the choice, that choice is made in all other kinds of writing besides the technical. Examined critically, Britton's specification is not specific enough.

UNIVERSALIST VIEW OF LANGUAGE

Thus far, I have been criticizing the definitions of "technical writing" and "writing technically" on many different grounds: that the definitions by inspection are imprecise, that experience limits such definitions, that various definers fail to distinguish technology and science, linguistic and epistemological objectivity, or the meaning and use of an utterance. The definers could probably reply to me by articulating more carefully what relationships they think hold between language, thought, science, technology, and reality. That they have not troubled to discuss these matters, however, is symptomatic of their underlying position on them. They do not think these relationships are problematic. I do. At the heart of our disagreement is a disagreement over language. They hold what George Steiner calls the "universalist" view of language; in this essay I argue for the opposite view, the "monadist." [15] Those taking the universalist view believe a sentence can mean a particular thing and that precisely that meaning can be understood; those taking the monadist believe that what someone means is indeterminate and can never be precisely understood. The universalist might describe language as a collection of data: the monadist a group of adumbrations.

Carolyn Miller has described the technical writing version of the universalist view as the "windowpane" theory of language, and she suggests that the theory comes from logical positivism, whose foremost exponent in English was A. J. Ayer [18]. In fact, the definers of technical writing and writing technically do inherit some of their attitudes from Ayer, but it is important to realize that he is no primogenitor. Both positivism and the windowpane theory spring from the tradition of Cartesian rationalism, which is hundreds of years old. Among their forefathers are Bacon, Locke, Burke, Spencer, Russell, and the early Wittgenstein. The assumptions that the definers hold are actually part of a system of assumptions held by all these men, a system which (in its barest possible outlines) is as follows: One, the world is out there. Two, by properly applying our minds, we can know it. Three, there is a best way of knowing the world (a "privileged access") which the nature of the world dictates. The world is an open book; the world is legible. Four, this best way of knowing the world is available to any intelligence. Five, it is thus independent of language and human quirks. Six, language is a way of using and telling this access, a coding of the world, but the decoder is operated by a prelinguistic knower. Seven, we are able to distinguish between correct and incorrect (true and untrue) uses of language because our way of knowing is independent of language. Eight, so distinguishing is difficult and we often fail at it. Nine, if we can purify language and our consciousness, we can formulate a perfectly correct language, a universal language, in which we would not make mistakes. Ten (often unstated), it is our responsibility to do so.

Only by assuming that the world is out there can the definers of "writing technically" believe that there are subjects out there to which readers can be brought closer. Only because they assume that the world is legible and that it can be coded in language can they believe that writing is capable of "help[ing] audiences approach subjects" (to use Stratton's terms). And only by believing that there is a best way of knowing the world, which is independent of language and human quirks, can they believe that the world can be known objectively. Finally, only by believing that the way can be coded in a perfectly correct language can they hope to rid technical writing of subjectivity. The assumptions held by the definers of "technical writing" — for whom it is the encounter with the text, not the world, which is problematic — are a subset of these. To see how, just substitute for "world," "text." The text exists independently; it can be read correctly and it is through this experienced reading that these definers can identify texts that genuinely belong to the corpus of technical writing.

Underlying the universalist position (and the definitions of "technical writing" and "writing technically" that it informs) is a profound dissatisfaction with language as it is now practiced, a dissatisfaction that is particularly evident in points eight, nine, and ten in the list of assumptions given above. The universalist, wishing to stand back and interrogate the world without implicating himself, finds himself frustrated at every turn by a degraded language, and by the fallen man who uses this language. (For the universalist, the failure of language and the failure of man indicate each other, so purifying language is a moral, as well as an intellectual imperative.) The best way to relieve the frustration and purify language is to divide it into objective and subjective, primary and secondary, fact and opinion, and eliminate the second term. Hence, the thrust toward objectivity, precision, and neutrality, which we have seen in the definers thus far, a thrust toward moral grace as well as intellectual honesty. Hence also their lack of concern for interpretive procedures, for once language is purified, interpretation will not be problematic.

It is this moral fervor which all those who have tried to build a universal language share. Perhaps inevitably, their architectural strategy has been much the same. All have sought to guarantee a sound moral base for their language by choosing to build upon some preexisting language form which for them had some moral cachet. The Gnostics, for instance, chose to reconstruct the language at Babel. Numerological analysis of Biblical phonemes being out of favor in the eighteenth century, rationalists built a language from the infallible signs of appearances, which were simultaneously made available to man and validated by a rational God. Again, in the twentieth century, a new attempt and a new language: this time, mathematics. Interestingly enough, the enemy for all was the fecundity of language, and that fecundity was a sign of man's fall. For the Gnostics, the fecundity stems from the failure at Babel and so is an actual relic of the fall. For Swift, on the other hand, it is not fecundity itself but man's ability to be untrue to appearances and speak "the thing which is not" which distinguishes him from the soft, rational Houyhnhms. For Russell and Wittgenstein, the endless extent of language made their project too vast for merely human capacities; again, it would take something better than man to make the language [15, pp. 49-235].

Ayer's logical positivism is an attempt to solve Wittgenstein's problem by limiting what is to count as a meaningful statement to statements derivable by formal procedures from statements about sense impressions. Statements such as "This pillow is good" are meaningless to the extent that "good" is not reducible to "soft" and "blue." The idea is obviously appealing to definers of technical writing; it probably accounts for the extraordinary word "data" in Harris's description of technical writing as a "data retrieval mechanism." [12, p. 137] But another offshoot from Wittgenstein and Russell has had an equally profound impact on thinking about technical writing: information theory. The power of this is not so much in the philosophy it provides as in the example. Computers and computer languages clearly use something which looks like language, which is based on the procedures of mathematics, and which transfers the language from donor to receptor perfectly. Technical writing should be so good. This example probably accounts for the "retrieval mechanism" in Harris's phrase; it certainly accounts for those flow charts for technical writing we've all seen, the ones with the boxes for the transmitter, channel, receiver, and noise. This seems to be what we do: write down information and have someone else pick it up, albeit imperfectly, because of the noise.

But the metaphors logical positivism and computer science provide the definers with are only metaphors and indeed rather unconvincing [19]. (Think about it. Even though a person may receive information from technical writing — so that the effect of technical writing is information transfer — does the nature of the effect in any way determine the way it is produced, that is, make information theory applicable to writing? The effect of art is pleasure, but that doesn't give us a theory of art.) That we do not criticize them for being only metaphors is perhaps not surprising. To the extent that the definitions have ever had any power to convince, it is because they participate in a drama now hundreds of years old, the drama of Western man confronting a malevolent other, the universe, and seeking the language and the tools to subjugate that other. It is a drama whose end — failure — is known. The universalist definitions account for that failure: language itself has broken under the weight of knowing placed on it. The definitions prescribe a remedy, make language stronger by making it like the currently fashionable theory of truth, in this case science. (It is well to remember that scientific writing, though it deals with scientific subjects, is not thereby made scientific any more than writing about music is musical.) Thus, it is easy for the definitions to justify their remedies by appealing to common sense, a common sense they need not question. The result, and it has been so at least since Descartes, is that such definitions suspect the experience and language of man.

If the universalist tradition could realize its project and create a universal language, then such suspicion would be warranted. Yet, as even the universalists acknowledge, it may not be possible. There are only two possible ways to build it up: start from existing formal languages or start from the universal constants of language behavior. As we've seen, science and mathematics might be such formal languages, the languages of sense-data. But most philosophers of science believe that they are not in fact formal, and even if they were, Quine has shown that they can't be built up [20]. A universal language might be built by finding the basic Chomskian deep structures which are actually wired into the brain and putting them together in the right way. Unfortunately, the available evidence suggests that there are no such structures. No language structure seems to be biologically inherent, the way the number of noses is.

If no universal language can exist, then the value of "purifying" language in its name should be reassessed. If we take each word only insofar as it contains information and refer each piece of information to other such pieces, we set up a clumsy interpretive system for ourselves. We must assert procedures for specifying context; we must account for and identify linguistic noise; we must write a technical lexicon. Moreover, we must accept preconditions for the project — a deracination of language, an implicit belief that man is fallen, and an automatic separation of epistemology and language — which are morally and pragmatically costly. And to what end?

THE MONADIST VIEW

The monadist alternative is to see language as it is actually used, rather than as a formal system, by readmitting its "tonal qualities" (Steiner's term).

> The directly informative content of natural speech is small. Information does not come naked except in the schemata of computer languages or the lexicon. It comes attenuated, flexed, coloured, alloyed by intent and the milieu in which the utterance occurs (and "milieu" is here the total biological, cultural, semantic ambience as it conditions the moment of individual articulation) [15, pp. 220-221].

The study of language becomes historical; it must ultimately take in each moment of being and the pressures shaping it. This seems sensible enough; we study technical writing by looking at how technical writers think technical writing, but the preconditions for this study — the monadist ideology — are difficult to those of us brought up in the Cartesian tradition. The monadist does not separate knowledge and language; he argues that one knows in language. Since there is no way of knowing without language — a human construct — there can be no privileged access to the world. Since language creates knowledge of the world, it is not fruitful to suspect language nor to diminish it. And since language is not suspect, neither is the man who makes it; man is not fallen. Each language use is a "rich expression of articulate being," a being which simply is [15, p. 51]. No preexisting language form is likely to be better than the one we have; formalized languages are useful in special situations, but they are not extensible. Interpretation, consequently, is very difficult, and meaning can never be fully understood. What we mean depends on our consciousness as we speak; "all communication 'interprets' between privacies." [15, p. 198]

What motivates this view of the world? Why shouldn't we try to distinguish between knowing and speaking, when so much of our intellectual apparatus depends on making such distinctions? To answer these questions, we must again look back, this time to Giambattista Vico, an eighteenth-century professor of law and science. It is Vico's great clairvoyance, says Steiner, that knowing and speaking are inseparable, "that man enters into active possession of consciousness, into active cognizance of reality, through the ordering, shaping powers of language." [15, p. 75] To believe this, of course, requires a radical reorganization of what one wants to count as real. Vico made such a reorganization. For him, what is real or true is what we make (the doctrine of *verum factum*). Thus laws, language, or history, which we make entirely, are the primary objects of knowledge, and the natural world, which we do not make, is entirely secondary. After all, Vico argues, what we know of the natural world we know through experiments, which we make. There is no uninterpreted knowledge of the natural world.

Vico's doctrine was not accepted by his own century, whose dispositions were elsewhere. It took the Romantic preoccupation with the past's constituting of the present and with the individual voice to create a world in which Vico made sense [15, pp. 49-235]. In that world, even the father of linguistics, Humboldt, could say that language and knowing were reciprocal. Steiner summarizes his ideas: "Language does not convey a pre-established or separately extant content, as a cable conveys telegraph messages. The content is created in and through the dynamics of statement." [15, p. 82] To Humboldt, this idea is inescapable; nothing else explains the variety of languages and the difficulties of translating them. So, too, for the twentieth century American linguists Edward Sapir and Benjamin Lee Whorf, the explanation of the differences in language was that "different linguistic communities literally inhabit and traverse different landscapes of conscious being." [15, p. 89] Whorf's most famous example is the Hopi language, in which, he claims, the Indians actually think time not as past, present and future, but as time-distance. Vico's thought, however, does not have its greatest consequence in linguistics. Coupled with the problem of how consciousness comes into being through language is the problem of how consciousness makes itself aware of the products of other consciousnesses, the problem of interpretation. Those who have grappled with this problem form a European tradition as distinguished as the universalist, but less familiar to Americans. The heirs of this tradition, Heidegger and Merleau-Ponty among others, have much to say about interpretation, which they view as the fundamental human activity [15, pp. 49-235].

Our version of Cartesian rationalism elides such radical problems of language production and interpretation by establishing pragmatic systems of interpretation and justifying them in common sense. For the monadist, however, the canons of common sense are what Steiner calls "axiomatic fictions," "conventions about 'reality-contents' of language . . . and about the accessibility of memory to grammatical coding." [15, p. 138] Axiomatic fictions claim to be absolute, but actually they provide a limited, indefensible view of the world. The descriptions of "technical writing" and "writing technically" which I have discussed are attempts to articulate these fictions. They are thus a description of language practice (including interpretive practice), not a formulation of the essential nature of technical writing. They bear the same relationship to a definition of technical writing as a description of Coach Woody Hayes' strategy has to a definition of football.

Such descriptions are, of course, definitive guides if everyone is playing Woody Hayes-style football. Even if the philosophic grounds for axiomatic fictions are crumbly, the group's decision to base its practice on them lend them a certain sturdiness, and make the group's injunctions on practice seem like common sense. My job in arguing a monadist view of technical writing (where the view seems quite out of place), is to show how the present axiomatic fictions do limit everyday practice — how they damage it or cause internal contradictions. I must ask what of value is left out by the prescriptions that make natural language resemble formalizable language. What, in other words, is the language so prescribed unable to do? If I cannot answer this question, my philosophical objections are irrelevant.

ALTERNITY

I cannot give a full answer here: yet the form of my argument and the people I refer to do indicate where a full answer can be found. I only have room to show that the prescriptions limit the vitality of the language used, thereby limiting the creativity of the writer and forcing us to establish in the writing human relationships which are mistaken and false. These prescriptions (objective, quantitative, univocal) propose to cure writing by eradicating ambiguity. What they actually do is confuse ambiguity (a property of denotations), vagueness (a confused intention) and what Steiner calls "alternity." [15, 21] Alternity is a characteristic of any language statement. It designates the fact that any statement, as it states what is, also brings into the domain of consciousness what isn't. Alternity is a source of vitality and creativity, because it means that using languages is always playing with the possible.

We play in several different ways simultaneously. As we use a word, for instance, we do not merely denote something, we also call up some of the linguistic history of the word, its associations, the way it is habitually used. More than that, we also call up a domain of words which are not used; when we say "red," we may also mean "not blue," or "not polka-dotted" (but we certainly don't mean "not elephants"). As we put words into sentences, we open up a world, which is rich because of its alternatives and unique because of what we deny. This sort of play is not merely important in literature or on some arcane philosophic plane; it is crucial in technical writing. As we write, we construct a way of looking at a thing which precludes other ways at least temporarily, announcing that this is the privileged access to the thing. We write design specifications and document maintenance procedures in part to ward off such illegitimate ways; we must, if only for legal reasons.

More fundamentally, we play as a way of becoming in the world, to exercise our human will. When I speak and believe it to be true, it can only be the truth because I know how to lie; I have considered the alternative; and I have chosen to behave in this way toward others and toward myself. No machine can speak the truth; it can only speak, because it does not make this choice. Our language also lets us play frequently with conditions other than the actual which are neither true or false, and so play with our hopes and fears. The past, the future, the conditional, and the hypothetical are constantly being set against the present when language is being used. (Note the orchestration of conditions in that last phrase "when — is — being — used.") Of course, as we play with these conditions, we do not necessarily involve others in it. Some of the play is private. I may associate a certain word with a friend who used it and so strain to use it myself just that I may remember or imitate. A word may surface from a private discourse, an internal expression of hope or hate. This privacy gives strength to the writer and to the listener, who rarely fails to appreciate it when a voice becomes individual or when a word strikes one of the listener's private chords. Perhaps a technical writer can indulge too much in private play, but strangely, the instrumental purposes of technical writing are rarely so finely tuned that it matters. In most technical writing, there is no editorial reason to choose between "squeeze between the palms" and "compress in the hands." The actions resulting will be the same. Yet for me the first image is more satisfying to write or think, and having it makes my job easier and less alienating.

The cause of this alternity, the reason it has developed and survived, is that it has specific functions within a group. Alternity makes participation in a group — at all levels — a dynamic activity. Alternity does this by making a language act both inclusive and exclusive, both shield and sword. At the level of consciousness, using a word (which is never our own) has admitted the other. Perhaps a better description, as autistic children know, is "has let the other invade." At best, accepting an outside word and using it is distressing. (We all know the turmoil of being unable to find the "right" word and being forced to accept another, and we know the attendant loss and denial.) Alternity defends against this invasion; it creates a zone of selfhood where we may become ourselves as we become the other. At the level of articulation, the inverse process occurs. As we use a word which others hear, we simultaneously enter the group (which of us has not felt relieved upon finally having talked at a party) and individuate ourselves. We give the words to the group, and yet they remain ours. Beyond these activities within a group, alternity allows our language acts to include members of the group and exclude the others. Language acts in this sense are like discussing baseball with the new one in a prisoner-of-war camp. Using the correct word shows we belong and tests whether he does. Does alternity operate in this way in technical writing? Take for one example, jargon, a sin to technical writers and technical writing teachers who wish that technical writing were not a collection of Balkan states. But is it a sin? Jargon may be owlish to us, but to students or engineers who use it so delightedly it is a ticket of admission to a group which they set against our own and prefer. Creating, employing, and preserving jargon is a means of self-preservation, not simply the mode of aggression we usually condemn it as.

According to the monadist view, alternity makes any group vital. Perhaps at the highest levels this is the most clear. Surely we agree with Orwell that a language rich in possibility commits us to democratic freedoms and threatens arbitrary authority. Such speech lets us find dissatisfactions and think of alternatives. That is why political repression aims at limiting speech, either by suppressing it entirely or by making it sere, vague, mechanical, unthinking, endlessly univocal.

How does ignoring the property of alternity affect the descriptions of technical writing? In three ways. First, because the descriptions ignore the delicate modes of group cohesion entailed in technical writing, they misconstrue the difficulty of interpreting one group to another, for instance engineers to managers. Writing for a lay audience, as another example, seems only to involve substituting the general for the precise word, the metaphor for the equation. In fact, it requires the translator (for that is what he or she is) to inhabit two groups at once, testing the practices of each against the other. Second, the definitions fail to give technical writing the responsibility it should have or to invest it with the consequent creativity. The belief that the world is legible largely accounts for this. When a technical writer places something before a group, he or she determines how it will be seen. (What reader of a John Deere manual would use a tractor for a backstop, as I saw some boys doing one day.) That determination is trivial if there is only one best way to see something. Third, the definitions fail to account for or even to describe a slackness in technical writing which is due to the fact that it is written to a limited future. Assuming that technical writing should disappear as it is read or acknowledging that it will disappear soon after gives a writer a few ways to play with it and little reason to establish selfhood in it.

The belief that technical writing should disappear has a graver consequence, because sometimes it shouldn't disappear. We tend to think that technical writing gives access to information about the world; a universalist holds that the access should be quick and efficient — usually logical. But in situations where the audience is going to be using the writing for a long time, it is not at all obvious that efficient access is paramount. Take access to streets in a city as an example — and as a metaphor for much technical writing. Generally speaking, street names and addresses are laid out systematically on a grid, so that residents or newcomers can find any place and the route to that place quickly. So it is in Los Angeles, where I come from. In cities like Boston, the street system is older than the idea of access, and the streets seem laid out randomly, at least to a newcomer. The result is chaos and confusion, occasionally, but also an increase in what city planner Kevin Lynch calls imageability [22]. According to Lynch, a city is highly imageable if it presents itself to the mind as a complex whole, which is understandable in many ways at once. A highly imageable city enriches the experience of the residents, for we learn its life as we learn to get around. I know that in Boston, Lynch's example of a highly imageable city, learning the city's ethnicities and history is part of learning the addresses. And in Boston, even physical access is humanized, for the only practical way of getting around is to get pretty close and then ask somebody. In a less imageable city, like Los Angeles, you can get no hint of the Korean neighborhood on 3rd Street from the map; street names record only the quirks of developers. Access, of course, is very simple: driveway to driveway. I came from Los Angeles to Boston, and Boston's system was difficult at first, and frustrating. But now I am grateful to it, for it gives contour to my experience.

A NEW DEFINITION OF TECHNICAL WRITING

I am not suggesting that we abandon methodical parts lists and label parts whimsically. I am not suggesting that we write precious ambiguities or take up obscurantism. I am suggesting that the injunctions of clarity, precision, logic, objectivity, and univocality, the injunctions which we have accepted in deference to and imitation of the technology we imagine our writing gives privileged access to, are not absolutes but axiomatic fictions of a particular group. What is technical about technical writing is technology, to the extent that technology defines certain human behaviors among certain human beings and defines a group. Hence I suggest the following definition of technical writing:

Technical writing is writing that accommodates technology to the user.

The key word is "writing": it should be understood in the monadist sense as a way of thinking and establishing human relations in a group. The word "accommodate" also suggests the invasive quality of technology (even to techno-logists) and the self-effacing role technical writing plays. ("Accommodate," curiously, allows its indirect and direct objects to be inverted with only a flick of the eye; in an invasion, who is accommodating whom, invader or invaded, technology or user, depends on the power of each.) "User" is appropriate rather than "reader," because technology is meant to be used; moreover, "user" reflects the fact that technical writing exists within a system which measures actions, people, and things by the criterion of use. "Technology" is more than an array of tools or procedures. It extends to the way human beings deploy themselves in the use and production of material goods and services. One may speak profitably of an economic strategy or an administrative formation as a technology.

The idea that by technology we mean a way that people, machines, ccr cepts, and relationships are organized is crucial to the definition, but at first glance it seems strange. We usually associate the word "technology" with machines or the ability to make machines, as in "computer technology." But this usage narrows our attention unnecessarily; the ability we speak of surely cannot be confined to a design, but must also include all concerned with creating and implementing the design. It is symptomatic, and I think instructive, that in its section on technology management the *Encyclopedia of Professional Management* argues that "private companies — multinational companies — are likely to be the most effective mechanisms for the spread and development of useful technology." [23, p. 1154] For the *Encyclopedia* a certain system of control is appropriate to technology; for me the two are a part of each other.

A second idea is that technology makes an essential difference to technical writing. Technical writing doesn't just happen to occur alongside technology; it is a technological product, a residue of technological management. Managers know this. It does not strike the editors of the *Encyclopedia* as odd, for instance, that they cross-reference "Research and Development Management" to "Writing for Business." Technical writing as a profession is a result of such management logic. It was invented after World War II in the aerospace and electronics industries, when very large tasks required extensive documentation, particularly in the proposal and design stages, and managers decided that these tasks could best be performed by separating the technical and writing functions. It may be argued that separation of difficult tasks is a natural response of any large organization, not something special to technology. But in fact, it, or even the less salient separation of the writing and engineering functions in a single job description, is the product of technological organization; the separation comes by analogy with the assembly line.

There are large organizations also concerned with the manipulation of the natural world in which the distinction is much less clear. I am thinking of academic science. In the scientific community, it would be considered an evasion of responsibility for a scientist to leave his or her writing to a scientific writer. (The only professional writing having to do with science, *per se*, is science writing, a species of journalism.) The organizational distinction, then, is very large; technology sees its technical writing as a thing to be quantified, controlled, and managed; academic science simply requires such competence to be part of the professional's tools. The distinction I made earlier between science and technology perhaps explains why. Scientific readers, engaged in a search for truth, are highly motivated, and they have a small arsenal of ways to test the writer's truth claim, the self-regulating mechanisms in the discourse. Technical readers have less exacting methods of testing a statement (they are not concerned with a writer's truth claim) and also make very different demands on it. The relationship of reader to text or writer to writing is thus like a loose joint, and so must be controlled and managed.

Under the universalist view, the fact that a group organizes its writing in a certain way does not say anything about the writing itself. In the monadist view it does, because the language practice of any group sets forth the limits of the group, the aims of the group, and the relationships that go on inside it. Technology, like any group, has particular ways to model the activity of human beings, particular categorizations of experience, particular modes of responsibility and control. Let me give an example. Most of this article was written while I was sitting in a Steelcase desk chair; the rest in an old-fashioned swivel desk chair which I got from a chairmaker. The Steelcase one came with a manual. The chairmaker did not provide one. Steelcase's manual is of more than semiotic interest, though that alone is considerable. (The manual proclaims the technology of chair-making, but so does the chrome and synthetic fabric. High-technology chairs do not sell unless they look technological.) The existence of the manual indicates more than a habit of documentation run wild, though this, too, is important. (I get the feeling the manual was included because everything before distribution had been documented, so why stop now?) The manual is not simply something to use if I need help. Its existence defines a particular relationship with me and projects a particular power over my experience. First of all, it proclaims the right to penetrate my experience, as it accomplishes the penetration. It models me as isolate. If I have trouble raising the chair, I should not turn to the mechanically minded professor next door or to my own common sense, I should turn to it. (True, I may be isolate, but that doesn't change my point.) Similarly, the manual also takes a certain line of responsibility and drops another. If I have trouble with the Steelcase chair, I go to the manual. If that fails, or I fail it, I then must take on the Steelcase Corporation. On the other hand, if I have trouble with the craftsman's chair, I first turn to myself or to a nearby friend. But I can always fall back on calling the craftsman, who I know will take responsibility. A principle of limited responsibility informs technological organizations; their writing enforces and establishes that principle.

Technology, in sum, not only uses language but employs its own axiomatic fictions; not only uses logic, but sets forth a rationality; not only perceives, but has its own way of knowing. The idea that technology has an ideology is difficult only because how technology thinks seems so obvious, so common-sensical; the idea would be easy if we were Hopi and studying technology from outside. Why has the ideology of technology become common sense? I find the most useful answer in the work of Herbert Marcuse and the Frankfurt School of philosophy. Several parts of the argument in Marcuse's *One-Dimensional Man* are particularly relevant to this discussion [24]. Marcuse argues, for instance, that the cooptation of science we have seen in some definitions of technical writing is integral to technological discourse. The key features of the scientific method as it was developed in the seventeenth century — they include the adoption of a value-free "objectivity," the constitution of the world into quantifiable and interchangeable things, qualities, and relationships (positivities), and the description of positivities in operational or instrumental terms so as to enable the manipulation of matter — the key features together form a discourse of technics, a *techno-logy*, which had no great authority in social and economic relations until the early nineteenth century, when it was brought into the discourse of production. Technological discourse then converted all things, natural or human, into functions, so that it could dominate man and matter simultaneously, using the same discourse to bring man into complicated systems of control and organization as it used to bring matter into complicated systems of manipulation. The conversion seemed like applying scientific logic to human beings, but the point of it was power for those wielding the logic. Marcuse thus calls it the "logic of domination."

Consider, for instance, how the logic of domination has coopted the idea of "objectivity." I have been arguing that in the definitions, no distinction has been made between epistemological and formal objectivity, when there is no necessary connection between the two, when the formal seems unnecessary and perhaps irrelevant and the epistemological seems problematic. Why then is objectivity so often stipulated in technical writing? Because technology demands a third kind of objectivity — instrumental objectivity or fungibility. If writing can speak with a single, third-person voice and pretend that this is the voice of everyman, the writing is likely to be uniform, and thus interchangeable.

The logic of domination operates in every such stipulation, whether it be objectivity, a scientific demeanor, or univocality that is stipulated. It must. We would probably not submit to such mechanization of our being, even though it brings us extraordinary material benefits, if the interchangeability of man and machine, the belief, for instance, that the question "will machines replace us?" makes sense, did not permeate our discourse. Thus Britton's dictum — convey one meaning and only one meaning — is not merely a guide to current practice in technical writing; it intends a subjugation of writing and writers. Dicta that remind the writer of the richness of language, whatever their truth, are very inconvenient in a testing laboratory. Alternity invests the writer with responsibility, responsibility which technology requires be in the hands of the manager. Alternity valorizes complex, personal communications, just the sort of thing to decrease productivity. Alternity makes quantifying language production silly. Yet how is one to plan, if one cannot set an output level?

Marcuse argues that most of technology's success comes from its ability to hide terms of the discourse which might be threatening to the discourse itself, terms like alternity. But his argument extends to the way technology is organized, and he thus explains the separation of functions described earlier. That there be a profession of technical writing is certainly one term of technology, and it is certainly an important one. Yet technical writers are pretty low on the corporate totem pole. They are not well paid nor held in great esteem. If a technical writer wants to get ahead, he or she tries to move as quickly as possible into management. Technical writers are production people. Yet technical writers must often get to know far more about what they write than anyone else. To do this, they perform managerial functions. They oversee the work of other sections, communicating frequently with many different areas of a company. They make frequent and discerning judgments about the products or processes. On the basis of these judgments, they frequently make *de facto* policy. They have power. Yet neither they nor management seem to be aware of this. Why? The belief that language is transparent and that there is a privileged access to the world clouds the issue. What a technical writer does is obvious and easy. Judgment, which is given to the manager, is a higher faculty than perception.

THE TRANSFER OF TECHNOLOGY

Technical writing moves outward — from designer to millwright, from engineer to manager, from distributor to customer. At each point, the reader is a user. (People do not read technical writing for fun but because they need to do a task.) At every point, the technology must be accommodated to the user or the user must be accommodated to the technology. Previous definitions call this process giving access to the user, but "accommodate" is more accurate. The ambiguity of the word "accommodate," as observed earlier, sets forth the mutuality and mutability of the power of relationships established by technical writing. Moreover, "accommodate" suggests that conversion of thing to function which is crucial to the discourse of technics. Technical writing appears to be concrete, but it is only concerned with the concrete. In fact it makes the concrete abstract; it replaces the obdurate thing with the manipulable concept. It thereby makes the strange, invasive, expensive, or inefficient into the familiar and useful. Most important, "accommodate," unlike "give access," reminds us that technical writing and the movement of technology are human relationships, with all the attendant feints. Viewing technical writing as access makes us blind to its rhetorical quiddity.

The criterion of use — put it in only if the reader can use it, read it only if I can use it — is the most important single governor on technical writing. In it are the grounds for Britton's confusion of meaning and use (the meaning of a bugle call and symphony may be different, though their use is the same). The word "use" is as difficult to understand or use as we have seen the word "meaning" is; yet in descriptions of technical writing it has been used in an equally simplistic, Gradgrindian sense. The use of the writing has been what the writing lets the user do efficiently. The criterion of use thus accounts for the barrenness of technical language. What is the use of fripperies in language, after all? But "use" need not be so demeaning. Can't joy in language communicate itself, and can't men or women on the job use joy? The criterion of use is one more gesture toward science, but in fact it reveals once more the difference between the two. If the criterion of use informs the structure of technical writing, then it undermines technical writing's ostensible status as the privileged access to a legible world. Technical writing gives what is useful, not what is known. The first question a technical writer asks is "Who is the reader?" not "What is the world?" and the answer to the first determines the answer to the second. Thus, the barrenness of technical writing is actually ironic. The gesture towards science gives technical writing a thirty-weight flavor, but technical writing's greatest success comes when it is swallowed easily and digested quickly.

THE IMPLICATIONS OF THIS DEFINITION

It may be charged that my definition evades the title question by displacing "technical" onto "technology." I criticize the other definitions for leaving fuzzy boundaries around "technical"; yet the boundaries around "technology" are by no means distinct. I admit this charge. My claim for the definition is not that it is ultimately accurate; it is that the definition shifts attention to where it should be shifted, to technological practices. The boundaries of that group cannot be distinct; the boundaries of no human endeavor are. Science and technology overlap; law and technology overlap; work and technology overlap. Yet even though they are fuzzy, the boundaries are more precise and more useful than the previous ones. The definition resolves problematic cases more accurately than the earlier ones: Velikovsky is not technological and not useful; environmental impact statements emphatically do accommodate technology to the user. Moreover, the definition does not let the boundaries be decided by one person's large experience. Technology is the subject of many disciplines: law, political science, history, management. The definition permits and even demands that we use such findings as they provide. The definitions we have seen are rules of thumb which serious and dedicated people have found useful for many years. My definition does not deny those definitions so much as it places them in context.

By questioning the philosophic basis of the prescriptions for technical writing, I am actually making my title question less meaningful. The title implies that language can be defined; my views of language say that such definitions are problematic — and mutable. The title implies that a procedure, presumably scientific, can be developed to answer the question; my criticism of previous definitions suggests that such procedures are misguided.

The definition suggests a different procedure for looking at technical writing. In this procedure, the piece of technical writing or the act of writing technically are two of several foci, which must also include the practice of the groups which the writer is writing to, writing for, and writing from, as well as the practices of the group in which the writer has located himself or herself. The procedure is in effect a natural history of technical writing. It looks at each thing in its domain both as an organism (which has a history) and as an entity (which is simply there). The procedure begins where someone conceives the need to accommodate, adducing the relationships of power and perception which generate it; and the procedure must end where the accommodation is completed. Along the way, the procedure follows the need and its traces in human relationships. Such a procedure is very difficult, for penetrating groups which you are not a member of requires learning a new way of thinking. It is likely that this new way will not be easy to generalize. The way they handle technical writing at Kodak is very different from the way they do at Corning, and each way is tied up with the corporation's organization, its self-image, its decisions about what is acceptable behavior, its valuations of judgment and knowledge, and so on. Despite the difficulties of this procedure, it provides the only means by which we can develop a full response to the question, "What's technical about technical writing?"

People come into technical writing from two directions; either they are technicians who are asked to write or writers asked to gain technical skills. As technical writers, they are likely to ask themselves what they are and what they do: obvious and necessary questions. The answers function as a definition of technical writing, and that definition helps the definer find an internal equilibrium and some direction for the future. The previous definitions of technical writing worked well to that end; they could make us feel very comfortable with technical writing, what it is and what it does. This definition does not. It questions the value of what we do; it suggests that our common sense misguides us much of the time. As a remedy, it requires that we abandon deeply held assumptions about how we know and write the world. Asking us to suspect ourselves leaves us without much equilibrium and with an uncertain future. But perhaps that future will give us writing which is more responsible, more creative, and more fulfilling.

ACKNOWLEDGEMENTS

This essay could not have been written without the help of many people. Jim Paradis, John Kirkman, and Bernard Avishai generously gave me meticulous and critical readings of various drafts, and the essay would not exist in its present form without their help. I am greatly indebted to Hubert L. Dreyfus, who of course is not responsible for any philosophical gaucheries in the piece. The technical writing group at Miami University in Oxford, Ohio, taught me much of what I know about technical writing, and the essay frequently states their ideas. Much of the argument was thrashed out in the hallways at Miami in long conversations with Brit Harwood. And without Judith Fryer, who gave me both intellectual support and sympathy during the whole time I wrote it, I would never have gotten started, nor would I have had the push to work it through.

REFERENCES

1. F. H. MacIntosh, Teaching Writing for the World's Work, in *The Teaching of Technical Writing*, D. H. Cunningham and H. A. Estrin (eds.), National Council of Teachers of English, Urbana, Illinois, pp. 23-33, 1975.
2. E. P. Dandridge, Notes Toward a Definition of Technical Writing, in *The Teaching of Technical Writing*, D. H. Cunningham and H. A. Estrin (eds.), National Council of Teachers of English, Urbana, Illinois, pp. 15-20, 1975.
3. R. Hays, What is Technical Writing?, in *The Teaching of Technical Writing*, D. H. Cunningham and H. A. Estrin (eds.), National Council of Teachers of English, Urbana, Illinois, pp. 3-8, 1975.
4. W. K. Sparrow, Six Myths About Writing for Business and Government, *The Technical Writing Teacher, 3*, pp. 49-59, 1976.
5. J. A. Walter, Technical Writing: Species or Genus?, *Technical Communication, 24*, pp. 6-8, 1977.
6. P. M. Kelley and R. E. Masse, A Definition of Technical Writing, *The Technical Writing Teacher, 4*, pp. 94-97, 1977.
7. R. Carter, Technical Writing: A Framework for Change, *The Technical Writing Teacher, 7*, pp. 39-42, 1979.
8. F. H. MacIntosh, Where Do We Go From Here?, *Journal of Technical Writing and Communication, 8*, pp. 139-145, 1978.
9. M. Rabinovitch, Technical Writing's Last Stand, *Technical Communication, 27*, pp. 23-25, 1980.
10. T. M. Sawyer, The Common Law of Science and the Common Law of Literature, in *The Teaching of Technical Writing*, D. H. Cunningham and H. A. Estrin (eds.), National Council of Teachers of English, Urbana, Illinois, pp. 185-191, 1975.
11. P. Skaggs, Teaching Business Communications: Journeywork or Humanistic Endeavor?, *The Technical Writing Teacher, 6*, pp. 66-68, 1979,
12. J. S. Harris, On Expanding the Definition of Technical Writing, *Journal of Writing and Communication, 8*, pp. 133-138, 1978.
13. C. R. Stratton, Technical Writing: What It Is and What It Isn't, *Journal of Technical Writing and Communication, 9*, pp. 9-16, 1979.
14. W. E. Britton, What Is Technical Writing? A Redefinition, in *The Teaching of Technical Writing*, D. H. Cunningham and H. A. Estrin (eds.), National Council of Teachers of English, Urbana, Illinois, pp. 23-33, 1975.
15. G. Steiner, *After Babel: Aspects of Language and Translation*, Oxford University Press, London, 1975.

16. J. Weizenbaum, *Computer Power and Human Reason*, W. H. Freeman, San Francisco, California, 1976.
17. H. Dreyfus, *What Computers Can't Do*, Harper and Row, New York, rev. ed., 1979.
18. C. R. Miller, A Humanistic Rationale for Technical Writing, *College English*, *40*, pp. 610-617, 1979.
19. D. N. Dobrin, What's Wrong with the Mathematical Theory of Communication?, *Proceedings of the 29th International Technical Communication Conference*, Society for Technical Communication, Washington, D.C., pp. E37-E40, 1982.
20. W. V. Quine, Two Dogmas of Empiricism, *From a Logical Point of View*, Harvard University Press, Cambridge, Massachusetts, 1953.
21. I. Scheffler, *Beyond the Letter: A Philosophical Inquiry into Ambiguity, Vagueness, and Metaphor in Language*, Routledge and Kegan Paul, London, 1979.
22. K. Lynch, *The Image of the City*, The M.I.T. Press, Cambridge, Massachusetts, 1960.
23. Technology, Management Implications, *Encyclopedia of Professional Management*, McGraw-Hill, New York, 1978.
24. H. Marcuse, *One-Dimensional Man*, Beacon Press, Boston, 1964.

Contributors

PAUL V. ANDERSON is Associate Professor of English at Miami University (Ohio), where he directs the master's degree program in technical and scientific communication. He has edited a monograph entitled *Teaching Audience Analysis and Adaptation* (Association of Teachers of Technical Writing, 1980), and his articles have appeared in several journals and essays collections. He also serves as a consultant to business and government.

CHARLES BAZERMAN is Associate Professor of English at Baruch College, City University of New York. He has published three books with Houghton Mifflin: *English Skills Handbook* (1977), *Reading Skills Handbook* (1978, 1982), and *The Informed Writer* (1981). He is currently engaged in a study comparing the notes and subsequent drafts of papers by the physicist Arthur H. Compton.

R. JOHN BROCKMANN is Assistant Professor of Technical Communication at Arizona State University. He is currently chairing the preparation of *The Case Method in Technical Communication: Theory and Models.* He specializes in computer documentation and has recently begun work on a stylistic history of patent writing.

DAVID N. DOBRIN is Assistant Professor of Technical Communication at the Massachusetts Institute of Technology. He has published on Dickens, Stoppard, and technical writing.

LESTER FAIGLEY is Assistant Professor of English at the University of Texas at Austin. He and Stephen Witte have recently published essays on revision and on cohesion, coherence, and writing quality. He is co-director of a project supported by the Fund for the Improvement of Postsecondary Education that is aimed at developing materials and instruments for assessing college writing programs.

LINDA FLOWER is Associate Professor of English at Carnegie-Mellon University. Her research has focused on thinking processes in writing and comprehension, supported by a grant from NIE, and on problems in writing public documents, as part of the Document Design Project at CMU. Her recent publications include *Problem-Solving Strategies for Writing* (Harcourt Brace Jovanovich, 1981). Her current work is focused on planning, revision, and document design for computer users.

DIXIE GOSWAMI is a director of the expository writing program at the Breadloaf School of English and is a consultant with the American Institutes for Research. With Lee Odell, she was co-investigator on a three-year study of writing in non-academic settings. She is also a member of the NCTE Commission on Composition and is the recipient of a Mina Shaughnessy fellowship.

ELIZABETH HARRIS is Assistant Professor of English at the University of Texas at Austin. She has published articles on technical writing and on historical scholarship in Anglo-Irish literature, along with a number of short stories. She is currently at work on a book entitled *A Theoretical Perspective on Scientific and Technological Discourse.*

JOHN R. HAYES is Professor of Psychology at Carnegie-Mellon University. He is interested in the analysis of complex human activities such as problem solving, writing, comprehension of text, and creativity. His text, *The Complete Problem Solver* (1981), is published by Franklin Institute Press. He has co-authored many articles on writing with Linda Flower.

ANNE HERRINGTON has administered a basic skills program at Johnson State College in Vermont and has directed writing-across-the-curriculum projects supported by the Fund for the Improvement of Postsecondary Education. She is presently researching the relationships between what the writing students are asked to do in undergraduate engineering courses and the writing they will do later on the job.

THOMAS N. HUCKIN is Assistant Professor of Linguistics in the Department of Humanities, and Assistant Research Scientist, English Language Institute, at the University of Michigan. He is co-founder and co-director of the University's annual summer conference/workshop on the teaching of scientific and technical English to non-native speakers and is co-author of *English for Science and Technology* (McGraw Hill, 1982).

CAROLYN R. MILLER is Assistant Professor of English at North Carolina State University. She has published essays on technical writing and rhetoric in *College English*, *Central States Speech Journal*, the *Journal of General Education*, and *Pre/Text*. She serves on the editorial board of *College Composition and Communication* and on the Executive Committee of the Association of Teachers of Technical Writing.

LEE ODELL is Professor of Language, Literature and Communication at Rensselaer Polytechnic Institute. He is co-editor of two NCTE publications, *Evaluating Writing* (1977) and *Research on Composing* (1978); trustee of the NCTE Research Foundation; and member of the editorial board of *College Composition and Communication*. Together with Dixie Goswami, he has just completed a three-year study, supported by NIE, on the nature and functions of writing in non-academic settings.

JAMES PARADIS is Associate Professor of Technical Communication at the Massachusetts Institute of Technology. He is author of *T. H. Huxley: Man's Place in Nature* (University of Nebraska, 1978), a study of Huxley's role as a nineteenth-century popularizer and partisan of science. He is co-editor of *Victorian Science and Victorian Values: Literary Perspectives* (New York Academy of Sciences, 1981), a collection of essays on the interrelations of science and literature in the nineteenth century.

DORIS QUICK is the director of in-service training for the Capital District Writing Program, and is Chair of the English Department at Burnt Hills, New York High School. She has conducted evaluations of school-wide writing programs in upstate New York. She is currently studying audience awareness of writers at four different age levels.

JACK SELZER is Assistant Professor of English at Pennsylvania State University. He teaches a variety of courses in literature and technical writing and helps to administer programs in business and technical writing. His articles and reviews have appeared in the *Journal of Business Communication*, *Philological Quarterly*, *English Literary Renaissance*, and the *Journal of Technical Writing and Communication*.

JAMES STEPHENS is Associate Professor of English at Marquette University, where he teaches courses in Renaissance literature. He is the author of *Francis Bacon and the Style of Science* (University of Chicago Press, 1976) and has published a number of articles on Renaissance prose and poetry. Currently, he is completing a book on the seventeenth-century physician-poet, Henry Vaughan.

HEIDI SWARTS is Research Assistant/Researcher at the Communications Design Center and Department of Psychology at Carnegie-Mellon University. Her research uses protocol analysis to examine both writers' and readers' processes. Her research interests include document design and the revision processes of expert and novice writers.

VICTORIA M. WINKLER is Assistant Professor of Rhetoric at the University of Minnesota, where she directs the undergraduate and graduate programs in technical communication. She has published articles in the *Journal of Communication, College Composition and Communication, ITCC Proceedings,* and two collections of essays on technical writing. She is the editor of *The Technical Writing Teacher* and is active in industrial consulting. She is currently conducting research in the use of peer instruction and peer evaluation in the writing classroom.

STEPHEN P. WITTE is Associate Professor of English at the University of Texas at Austin. He conducts courses in writing, research in composition, and the teaching of writing. He is currently doing research on writing course and program evaluation; topical structures in texts of different types; revision; and topical development in the texts of elementary, secondary, and college students.

JAMES P. ZAPPEN is Assistant Professor of Humanities in the College of Engineering at the University of Michigan. He has published articles on Thomas Hobbes and on the psychotherapist Carl R. Rogers, and he is currently at work on a goal-oriented rhetoric for the environmental impact statement.